Reverberations of the Exodus in Scripture

Reverberations
of the Exodus in Scripture

Edited by
R. Michael Fox

PICKWICK *Publications* · Eugene, Oregon

REVERBERATIONS OF THE EXODUS IN SCRIPTURE

An earlier version of some portions of chapter 8 appeared in David I. Starling, *Not my People: Gentiles as Exiles in Pauline Hermeneutics*, BZNW (Berlin: de Gruyter, 2011) 167–94. Those portions are included here with the kind permission of the original publishers.

Pickwick Publications
An Imprint of Wipf and Stock Publishers
199 W. 8th Ave., Suite 3
Eugene, OR 97401

www.wipfandstock.com

ISBN 13: 978-1-62032-576-6

Cataloguing-in-Publication data:

Reverberations of the exodus in scripture / edited by R. Michael Fox.

xx + 210 pp. ; 23 cm. Includes bibliographical references.

ISBN 13: 978-1-62032-576-6

1. Exodus, The—Biblical teaching. I. Title

BS1199 E93 R37 2013

Contents

Contributors

Hélène M. Dallaire is Associate Professor of Old Testament and Director of Messianic Judaism programs at Denver Seminary. She authored the commentary on "Joshua" in the revised edition of the *Expositor's Bible Commentary* series. Current projects include a textbook entitled *Biblical Hebrew: A Living Language* (Eerdmans), *The Syntax of Volitives in Biblical Hebrew and Amarna Canaanite Prose* (Eisenbrauns), and a commentary on "Joshua" in the new series, *Hearing the Message of Scripture* (Zondervan).

Nevada L. DeLapp teaches Classical Greek at St Peter's Classical school in Fort Worth, TX. He has also taught courses in Biblical Hebrew at Brite Divinity School. His forthcoming monograph investigates ways in which 16th and 17th century Reformed authors read and used the stories of David and Saul as they struggled with the question of armed resistance against tyrants.

Daniel J. Estes is Distinguished Professor of Old Testament at Cedarville University. He has lectured in Israel, Hong Kong, Hungary, England, and Greece. His numerous publications include commentaries on Song of Songs (IVP Academic) and Job (Baker) as well as *Handbook on the Wisdom Books and Psalms* (Baker), which will soon be translated into Chinese. He is presently working on a commentary on Psalms (Broadman & Holman).

R. Michael Fox has taught courses in Biblical Studies and Biblical Hebrew at Texas Christian University and Southwestern Baptist Theological Seminary. He has also pastored churches in Arkansas and Missouri. His articles, essays, and reviews appear in a variety of scholarly publications.

Radu Gheorghita is Associate Professor of Biblical Studies at Midwestern Baptist Theological Seminary. He has also taught at Emmanuel Bible Institute and the University of Bucharest in Romania. His prior publications, including *The Role of the Septuagint in Hebrews* (Mohr Siebeck), focus on the Septuagint and the use of the Jewish Scriptures in the New Testament. He is passionate about scripture memorization, especially in the original languages.

Joshua L. Mann is a PhD candidate at the University of Edinburgh. He has published articles in scholarly journals, served as assistant editor for the *Midwestern Journal of Theology*, and taught courses in the areas of New Testament and Hermeneutics at Midwestern Baptist Theological Seminary and Calvary Bible College. He is also the owner and editor of JoshuaLMann. com, an academic biblical studies website.

Eugene H. Merrill is Distinguished Professor of Old Testament Studies at Dallas Theological Seminary. His prior publications include *Everlasting Dominion: A Theology of the Old Testament* (Broadman & Holman), *Kingdom of Priests: A History of Old Testament Israel* (Baker), and numerous articles, essays, commentaries, and translation projects.

Denise R. Morris is a writer and editor with an M.A. in Old Testament Biblical Studies from Denver Seminary. Her thesis focused on a theology of faith in action as seen through the exodus. She has written numerous Bible curricula and has extensive experience writing and teaching on biblical studies and the Christian worldview. She has taught courses on the history and literature of ancient Israel at Colorado Christian University.

Robin Routledge is Academic Dean and Senior Lecturer in Old Testament at Mattersey Hall in England. He is the author of numerous scholarly articles and essays, as well as *Old Testament Theology: A Thematic Approach* (IVP/ Apollos). He brings a wealth of pastoral and pedagogical experience to his research and has taught Masters' courses in Prague (International Baptist Theological Seminary) and Brussels (Continental Theological Seminary). His article "'God's Spirit' in Genesis 6:1–4" recently received an award for excellence from the Foundation for Pentecostal Scholarship.

David I. Starling is senior lecturer in New Testament and Theology at Morling College in Sydney, Australia. His publications on the use of the Old Testament in Paul's letters include *Not My People: Gentiles as Exiles in Pauline Hermeneutics* and a number of articles in journals including *Novum Testamentum*, *Journal of Theological Interpretation*, *Reformed Theological Review*, and *Journal for the Study of Paul and His Letters*.

Joshua E. Williams is Assistant Professor of Old Testament at Southwestern Baptist Theological Seminary. Along with articles appearing in scholarly journals such as *Southwestern Journal of Theology*, he is a contributor to the *Baker Illustrated Bible Dictionary*.

Thomas N. Willoughby is a PhD candidate at Midwestern Baptist Theological Seminary (MO). He has taught extensively for Midwestern over the past five years in the area of Biblical Studies. He also teaches regularly for Charleston Southern University and Criswell College. His recent scholarly activities include lectures on John's Gospel at Midwestern, Princeton Theological Seminary, and Criswell.

Acknowledgments

I WOULD LIKE TO thank the patient staff at Pickwick Publications, who never once shied away from my constant barrage of questions (and I do mean constant). I would also like to thank the contributors for working with me to develop this volume. I appreciate not only their diligence in seeing this project to completion and their excellent scholarship, but also (perhaps especially) their cordiality displayed throughout the process. Put simply, the pleasure has been mine. I hope this volume not only helps readers of the Bible understand the role, significance, and centrality of the exodus event in the larger canon, but also that it demonstrates the advantages of collaborative scholarship for this type of endeavor.

Furthermore, I wish to acknowledge the support of my loving family:

Rachel—Who knew where forgetting one's watch would lead? Thank you for everything.

James—You constantly remind me that there is fun to be had in this world, and lots of it if you try. Thank you.

Jonah—By God's grace your big, bright, hazel eyes regard me as a hero, and I am better for it. Thank you.

Introduction

R. Michael Fox

Scholars were investigating the use of the OT in the NT long before that specialization found the place of prominence that it presently enjoys.[1] Although it may seem a curious launching point for such a discussion, an important moment for this trajectory in critical scholarship was the arrival of E. P. Sanders's *Paul and Palestinian Judaism,*[2] which readers may note is not, strictly speaking, even about inner-biblical studies.[3] With this investigation, Sanders ushered forth something of a paradigm shift in NT interpretation and, even wider, biblical studies in general. One legacy of this work is that critical scholars typically no longer investigate the Pauline corpus exclusively against Greco-Roman backgrounds. Instead, Sanders brought early Jewish works to the foreground and sought to understand Paul's letters and theology in light of those texts. Although many today would agree that Sanders was a bit extreme on some points and perhaps a bit reactionary overall, his influence upon some of the most significant works of the last couple decades is unquestionable.[4] In short, *Paul and Palestinian Judaism*

1. E.g., C. H. Dodd, *According to the Scriptures: The Sub-Structure of New Testament Theology* (London: Nisbet, 1952); Earle E. Ellis, *Paul's Use of the Old Testament* (Edinburgh: Oliver & Boyd, 1957); R. T. France, *Jesus and the Old Testament: His Application of Old Testament Passages to Himself and to His Mission* (Downers Grove, IL: IVP, 1971).

2. E. P. Sanders, *Paul and Palestinian Judaism: A Comparison of Patterns of Religion* (Philadelphia: Fortress, 1977).

3. Indeed, the candidates for a launching point are numerous. It would also be valid to begin with seminal literary-critical works, e.g., Julia Kristeva, *Séméiôtiké: recherches pour une sémanalyse* (Paris: Seuil, 1969); Kristeva, *La Révolution du langage poétique* (Seuil, 1974). I think Sanders's contribution—though perhaps not in an obvious fashion—is a good choice here because it streamlines the effort (as we shall see) to make the point that the field has developed in such a way that works tend to focus on the OT in the NT *or* OT inner-biblical studies, but generally not a synthesis of both.

4. See, for instance, the influence of Sanders in N. T. Wright, *The New Testament and the People of God*, vol. 1 of *Christian Origins and the Question of God* (Minneapolis: Fortress, 1992), 244–79; and in James D. G. Dunn, *The Theology of the Apostle Paul*

proves to be a major work of influence and an outright watershed in the areas of NT and Christian origins.

In the wake of *Paul and Palestinian Judaism*, it became apparent that consideration of OT texts and themes for NT interpretation was not merely a pre-critical exercise useful only in confessional contexts or for biblical theology of the conservative variety. Biblical scholars had to make room for and further take into account the influence of the Jewish scriptures and the Second Temple religious milieu upon first-century Judaism and the early church. Thus a major impact of Sanders's program upon inner-biblical studies is that it allowed such works as those by Richard Hays and Christopher Stanley[5] to garner a more sizable hearing from the guild since they were giving attention to Paul's Jewishness, not merely reading Paul within the confines of the Christian canon.[6]

Presently, the area of inner-biblical studies in critical scholarship is experiencing something of a golden age. The major trailblazer in recent years by virtue of output is Steve Moyise, who has written multiple introductions on the OT in the NT and has edited and contributed to several studies investigating the use of single OT books throughout the NT literature.[7] Stanley Porter has been actively involved in similar projects.[8] The appearance of works closer to the popular level[9] and the publication of a biblical theology

---

(Grand Rapids: Eerdmans, 1998), 334–89.

5. Richard B. Hays, *Echoes of Scripture in the Letters of Paul* (New Haven: Yale University Press, 1989); Christopher D. Stanley, *Paul and the Language of Scripture: Citation Technique in the Pauline Epistles and Contemporary Literature*, SNTSMS 74 (Cambridge: Cambridge University Press, 1992).

6. That is not to imply that global Christianity is in full agreement on the biblical canon.

7. See, e.g., Steve Moyise and Maarten J. J. Menken, eds., *Deuteronomy in the New Testament: The New Testament and the Scriptures of Israel*, LNTS (London: T. & T. Clark, 2007); Moyise and Menken, eds., *Isaiah in the New Testament* (London: T. & T. Clark, 2007); Moyise, *The Old Testament in the New: An Introduction* (London: Continuum, 2001); Moyise, *Evoking Scripture: Seeing the Old Testament in the New* (London: T. & T. Clark, 2008); Moyise, *Paul and Scripture: Studying the New Testament Use of the Old Testament* (Grand Rapids: Baker, 2010).

8. E.g., Stanley E. Porter, *Hearing the Old Testament in the New Testament*, MNTS (Grand Rapids: Eerdmans, 2006); Thomas L. Brodie, Dennis R. MacDonald, and Stanley E. Porter, eds., *The Intertextuality of the Epistles: Explorations of Theory and Practice*, NTM 16 (Sheffield: Sheffield Phoenix, 2006); Stanley E. Porter and Christopher D. Stanley, eds., *As It Is Written: Studying Paul's Use of Scripture*, SBLSymS 50 (Atlanta: SBL, 2008).

9. See the point/counterpoint discussion in Kenneth Berding and Jonathan Lunde, eds., *Three Views on the New Testament Use of the Old Testament* (Grand Rapids: Zondervan, 2007).

focusing on this perspective by a prominent evangelical scholar[10] are indications that this niche is emerging as a central focus in biblical studies.

Yet, one gets the sense that there are still uncharted waters. Although studies in this area display variety regarding hermeneutical perspectives and presuppositional starting points, there is generally a primary concern for how the NT uses OT texts and themes.[11] The model can at times be a very straightforward one.

There is room in this area for a greater emphasis on consideration for how an OT text or theme had already been reused and previously interpreted in the OT itself *before* it appeared in the NT. Not everyone agrees with his model for dating Israelite traditions, but it is difficult to argue with Michael Fishbane's premise that OT/HB books engaged in inner-biblical exegesis; and I would add—with an eye towards the present study—they were doing so centuries before the NT writers came onto the scene.[12] Fishbane's influence is evident in works like Benjamin Sommer's study on inner-biblical allusions in Isa 40–66.[13] Another important work in this vein appeared when Mark Boda and Michael Floyd made available in print the 1973 thesis of Rex Mason on inner-biblical allusions in Zech 9–14. Although Mason's thesis originally appeared prior to Fishbane's study, Boda and Floyd's edition includes nine additional chapters by leading scholars on method and critical issues.[14] Without getting too exhaustive, one can see that there is certainly an arc of scholarship focusing on how texts in the OT itself engage other OT texts, themes, and traditions.[15]

10. G. K. Beale, *A New Testament Biblical Theology: The Unfolding of the Old Testament in the New* (Grand Rapids: Baker, 2011).

11. E.g., Darrell L. Bock, *Proclamation from Prophecy and Pattern: Lucan Old Testament Christology*, JSNTSup 12 (Sheffield: JSOT Press, 1987); Sylvia C. Keesmat, "Exodus and the Intertextual Transformation of Tradition in Romans 8.14–30," *JSNT* 54 (1994) 29–56; William N. Wilder, *Echoes of the Exodus Narrative in the Context and Background of Galatians 5:18*, StBL (New York: Lang, 2001); J. Severino Croatto, "Jesus, Prophet like Elijah, and Prophet-Teacher like Moses in Luke-Acts," *JBL* 124, no. 3 (2005) 451–65; Rodrigo J. Morales, *The Spirit and the Restoration of Israel: New Exodus and New Creation Motifs in Galatians*, WUNT 2/282 (Tübingen: Mohr/Siebeck, 2010).

12. See, e.g., Michael Fishbane, *Biblical Interpretation in Ancient Israel* (Oxford; New York: Clarendon, 1985); Fishbane, "Jeremiah IV 23–26 and Job III 3–13: A Recovered Use of the Creation Pattern," *VT* 21, no. 2 (1971) 151–67; Fishbane, "The 'Exodus' Motif/The Paradigm of Historical Renewal," in *Text and Texture: A Literary Reading of Selected Texts*, ed. Fishbane (Oxford: One World, 1998) 121–40.

13. Benjamin D. Sommer, *A Prophet Reads Scripture: Allusion in Isaiah 40–66*, Contraversions (Palo Alto, CA: Stanford University Press, 1998).

14. Mark J. Boda and Michael H. Floyd, eds., *Bringing out the Treasure: Inner Biblical Allusion in Zechariah 9–14*, JSOTSup 370 (London: Sheffield Academic, 2003).

15. See also, e.g., Bernhard W. Anderson, "Exodus Typology in Second Isaiah," in

The present study is an attempt to stand on the shoulders of the giants in this blossoming field and experiment with its presentation and methodology. This volume falls in the trajectory of scholarship that includes all the secondary literature mentioned above (and many more), but it builds on it in an attempt to do something a bit different. This project looks at a central biblical event—the exodus from Egypt—as it recurs in various texts and in various ways in *both* the Old and New Testaments. That quality is crucial. What emerges from this study is a stronger sense that, when the NT writers made use of the exodus, they were reusing and re-appropriating a story that already had a long history of being reused, re-appropriated, and re-actualized by communities who viewed themselves as the people of God and the heirs of his covenant promises. To put it another way, the echoes of and allusions to the exodus event in the NT are just further reverberations in scripture of this sacred, central, and formative story.

This characterization is not to imply that previous studies have completely neglected this line of thinking. Indeed, some works demonstrate acute awareness that their NT texts under consideration interact with OT texts that are themselves interacting with prior texts and/or traditions; and, some of these studies even focus on the exodus.[16] The present study, however, is different in that several books in both testaments receive their own, individual treatment by specialists. The reader, then, gets to see several presentations and examples of how the exodus event keeps emerging in new contexts throughout the canon, with the advantage that each of those contexts is the primary focus of its individual treatment within the larger work.

This project is merely a sampling. Cataloguing and commenting upon every allusion to or citation of the exodus event would require endless volumes, if it is even possible at all. The texts under consideration were selected for two primary reasons. First, and at risk of being obvious, these texts exhibit points of contact with the exodus event which merit further exploration and contribute to the larger picture of the exodus constructed in this volume.

Israel's Prophetic Heritage: Essays in Honor of James Muilenburg, eds. Anderson and Walter Harrelson (New York: Harper & Brothers, 1962), 177–95; Amos Frisch, "The Exodus Motif in 1 Kings 1–14," *JSOT* 81 (2000) 3–21; Rebecca G. S. Idestrom, "Echoes of the Book of Exodus in Ezekiel," *JSOT* 33, no. 4 (2009) 489–510; Lee Roy Martin, "'Where are all his wonders?' The Exodus Motif in the Book of Judges," *JBPR* 2 (2010) 87–109.

16. See, e.g., William J. Webb, *Returning Home: New Covenant and Second Exodus as the Context for 2 Corinthians 6:14—7:1*, JSNTSup 85 (Sheffield: JSOT Press, 1993); Rikki E. Watts, *Isaiah's New Exodus in Mark*, BSL (Grand Rapids: Baker Academic, 1997); David W. Pao, *Acts and the Isaianic New Exodus*, BSL (Grand Rapids: Baker Academic, 2002). Works investigating NT usage of the OT "new exodus" must deal with the exodus in the Torah by default.

Second, of course, specialists regarding specific biblical books or genres were available to work on those texts. Indeed, those involved in this project consider the collaborative nature of this endeavor to be one of its greatest strengths. The contributors represent a diverse cross section of biblical scholarship and Christian traditions and hail from three different continents.

A keen eye will also detect that there is diversity across the various, individual treatments as well. The first and last chapters are broader than the rest and provide more sweeping treatments, though they both have different emphases, tasks, and procedures. The foci of the chapters in between include theological treatments, further developments of previous scholarly insights, critiques of prior scholarship, new ideas and insights, and so forth. What *Reverberations of the Exodus in Scripture* offers, then, is a sampling of scholarly investigations into key texts leading to a robust portrait of the exodus event as it emerges in various places in both the OT and the NT.

Soli Deo Gloria

Abbreviations

AASF	Annales Academiae Scientiarum Fennicae
AB	Anchor Bible
ABD	*The Anchor Bible Dictionary*. 6 vols. Ed. David Noel Freedman. Garden City, NY: Doubleday, 1992
AJPS	*Asian Journal of Pentecostal Studies*
AnBib	Analecta Biblica
ANET	*Ancient Near Eastern Texts Relating to the Old Testament*. Ed. James B. Pritchard. 3rd ed. Princeton: Princeton University Press, 1969.
Ant.	*The Jewish Antiquities* (Josephus)
AOS	American Oriental Series
AUS	American University Studies
b. Sand.	Babylonian Talmud: Sanhedrin
BA	*Biblical Archaeologist*
BASOR	*Bulletin of the American Schools of Oriental Research*
BBR	*Bulletin of Biblical Research*
BDB	Francis Brown, S. R. Driver, and Charles A. Briggs. *Hebrew and English Lexicon of the Old Testament*. Oxford: Clarendon, 1907
BECNT	Baker Exegetical Commentary on the New Testament
BI	*Biblical Interpretation*
BJ	*Bellum Judaicum* (Josephus)
BNTC	Black's New Testament Commentary
BR	*Biblical Research*

BRS	The Biblical Resource Series
BSac	*Bibliotheca Sacra*
BSL	Biblical Studies Library
BZAW	Beihefte zur Zeitschrift für die alttestamentliche Wissenschaft
BZNW	Beihefte zur Zeitschrift für die neutestamentliche Wissenschaft
CBQ	*Catholic Biblical Quarterly*
CBQMS	Catholic Biblical Quarterly Monograph Series
CBR	*Currents in Biblical Research*
CJT	*Canadian Journal of Theology*
ConBOT	Coniectanea Biblica: Old Testament Series
COS	*The Context of Scripture*. Ed. William H. Hallo and K. Lawson Younger. 3 vols. Leiden: Brill, 1997
CTM	*Concordia Theological Monthly*
DSD	Dead Sea Discoveries
ECC	Eerdmans Critical Commentary
EKKNT	Evangelisch-katholischer Kommentar zum Neuen Testament
ESV	English Standard Version
ET	English Text
ExpTim	*Expository Times*
HALOT	*The Hebrew and Aramaic Lexicon of the Old Testament*. Ed. Ludwig Koehler and Walter Baumgartner. Rev. Walter Baumgartner and Johann Jakob Stamm. Trans. M. E. J. Richardson. Leiden: Brill, 2001
HB	Hebrew Bible
HBM	Hebrew Bible Monographs
HNTC	Holman New Testament Commentary
HSM	Harvard Semitic Monographs
ICJ	*International Congregational Journal*
Int	*Interpretation: A Journal of Bible and Theology*
Int	Interpretation

IRT	Issues in Religion and Theology
JANER	*Journal of Ancient Near Eastern Religions*
JANESCU	*Journal of the Ancient Near Eastern Society of Columbia University*
JATS	*Journal of the Adventist Theological Society*
JBL	*Journal of Biblical Literature*
JBPR	*Journal of Biblical and Pneumatological Research*
JBQ	*Jewish Bible Quarterly*
JETS	*Journal of the Evangelical Theological Society*
JITC	*Journal of the Interdenominational Theological Center*
JPTSup	Journal of Pentecostal Theology Supplement Series
JQR	*Jewish Quarterly Review*
JSNT	*Journal for the Study of the New Testament*
JSNTSup	Journal for the Study of the New Testament Supplement Series
JSOT	*Journal for the Study of the Old Testament*
JSOTSup	Journal for the Study of the Old Testament Supplement Series
JSS	*Journal of Semitic Studies*
LCBI	Literary Currents in Biblical Interpretation
LNTS	Library of New Testament Studies
LXX	The Septuagint
MJT	*Midwestern Journal of Theology*
MLBS	Mercer Library of Biblical Studies
MNTS	McMaster New Testament Studies
MT	Masoretic Text
NA27	*Novum Testamentum Graece.* Ed. B. and K. Aland et al., after Erwin Nestle. 27th ed. 1993. Stuttgart: Deutsche Bibelgesellschaft, 2001
NAC	New American Commentary
NASB	New American Standard Bible
NCBC	New Cambridge Bible Commentary

NICNT	New International Commentary on the New Testament
NICOT	New International Commentary on the Old Testament
NIDOTTE	*New International Dictionary of Old Testament Theology and Exegesis*. Ed. Willem A. VanGemeren. Grand Rapids: Zondervan, 1997
NIV	New International Version
NIVAC	NIV Application Commentary
NKJV	New King James Version
NovT	*Novum Testamentum*
NovTSup	Supplements to Novum Testamentum
NRSV	New Revised Standard Version
NSBT	New Studies in Biblical Theology
NT	New Testament
NTM	New Testament Monographs
NTS	*New Testament Studies*
OT	Old Testament
OTL	Old Testament Library
OTS	Old Testament Studies
PNTC	Pillar New Testament Commentary
ResQ	*Restoration Quarterly*
RevExp	*Review and Expositor*
RSV	Revised Standard Version
SBLMS	Society of Biblical Literature Monograph Series
SBLRBS	Society of Biblical Literature Resources for Biblical Studies
SBLSCS	Society of Biblical Literature Septuagint and Cognate Studies
SBLSymS	Society of Biblical Literature Symposium Series
SBTS	Sources for Biblical and Theological Study
SJT	*Scottish Journal of Theology*
SNTSMS	Society for New Testament Studies Monograph Series
StAC	Studies in Antiquity and Christianity

StBL	Studies in Biblical Literature
SWJT	*Southwestern Journal of Theology*
TB	Babylonian Talmud
TBC	Torch Bible Commentaries
TDOT	*Theological Dictionary of the Old Testament*. Ed. G. Johannes Botterweck and Helmer Ringgren. Trans. Geoffrey W. Bromiley et al. 14 vols. Grand Rapids: Eerdmans, 1974–2004
TOTC	Tyndale Old Testament Commentaries
TrinJ	*Trinity Journal*
TS	*Theological Studies*
TU	Texte und Untersuchungen
TynBul	*Tyndale Bulletin*
UBS4	*The Greek New Tesetament*. Ed. B. and K. Aland et el. 4th ed. 1993. Stuttgart: United Bible Societies, 1998
USQR	*Union Seminary Quarterly Review*
VT	*Vetus Testamentum*
WBC	Word Biblical Commentary
WO'C	Bruce K. Waltke and M. O'Connor. *An Introduction to Biblical Hebrew Syntax*. Winona Lake, IN: Eisenbrauns, 1990
WTJ	*Westminster Theological Journal*
WUNT	Wissenschaftliche Untersuchungen zum Neuen Testament
ZAW	*Zeitschrift für die alttestamentliche Wissenschaft*

1

The Meaning and Significance
of the Exodus Event

Eugene H. Merrill

Introduction

Judaism, both ancient and modern, has univocally spoken of the exodus
of its forebears and the ensuing Mosaic Covenant with them as the greatest,
most theologically significant event in all its 4,000 year history.[1] Walther
Eichrodt proposes, "The foundation of an enduring covenant order appears
as the purpose and consummation of the mighty deliverance from Egypt."[2]
The spring festival known as *Pesach* (Passover) celebrates this mighty act of
God as fundamental to Jewish deliverance and sustenance.[3] Judith Plaskow

1. See, e.g., the assessment by Abraham J. Heschel, *The Prophets: An Introduction*
(New York: Harper & Row, 1962) 43: "The central manifestation of the love and om-
nipotence of God, cherished and remembered in Israel, was the exodus from Egypt."
Speaking of the Song of Moses, the poetic interpretation of the event (Exod 15:1–21),
Benno Jacob elegantly declares, "One might well call it the national anthem of Israel"
(*The Second Book of the Bible: Exodus* [Hoboken, NJ: KTAV, 1992] 424).

2. Walther Eichrodt, *Theology of the Old Testament*, trans. J. A. Baker (Philadelphia:
Westminster, 1961) 1:37–38.

3. Its ritual text, the Haggadah, makes this clear when speaking of the *matzot* or
unleavened bread at the very beginning of the liturgy: "This is the bread of affliction
that our fathers ate in the land of Egypt" and in answer to the children's questions as to
its meaning declares: "We were slaves to Pharaoh in Egypt, and the L-rd, our G-d, took
us out from there with a strong hand and with an outstretched arm . . . Even if all of us
were wise, all of us understanding, all of us knowing the Torah, we would still be obli-
gated to discuss the exodus from Egypt, and everyone who discusses the exodus from

notes, "On this most widely celebrated of Jewish holidays, families gather together not to memorialize the Exodus from Egypt but to relive it."[4] It, with its message of redemptive grace, is to the Jew what Passion Week is to the Christian, with its intense focus on the vicarious suffering, atoning death, and triumphant resurrection of Jesus the Christ. In fact, it is the symbol of redemption from oppression at the hands of a cruel dictator to the glorious freedom of independent nationhood; from only dim memories of the patriarchs who, more than four centuries earlier, had been recipients of God's gracious promises to standing now on the verge of seeing those promises fulfilled in a covenant relation with Him; and from alienation from the land God had first ceded to Abraham to a pilgrimage to that land in which all other promises would find fruition.[5] Geerhardus Vos equates exodus and redemption in his pithy observation, "The exodus from Egypt *is* the Old Testament redemption."[6]

However, one must not forget the purpose for Israel's descent into Egypt in the first place. As is often the case, reasons for God's structuring of the affairs of life and history cannot always be perceived by human minds and often seem inimical to personal well-being or even to God's self-interest; but, reasons also exist that only God can perceive, those for blessing and wholeness that remain hidden until retrospection brings clarity. Shortly before Joseph's elevation to prominence in the Egyptian government, the pharaoh dreamed of a famine that would come upon the land and for seven years would reduce the so-called "bread-basket of the world" to a barren desert (Gen 41:25–36). Joseph counseled the king to store up the bumper crops that would precede that agricultural calamity. This done, Egypt had abundance and to spare, so much so that neighboring peoples flocked there to secure the grain necessary for survival (41:47–57). Among them were Jacob and his larger family who, through the good offices of Joseph whom God had sent ahead for that very purpose, procured sufficient goods for the years of famine that yet remained. Egypt thus became a place of security and plenty to which the nascent nation of Israel eventually emigrated (46:1–7).

Egypt at length is praiseworthy." See "Maggid—Retelling the Passover Story," accessed February 2013, http://www.chabad.org/holidays/passover/pesach_cdo/aid/1737/jewish/Maggid.htm.

4. Judith Plaskow, "Standing Again at Sinai," in *Contemporary Jewish Theology: A Reader*, eds. Elliot N. Dorff and Louis E. Newman (New York, Oxford: Oxford University Press, 1999) 257.

5. For an extended discussion of the exodus as a symbol of liberation, see Bruce K. Waltke, *An Old Testament Theology* (Grand Rapids: Zondervan, 2007) 389–93. He proposes the following four: (1) Exodus of the Patriarchs from Egypt and Mesopotamia; (2) Exodus from Egypt; (3) Exodus from Babylon; (4) Exodus of the Church.

6. Geerhardus Vos, *Biblical Theology* (Grand Rapids: Eerdmans, 1954) 124.

What Joseph's brothers had intended to be a means of disposing of him ironically turned out to be their ticket to national survival (45:5, 7–8; 50:20).

A deeper and more important (but less obvious) explanation for the descent was the moral and spiritual decline of Jacob's family in the hostile, pagan world in which they lived. This is illustrated by examples such as Esau's marriage to a Hittite woman (Gen 26:34–35), Jacob's negotiations with Hamor the Hivite (34:1–17), Reuben's sexual encounter with his father's concubine Bilhah (35:22), and, most serious of all, the sordid behavior of Judah, ironically the son of the messianic hope (49:10). He married a Canaanite (38:2), sired three wicked sons who died at God's hand for their failure to observe proper marriage customs (38:7–11),[7] and seduced his own daughter-in-law Tamar by whom he fathered twins named Perez and Zerah (38:27–30).[8]

The cumulative effect of all this was the imperative for Israel to move from the temptations of Canaanite idolatry to a land where the nation could find incubation and thus an environment more conducive to its development into a Yahwistic light among the nations. The Israelite settlement, apparently peaceful as long as Joseph lived and even later (ca. 1876–1580 BCE), gave way to arduous labor and loss of freedom, measures designed not to punish Israel so much as to discipline it for the rigors of desert life and conquest that lay ahead. When that appeared to have been achieved, the exodus from Egypt under Moses was put into effect.

The Setting of the Book of Exodus

The proper understanding of any piece of literature, particularly historiographical narrative, is largely dependent on the reader's understanding of the places, times, and circumstances of the author. In addition, in an ideological or tendentiously "slanted" work (such as the OT), one must attempt to discover how and why the piece was written and why it was placed where it is in a given collection of works. Thus, Exodus must be read with due regard to its (1) canonical, (2) historical, and (3) theological environment.

---

7. The custom referred to was the so-called "levirate law," which mandated a widow to have sons by her husband's brothers who could carry on the name of the deceased husband (cf. Deut 25:5–10; Matt 22:23–33). "Levir" is Latin for "brother-in-law" and has nothing to do with the term "Levite."

8. Once again the mercy of God is seen not in excusing sin but in overriding its consequences. In this case, Perez became the covenant son of Judah and the transmitter of the Abrahamic promise in the line that passed through David (Ruth 4:18–22; 1 Chr 2:1–15; Matt 1:1–6).

Canonical Setting of the Book

In every canonical list—ancient or modern, Jewish or Christian—Exodus occupies the second spot, immediately after Genesis. This is evident not only by the very fact of its traditional attestation as such,[9] but by the literary bridging between the two books. Genesis ends with reference to Abraham, Isaac, and Jacob and the promise given them that they would be brought up out of the land of bondage (Gen 50:24; cf. 15:12–16; 46:4); and, Exodus begins with the words ואלה שמות בני ישראל, "these are the names of the sons of Israel," referring, of course, to those at the end of Genesis and their descendants. This linkage plus the smooth narrative transition between the two books joins them in both a logical and historical sense. As for the name of the book, Exodus derives from the Greek ἔξοδος mediated through the Latin *exodus*. The Greek term does not occur in Exodus, but it does in LXX Pss 104:38 [HB 105:38] and 113:1 [HB 114:1] as well as in the NT in Heb 11:22. Its most central historical event is thus captured in these versions by the title assigned by them to the book.

Historical Setting of the Book

According to the book's own assertions (Exod 1:1; 17:14; 24:4; 34:4, 27–29), it was written by Moses sometime after the exodus, the precise date impossible now to discern.[10] It clearly could not be earlier than the completion of the erection of the Tabernacle since it describes this as an eye-witness

9. See TB Baba Bathra 14b. See also Roger Beckwith, *The Old Testament Canon of the New Testament Church* (Grand Rapids: Eerdmans, 1985) 127–28.

10. Most scholars who accept the historicity of the exodus at all date the event in the time of Rameses II, probably ca. 1250 BCE. This "late date" view is opposed by many evangelical scholars who favor the "early date" position that argues, on the basis of the Bible's own chronological data taken at face value, that it took place ca. 1440 BCE. For arguments supporting the earlier date, see Michael A. Grisanti, "The Book of Exodus," in *The World and the Word: An Introduction to the Old Testament*, eds. Eugene H. Merrill, Mark F. Rooker, and Michael A. Grisanti (Nashville: Broadman & Holman, 2011) 194–207. As for the date of the composition of the book, historical-critical scholarship has, since the early 19th century, denied the work to Moses, assigning it rather to anonymous compilers of traditions collected eventually as sources labeled either J (German Jahwist), E (Elohist), or P (Priestly), to be dated 950–850, 750, and 450 BCE, respectively. For a recent treatment of the issue from this standpoint, see Joseph Blenkinsopp, *The Pentateuch: An Introduction to the First Five Books of the Bible* (New York: Doubleday, 1992) 141–60. For adherents to the traditional, earlier, Mosaic authorship and dating, see Oswald T. Allis, *The Five Books of Moses* (Philadelphia: Presbyterian & Reformed, 1949) 5–14; Tremper Longman III and Raymond B. Dillard, *An Introduction to the Old Testament* (Grand Rapids: Zondervan, 2006) 51, 65–68; Grisanti, *The World and the Word*, 190–92.

account (Exod 40:17),[11] nor could it be later than Moses' address to the assembly of Israel recorded in Deut 1:1–3 inasmuch as Moses died shortly thereafter.[12] The Masoretic chronology dates the exodus to the latter part of the 15th century BCE, the Late Bronze age in archaeological terms.[13] After the exodus, the Israelites trekked for three months to Mt. Sinai in the south Sinai Peninsula where the Lord revealed to Moses and the people the terms of the covenant described generally as either the Mosaic or Sinaitic Covenant (Exod 19:1). The latter term is preferable in that the covenant later reaffirmed and updated at the Plains of Moab is also Mosaic and therefore should be described as the Deuteronomic Covenant to distinguish it from the one revealed at Sinai.[14]

11. Moses records the datum that the tabernacle was completed on the first day of the second year (since the exodus, the bench mark for all subsequent dated events). The date of the Passover just prior to the exodus was Nisan 14, from that time forward to be reckoned as the first month of the year (Exod 12:2, 6). Exactly seven days later (Nisan 21), Israel commenced its departure for Canaan (12:18, 28, 41), arriving at Sinai three months later on precisely Sivan 21. They remained at Sinai until Iyar 20, the second month of the following year (Num 10:11).

12. Several reflective statements in the book suggest that Moses composed it after arrival in the Transjordan but that a few glosses were later added by someone else (e.g., Exod 16:35).

13. By "Masoretic chronology" is meant the figures in the Hebrew text taken at face value and not as ciphers or symbols of something else. E.g., the number 40 or any of its multiples such as 20 or 80 are common in the OT and not just in narrative where one might most expect a figurative meaning. Thus, the flood waters were on the earth for 40 days and 40 nights (Gen 7:4, 12); Isaac was 40 when he married (Gen 25:20), as was Esau (26:34); Israel was in the desert for 40 years (Exod 16:35); Moses was on the mountain for 40 days and nights (24:18); the land had rest in the days of the judges for periods of 40 years (Judg 3:11; 5:31; 8:28); and David and Solomon both reigned 40 years (2 Sam 5:4; 2 Kgs 11:42). The NT also records that Jesus fasted for 40 days and 40 nights (Matt 4:2) and appeared to the people for 40 days following his resurrection (Acts 1:3). Unless and until figures like these can be proved to be only symbolic and not literal, no amount of manipulating or factoring them in various ways will do. See John James Davis, *Biblical Numerology* (Grand Rapids: Baker, 1968); Robert D. Johnston, *Numbers in the Bible: God's Unique Design in Biblical Numbers* (Grand Rapids: Kregel, 1990); Susan Lampitt, "Decoding the Bible," *ExpTim* 115, no. 8 (2004) 278–79; Aron Pinker, "The Number 40 in the Bible," *JBQ* 22, no. 3 (1994) 163–72; Maureen Tilley, "Typological Numbers—Taking a Count of the Bible," *BR* 8, no. 3 (1992) 48–49.

14. The purpose of the two renditions of the Mosaic Covenant was not to create a people for the Lord but to call that already elect and existing nation to the function of servant-hood, to be "a priestly kingdom and a holy [i.e., a separated] nation" (Exod 19:4–6). This is evident from both the unilateral nature of the covenant and from Israel's later identity as a servant of YHWH (Isa 41:8; 43:10; 44:1; 45:4). For an analysis of this so-called Suzerain-Vassal Treaty form see K. A. Kitchen, *The Reliability of the Old Testament* (Grand Rapids: Eerdmans, 2003) 283–99.

Following Joseph's rise to power in the reign of Sesostris II (1897–1878) of Dynasty 12, his father Jacob with his clan was welcomed into Egypt, probably by Sesostris III (1878–1843).[15] Jacob died ca. 1860, but one might assume that Egyptian hospitality extended at least through the tenure of Amenemhet III (1842–1797), shortly after Joseph's death in 1806, and probably until the time of the founding of Dynasty 18 ca. 1570 BCE.[16] The book of Exodus is set against the latter dynasty, a totally different environment from that of the patriarchs. Dynasty 12 had been gradually overthrown by the hated Hyksos invaders who occupied the Egyptian Delta through Dynasties 13–17 until they were defeated and expelled from Egypt by the founders of Dynasty 18, a native Egyptian royal house, in the so-called Middle Kingdom period (1570–1320).

According to the Masoretic chronology, Moses was born in 1526, probably in the reign of Amenhotep I (1546–1526). He is likely the pharaoh who "did not know Joseph" (Exod 1:8) and who instituted the harsh measures described in Exod 1.[17] These included forced construction labor using clay bricks that the Israelites themselves manufactured, all the while being mistreated (פרך, 1:13) and with bitterness (מרר, 1:14). But Pharaoh's greater concern was the burgeoning population of the Hebrews that seemed likely to outstrip that of the native Egyptians if nothing were done to bring

---

15. Egyptian chronology is still in a flux because of the lack of data or the inability so far to interpret them univocally. The dates proposed here are mainly from the *Cambridge Ancient History*, 3rd ed., vol. 1/2 (Cambridge: Cambridge University Press, 1973) 308, 315–21. For recent discussions see William Adler, "Moses, the Exodus, and Comparative Chronology," in *Scripture and Traditions*, eds. Patrick Gray and Gail R. O'Day (Boston: Brill, 2008) 47–65; Rodger Dalman, "Egypt and Early Israel's Cultural Setting: A Quest for Evidential Possibilities," *JETS* 51, no. 3 (2008) 449–88; Erik Hornung, Rolf Krauss, and David Warburton, *Ancient Egyptian Chronology* (Leiden: Brill, 2006); William Ward, "The Present State of Egyptian Chronology," *BASOR* 288 (1992) 53–66.

16. For these dates and their justification see Eugene H. Merrill, "Fixed Dates in Patriarchal Chronology," *BSac* 137 (1980) 241–51. The entire scenario is altered if one accepts a late exodus date of the mid-13th century or so. In this case, all dates proposed here must be lowered by 200 years, resulting, among other things, in a 19th Dynasty background, that is, the so-called "Ramesside" era (1320–1223). The pharaoh "who did not know Joseph" is then identified with Rameses II (1304–1236). For the fallacy of this identification, see Merrill, "Rameses II and the Date of the Exodus: A Case of Mistaken Identity," in *Homeland and Exile: Biblical and Ancient Near Eastern Studies in Honour of Bustenay Oded*, eds. Gershon Galil, Mark Geller, and Alan Millard (Leiden: Brill, 2009) 533–45.

17. Not to "know" Joseph in context here obviously does not mean not to know him face to face, but to have lost sympathy for the Hebrew people and even to have become hostile toward them, perhaps because of the erroneous assumption on their part that the Hyksos and Hebrews were one and the same people or at least were in league. See Douglas K. Stuart, *Exodus*, NAC 2 (Nashville: Broadman & Holman, 2006) 62–63.

it under control. Hence, the policy of infanticide was conceived that mandated that every Hebrew baby boy must be slain from then on (1:16). This included Moses and explains why escape was the only viable option for not only Moses and the whole nation but all the baby boys born after the edict had been made (1:17–22).[18]

The deliverance of Moses from death by means of a basket in the river is reminiscent in some ways of Noah's deliverance by a boat from universal judgment and also foreshadows the exodus of the people of Israel from even more extreme circumstances, a deliverance which, ironically, none other than Moses would lead. The crossing of the Jordan under Joshua's leadership forty years later repeats the exodus in some respects, but more properly should be called an "eisodus" inasmuch as Israel was then entering a land and not escaping from one.[19] Thus, salvation from a watery abyss over which YHWH has absolute control seems to constitute a kind of metaphor through which YHWH displays his sovereignty over the destructive forces of evil on behalf of those whom he has chosen for salvation and service. This notion must now receive consideration as a central theological theme throughout sacred history.

Theological Setting of the Book

Preparation for exploring this matter of the setting of the book of Exodus and the exodus event requires brief attention to antecedent acts of God that saved and perpetuated the race in times of peril. This is hinted at already in the creation account of Gen 1 in which the unruly sea was restrained as it were and its boundaries set in place (Gen 1:9–10).[20] This permitted life to exist on the land, microcosmically set in the garden over which mankind was appointed

18. Aaron was exempted from this, evidently because he was three years older than Moses and therefore was eliminated from this bloody rampage (Exod 7:7).

19. Brevard S. Childs, *The Book of Exodus*, OTL (Philadelphia: Westminster, 1974). Childs, however, dates the conquest narrative earlier then the Song of Moses (p. 244).

20. This observation is in no way intended to support the notion entertained by some scholars that the creation account of Gen 1 is a primitive legendary tradition (*Chaoskampf*) scrubbed clean of offensive pagan polytheism. See most famously Hermann Gunkel, *Genesis*, trans. Mark E. Biddle (Macon, GA: Mercer University Press, 1997) 103–33. Gunkel's work was done in the waning years of "Pan-Babylonianism" when the OT creation and flood texts especially were thought to reflect ANE epical literary influence. See also John I. Durham, *Exodus*, WBC 3 (Waco, TX: Word, 1987) 203, citing the view of J. Pederson; Umberto Cassuto, *Commentary on Exodus*, trans. Israel Abrahams (Jerusalem: Hebrew University, 1967) 177–81. For caution in making improper use of these ancient Near Eastern parallels, see R. K. Harrison, *Introduction to the Old Testament* (Grand Rapids: Eerdmans, 1969) 47–48.

steward in God's service of dominion (2:8, 15; cf. 1:26–28). Gerhard von Rad draws attention to the Creation-Exodus intertextuality as follows:

> This confession [of Deut 26] received a peculiar enlargement when elements of the Creation myth, the struggle with Chaos, were welded into it. This procedure was suggested by the common appearance of the catchword "sea" both here and in the creation myth. Jahweh "rebuked" the Red Sea (Ps. CVI.9) in the same way as he had done in its time to the sea of Chaos, and like the latter it "fled" (Ps. CXIV.3). The event thus took on primeval dimensions, and was transferred from its historical setting to the beginning of its history; indeed it stood for Israel at the beginning of her whole existence.[21]

Many other passages reflect on this or on other aspects of YHWH's lordship over the waters that enables him to deliver his people from destruction or, on the other hand, to be an instrument of his judgment (cf. Job 9:8; 26:10; 38:8–11; Pss 24:2; 29:3, 10; 33:6–7; 74:12–17; 89:8–10; 104:5–7; Prov 8:29; 30:4; Isa 40:12; 50:2; 51:9; 54:9; Jer 5:22; Amos 5:8; 9:6; Nah 1:4; Hab 3:15; Matt 8:26–27; Rev 21:1).

More to the point of the circumstances of Israel's oppression under Pharaoh is YHWH's promise to Abraham as an aspect of the Abrahamic Covenant that his descendants in days to come would become slaves to a foreign power that would hold them in servility for four hundred years.[22] He would then release them by punishing their overlords, after which they could escape (Gen 15:12–14). The theological center-point of Exodus is the cluster of events that followed the promised release, namely (1) the formation of an inchoate people into a nation; (2) the invitation to Israel to become an instrument of mission by accepting the terms of a covenant designed for that purpose; and (3) the guidelines of the covenant by which the chosen nation must live in order to be a "light to the Gentiles" (Isa 49:6). By virtue of descent from Abraham, Israel was already the people of YHWH (Exod 2:23–24; 3:7, 10; 5:1, passim). More than that, they were his son, the one nation from all the earth worthy to be called God's son (Exod 4:22–23; cf. Deut 7:6–8; Isa 63:16; 64:8; Hos 11:1). The exodus, then, was not designed to create a new people, but to take an existing people, Israel, and to make of that people an intermediary between God and the world of

21. Gerhard von Rad, *Old Testament Theology*, trans. D. M. G. Stalker (New York: Harper & Row, 1962) 1:178.

22. The verb employed to denote their plight is עָנָה, "oppress, humiliate" (Gen 15:13). It is true, of course, that until Joseph died (ca. 1800) the conditions in Egypt were benign, but there came a time following his demise that there sat on Egypt's throne a pharaoh "who did not know Joseph" (Exod 1:8). See discussion above, note 14.

nations, one that by its example and teachings would persuade them also to seek him. Hamilton succinctly makes the point, "Israel's misery is not the Lord's primary motivating factor [for the exodus]. Rather, it is to fulfill the covenant he has made with Abraham, Isaac, and Jacob, of which Genesis speaks."[23] Peter Gentry concurs, but adds the important idea, "Through covenant, God will bring his blessing and establish his rule in the lives of his people and, through them, to the rest of the world."[24]

From that time forward, the concept of exodus from Egypt was recollected and reinterpreted as a paradigmatic event to describe God's saving work on behalf of Israel and, indeed, of all people, especially in eschatological contexts.[25] The psalms are particularly rich in appropriating the motif. Psalm 66 extols the greatness of God, singling out that "he turned the sea to dry land so that they [Israel] went across the river by foot" (Ps 66:6). Here the word for river (נהר) clearly refers to the Reed Sea[26] as its synonymously parallel "sea" (ים) does (cf. Exod 14:21). Another celebration of the mighty deeds of YHWH occurs in Ps 77:15–16 (HB 77:16–17): "You redeemed your people by your arm, the descendants of Jacob and Joseph; the waters saw you, O God, the waters saw you and quaked; even the great deep (תהומות; cf. Gen 1:2; Exod 15:8; Ps 104:6) trembled." Psalm 78:13 similarly points out with reference to the exodus, "YHWH parted the sea and allowed them to pass over; he made the water heap up like newly ploughed soil."

The prophets too availed themselves of the imagery conjured up by the exodus miracle. Speaking of the looming Assyrian threat, Isaiah says that YHWH of Hosts will do to them what he did in the ancient past to the Egyptians: "His scepter he will extend over the sea just as he wielded it with regard to Egypt" (Isa 10:26; cf. Exod 14:16, 21). Turning to a second exodus, Isaiah speaks of it to the future exilic community as a cause for comfort (Isa 40:1). Her times of oppressive labor and of double punishment for her

---

23. Victor P. Hamilton, *Exodus: An Exegetical Commentary* (Grand Rapids: Baker, 2010) xxii.

24. Peter J. Gentry and Stephen J. Wellum, *Kingdom through Covenant: A Biblical-Theological Understanding of the Covenants* (Wheaton, IL: Crossway, 2012) 388.

25. Eugene H. Merrill, "Pilgrimage and Procession: Motifs of Israel's Return," in *Israel's Apostasy and Restoration: Essays in Honor of R. K. Harrison*, ed. Avraham Gileadi (Grand Rapids: Baker, 1988) 261–72.

26. The nomenclature "reed" is the proper translation of Hebrew סוף (*HALOT* 747; cf. Isa 19:6; Jon 2:6). However, it is not an indication of the depth of the water but a description of the shoreline of a body of fresh water that was everywhere infested with (papyrus) reeds. The name "Red Sea" originated in the Greek ἐρυθρα θάλασσα; thus LXX and NT. For the issue of Reed Sea/Red Sea, see Bernard F. Batto, "The Reed Sea: Requiescat in Pace," *JBL* 102 (1983) 27–35.

transgressions will come to an end (40:2).[27] The prophet further notes that YHWH is the one "who provides a way through the sea and a path through the mighty waters" (43:16). Borrowing mytho-poetic imagery, the same prophet likens the Reed Sea to the primeval monster Rahab who, like Tiamat in Sumero-Babylonian epic, was cut in half to form the heavens and the earth.[28] Canaanite mythology views Baal's accession to kingship as a result of his conquering hostile forces including Yammu (i.e., the sea).[29] In Israel's case, it was YHWH who "slew" the monstrous sea, thus "drying up the sea, even the great deep" (תהום, Isa 51:9–10; cf. 63:11–13). The clearest remaining passage is Zech 10:10–12, in which this post-exilic prophet predicts a future day when YHWH will enable restored Israel to cross the sea; but, it will be an arduous crossing that requires a fatal blow against the waves so that all the sea's depths can be dried up (Zech 10:11).

It is therefore no overstatement to conclude that the exodus event is the single most important historical and theological event in the OT and that it occurred at precisely the right time in history to be most effective. YHWH's destruction of the army of the mightiest nation on the earth at the time, the political and military malaise of the Mesopotamian powers in the Late Bronze Age that rendered the Assyrians and Babylonians incapable of intervention in international affairs, and the weakness of the Canaanite city-states because of the iron heel of the Egyptian 18th Dynasty prior to the exodus all provided a vacuum of power and influence that allowed Israel to fulfill its covenantal destiny.

27. In the context of bondage, especially with clear reference to the Egyptian sojourn, the noun צבא here clearly is best understood as compulsory labor (thus *HALOT* 995).

28. This is recounted in an epic known as Enuma Elish. See conveniently *ANET* 72–99, as well as *COS* 1.390–402. An excellent work that compares and contrasts the Genesis account of creation with others is Alexander Heidel, *The Babylonian Genesis*, 2nd ed. (Chicago: University of Chicago Press, 1951). In addition to Enuma Elish, Heidel draws attention to other Babylonian mythic creation texts such as "The Slaying of the Labbu" (pp. 141–43) and "The Adapa Legend" (pp. 147–53). The most important Egyptian creation myth is in "The Memphite Theology" text (*COS* 1.21–23). This shows comparatively little resemblance to the Genesis accounts.

29. The Ba'lu Myth reads: "You, your name is 'Ayyamurru; 'Ayyammuru, expel Yammu, expel Yammu from his throne, Naharu from his seat of sovereignty. You'll whirl in Ba'lu's hand, like a hawk in his fingers, Strike Prince Yammu on the head, Ruler Naharu on the forehead" (*COS* 1.249).

The Importance of the Exodus Event in the Torah

The exodus deliverance was so important to Israel that it was incorporated into Deuteronomy's version of the Decalogue as the motive clause for the observance of the Sabbath:

> Observe the Sabbath day to set it apart[30] . . . and remember that you were a slave in the land of Egypt and the Lord your God brought you out from there by a mighty hand and by an outstretched arm. Therefore, the Lord your God commanded you to keep the Sabbath day (Deut 5:12–15; translation mine).

The differences in the two motive clauses—Exod 20:11 and Deut 5:15—are of utmost theological importance because they demonstrate the possibility, indeed necessity, of applying various biblical texts to varying and developing situations.[31] In this case, the most significant event in the memory of the recently delivered people of Israel was creation itself by their omnipotent God, a display of power reenacted in the exodus and articulated most brilliantly in the Song of Moses (Exod 15:1–18). There YHWH, the creator of the sea, uses the sea as his instrument of destruction of the mighty Egyptian forces (15:1, 4, 5, 8, 10; cf. Gen 1:2, 7). Using the relatively rare "deeps" (תהומות, Exod 15:5, 8) reflects the language of Gen 1:2, "the face of the deep" (פני תהום).

On the other hand, the Deuteronomy version of the Sabbath commandment focuses on the exodus itself as the fundamental reason for setting aside the seventh day. The emphasis thus shifts from creation to redemption. It is because the Israelites were slaves in Egypt, forced to work without compensation and rest, that they must not treat their own slaves and servants in such a manner.[32] God had released them from the oppres-

---

30. The differences in the use of technical terms are not greatly significant but should be noted here for at least fine nuancing: (1) whereas לְקַדְּשׁוֹ, a piel inf cst, introduces a purpose clause, the form in Exod 20:11 (וַיְקַדְּשֵׁהוּ), a qal pret 3ms, reflects a past action with YHWH as subject; (2) Deut 5:15 enjoins the hearer to remember זָכַרְתָּ, qal impv ms; Exod 20:8 employs the inf. cst of the same verb as an impv; (3) finally, Deut 5:12 urges the hearer to keep (שָׁמוֹר) the sabbath (inf cst), but Exod lacks any such notion in its motive clause.

31. Application to the NT and the Church is in other chapters of this work.

32. The common Hebrew term for servant or slave is עֶבֶד, a term far removed from the concept of slavery in the Greco-Roman world or in the days of European and American colonialism. In the great majority of cases it refers to bond-servants, that is, men or women forced into servitude because of loans necessitated by financial distress or simply because of a lack of ability to become or remain financially independent for whatever reason. For important regulations governing such a status, see Exod 21:2–11, 26–27; Deut 15:7–18. The slave, on the other hand, was considered personal property to be bought or sold. Unlike the bond-servant, he could not be a fellow Israelite but a

sion of slavery, so the Israelites must at the least provide a day off for those under their control and care. The Sabbath, then, provided an appropriate occasion to reflect on God's redemptive act on Israel's behalf and to imitate God's gracious intervention by granting to their fellow human beings respite from their onerous burdens.[33]

The differences between the motive clauses in Exod 20 and Deut 5 provide opportunity to make two important hermeneutical and theological points: (1) Both versions stress that a Sabbath day must be kept; but, (2) the rationale for the observance may change. In Exodus, the major event of world history to that point was creation itself. In Deuteronomy, however, the event that eclipsed even creation was Israel's recent and miraculous deliverance from Egyptian slavery to the lordship of the Creator. The one celebrated the beginnings of all things, the other the celebration of Israel's nationhood and call to be YHWH's agent of redemption. To carry this forward, the Christian sets aside a day to remember appropriately the third and most glorious event of all, the triumphant resurrection of Jesus Christ. The day has changed (now the first day of the week), and the motive clause has as well (because he rose again to justify the children of God to exercise their God-given privileges inherent in being the image of God). A NT version of the fourth commandment could now read something like this:

> Remember the first day to make it exceptional; on all other days
> go about your daily lives, but on the first day of the week
> Jesus rose from the dead. Therefore, the Lord has blessed the
> first day and set it apart.[34]

Less significant (but important) linkages to the exodus occur already in Lev 26 where covenant obedience is urgently demanded by Moses on the basis of YHWH's having broken the bondage of Egyptian slavery by delivering his people from their overlords (Lev 26:13). If they do so, they

---

foreigner or alien, usually a prisoner of war and the like. Nevertheless, even they must be treated humanely and with dignity (cf. Lev 25:42, 44; Deut 21:14; 23:15; 24:7).

33. One should also note that this tradition of remembering the Sabbath day because of the most recent event in Israel's salvation history carries forward into the NT church whose most significant (indeed, foundational truth) was the resurrection of Jesus Christ on the first day of the week; hence, the church's observance of Sunday with its implicit motive: "because Jesus rose from the dead" (cf. Acts 20:7; 1 Cor 16:2; Rev 1:10). For remembrance as an important theological concept, see Eugene H. Merrill, "Remembering: A Central Theme in Biblical Worship," *JETS* 43, no. 1 (2000) 27–36.

34. There is, of course, no mandate in the NT to set aside Sunday or any other day for public worship. However, apostolic practice and the sanction of tradition have made it crystal clear that the earliest church understood the obsolescence of the OT practice and joyfully embraced the new thing that had taken place in Jesus Christ (Acts 20:7; 1 Cor 16:2; Rev 1:10).

can expect the blessings of the Abrahamic covenant that promised mul-
tiplication in number and the presence of YHWH walking among them
(26:9–12). Covenant disloyalty, however, would result in just the opposite: a
return to bondage, deprivation, and the absence of their God among them
(26:14–33). Only an exodus-like redemption would bring them back again
to their land (26:42–45).[35] Numbers also recollects the exodus as it appeals
to YHWH, the God of the exodus, in times of national peril. He is identified
as "YHWH your God who brought you out (יצא) of the land of Egypt to be
your God" (Num 15:41; cf. 20:16; 23:22).

Returning to Deuteronomy, one is hardly surprised to find frequent
reference to the exodus. In summarizing events from the revelation at Sinai
to the assembly at the plains of Moab, Moses harked back to the exodus as
a deliverance of Israel from the "iron furnace" of Egypt, thus enabling them
to enter into covenant with YHWH (Deut 4:20). This demonstrated his in-
comparability amongst the alleged gods of the nations, for what other nation,
Moses asked, had ever been delivered in such a manner (4:34). Such a God
deserved their undivided loyalty, a point reinforced over and over by recalling
the mighty exodus event (6:12, 21–23; 11:1–4; 13:5; 29:2–3). It was the exodus
also that testified of his choice of Israel to be a special people (7:8–9), which
should remind them of their need to express devotion to him in worship
(8:11, 14; 26:5–11). More than that, they should manifest mutual love and
care for one another because YHWH cared for them enough to redeem them
(פדה, 9:26; 21:8) from Egyptian bondage. They should show each other the
same mercy and beneficence (15:15; 24:22). In times of insuperable obstacles
and perils, they must recollect what God did to the mightiest nation on earth
when he defeated Egypt and released his people from its grasp (20:1).

Not entirely lacking in Deuteronomy is the exodus as a model for times
to come when and if the nation repents of its sin and returns to YHWH. He
will reverse their captivity and bring them into their land once more (Deut
30:3–5). Interestingly, this new exodus and conquest will feature circumcision just as under Joshua (Josh 5:2–9). The future circumcision, however,

35. The concept of redemption is an important theological datum associated with
the exodus but in the sense not of atonement for sin, which is the more common application, but of ransom from involuntary detainment. The two major Hebrew verb
lexemes for "redemption" are גאל and פדה, commonly used in synonymous parallelism
(Lev 27:27; Isa 35:10; 51:10–11; Jer 31:11; Hos 13:14; Ps 69:18 [HB 69:19]; cf. *HALOT*
169, 911–12, respectively; *NIDOTTE* 1:789–94, 3:578–83 respectively). For an excellent
treatment of these and other technical terms associated with the redemptive aspect
of the exodus, see Walter Brueggemann, *Theology of the Old Testament: Testimony,
Dispute, Advocacy* (Minneapolis: Fortress, 1977) 174–76. He proposes (correctly) that
YHWH is the subject of all these verbs of action clustered around the event. Moses and
Israel essentially had no part to play in their own redemption (76).

will not be of the flesh but of the heart, signifying a renewal of the covenant, this one interiorized and not merely external (Deut 30:6; cf. Jer 31:31–34; 32:6–40, 44; Ezek 36:22–31).

The Importance of the Exodus Event in the Former and Latter Prophets

References to the exodus in the Prophets are of two kinds: (1) the literal and historical deliverance from Egypt and (2) a future, usually eschatological reference to an exodus yet to come, especially in the context of the exile and return of God's people to the land.

The Historical Exodus

The book of Joshua (unsurprisingly) recounts the exodus as a display of YHWH's great salvific power. Rahab, a Canaanite, lamented at the prospects for her people on the basis of rumors she had heard about the parting of the Red Sea and the subsequent victories Israel had enjoyed over the peoples of the Transjordan (Josh 2:10–11). The prevaricating Gibeonites had also heard these reports of Israel's God and all he did to Egypt and thus made covenant with Israel (9:9–10). In his farewell address, Joshua recited YH-WH's mighty deeds in rescuing the people from onerous bondage in Egypt by a miraculous deliverance (24:5–7). Judges recollects God's supernatural work on Israel's behalf, especially in the cliché, "I/he brought them up/out of Egypt" (hiphil of עלה, "go up" or of יצא, "go out," Judg 2:1, 12; 6:8, 13).

Samuel also used the exodus miracle as a reminder of the past in his case harking back to the day when YHWH was king and Israel had no yearning for another (1 Sam 10:18; 12:6–8). Later, in response to David's desire to build YHWH a temple, YHWH pointed out that, since the exodus, no temple was necessary. Why should one be required now (2 Sam 7:6, 23 [see 1 Chr 17:5]; cf. 1 Kgs 8:16)? The book of Kings likewise reflects on the fact that the work of salvation from Egypt was God-initiated (thus again עלה, 1 Kgs 12:28; 2 Kgs 17:7, 36; or יצא, 1 Kgs 8:16, 21, 51, 53; 9:9). Upon the accession of Solomon and his plan to build a temple, the exodus served as the chronological benchmark according to which the founding of the temple could be dated (1 Kgs 6:1). It also was the basis of appeal to Israel to avoid idolatry and remain true to the covenant made at Sinai, an act of redeeming grace that must be recalled by a people prone to go astray from the one who had sovereignly chosen them to be a kingdom of priests and a holy nation (Deut 7:8; 18:5; 1 Chr 17:21;

2 Chr 7:22; Neh 1:10; 9:18; Jer 2:6–7; 7:22–26; 11:4, 7; 32:21–23; Ezek 20:5–17; Hos 12:9–14; Amos 2:9–12; Mic 6:1–5).

The latter prophets attempted to teach covenant obedience by reminiscing on the exodus and the blessings it brought but also the terror that adhered to those who disbelieved in YHWH and were tempted to become disloyal. Isaiah threatened Assyria with the same judgment that Egypt suffered when Pharaoh refused to let God's people go (Isa 10:26). Jeremiah reminded his own disobedient generation of what YHWH had done at the Reed Sea, using the formulaic verbs עלה and יצא as in the former prophets (Jer 16:14; 23:7; 32:20–21; 34:13). Daniel appealed to YHWH to replicate what he had done in saving Israel from Egypt (יצא) by saving the Jewish community for which he felt special responsibility (Dan 9:15). Hosea records YHWH's self-predication, "I am YHWH your God from Egypt," coupled with the threat that Israel will return there short of repentance (Hos 12:9; cf. 13:4). He adds, "by a prophet [i.e., Moses] YHWH brought Israel up out of Egypt" (12:13). Amos speaks in virtually the same terms (Amos 2:10) but adds a note about Israel's having been chosen by YHWH, evidence of which was the exodus (3:1; cf. 9:7). Micah extends this refrain by adding the concept of redemption (פדה) as the purpose of the exodus (Mic 6:4).

The Paradigmatic and Eschatological Exodus

A great number of OT passages view the exodus as the supreme model of salvation against which future acts of God's redemption should be compared and understood. John Goldingay felicitously puts the matter of recapitulation as follows:

> What God intends to do is described in terms of the renewing of the old. That is so for epistemological reasons. God can enable people to understand what the new will be like only by describing it in terms of what they know. But it is also thus for theological or substantial reasons. God can act in the future in ways that take forward what God has done in the past. This new act will be an expression of God's faithfulness. The new "does not annihilate the old but gathers it up and creates it anew."[36]

Isaiah saw a day when Israel would again return from Egyptian (and Assyrian) exile akin to the exodus of old (Isa 27:12–13; 40:3–5; 43:1–7, 14–21; 44:21–23; 48:20–22; 49:8–13; 51:9–11). He, too, drew attention to the

---

36. John Goldingay, *Old Testament Theology, Israel's Faith* (Downers Grove, IL: IVP 2006) 2:426, citing partly Gerhard von Rad, *Old Testament Theology* (Edinburgh: Oliver & Boyd, 1965) 2:1.

redemptive aspect of the exodus (גאל), comparing that which lay ahead and would cost them nothing to that of the past when YHWH freely granted them release from Egypt (52:3–4; cf. 63:9).

Jeremiah, an eye-witness to the Babylonian destruction of Jerusalem and the Temple and the deportation of thousands of his fellow citizens, likewise saw a day when Judah would be freed from exile and would return to the land in a second exodus (Jer 16:14–15; 23:5–8). Just as the first exodus allowed Israel to enter into covenant with YHWH, so the second would be foundational to the new covenant (31:11, 31–34). The same eschatological and redemptive theology was espoused by Hosea (Hos 2:14–20; 11:1, 11; 13:14). Amos's basis for his proclamation of the restored house (i.e., dynasty) of David (Amos 9:14–15) rested on an exodus to come (9:14–15). The same is true of Haggai (Hag 2:4–9) and Zechariah (Zech 10:8–12). As YHWH had in Moses' day performed a great act of salvation from onerous Egyptian bondage and had constituted a covenant nation, thus he would do for the descendants of these ancient forebears. He would free them from captivity, return them to their own land, and reconstitute them as a nation once more by a new covenant that they could keep (Jer 31:27–40; 33:14–26; cf. Ezek 36:22–36).[37]

The Importance of the Exodus Event in the Poetic and Wisdom Literature

Poetry (Psalms)

Harking back to creation, the poet in Ps 33:7 extolls YHWH as the one who "gathered the waters of the sea into a pile" and restrained the great deep in his storehouses. Speaking clearly of the exodus and Reed Sea, Ps 77:16 [HB 77:15] declares, "The waters saw you, O God, the waters saw you and were fearful; the great deep also trembled" (cf. 77:15 [HB 77:14]). Psalm 104:6–7 says of the primordial earth, "You [YHWH] covered it with the deep as with a garment; the waters stood above the mountains. When you rebuked them they fled; at the sound of your voice they ran away" (cf. Ps 106:9). Most striking is Ps 148:7, "Praise YHWH from the earth [i.e., likely here, the underworld or Sheol]; (you) תנינים and all (you) תהמות." The former is generally translated "sea creatures" or the like and the latter "great deep." The parallelism suggests here that the great deep can also be considered

---

37. Gentry, *Kingdom through Covenant*, 433–564.

zoomorphically as a monster of some sort, but no case can be made (in this instance) that either Hebrew or ANE mythology is in view.[38]

The poets, however, also drew attention to Israel's unfaithfulness to YHWH despite the exodus and subsequent displays of his power and grace. They forgot about his power in unleashing the plagues against Egypt (Ps 78:42a, 43–48) and the redemption from bondage exercised on their behalf (Ps 78:42b [פדה], 53–49). A similar sentiment is expressed in Ps 106:7–8, 13 (cf. 106:10, גאל).

Wisdom

The wisdom literature also reflects the mighty hand of YHWH who re-strains and controls the waters. Personified Wisdom says that she was there when YHWH established the heavens and when he circled in the "face of the deep," thus allocating its boundaries (Prov 8:27). Elsewhere YHWH is said to have "broken up the deeps" (3:20). Job 38:30 speaks of YHWH's im-mobilizing the great deep by freezing it! This book also asserts that even the great beast Leviathan is able to "make the great deep boil" merely by passing through it (Job 41:31–32 [HB 41:23–24]).

Conclusion

Of all the strands of historical and theological significance that run their course through the OT and NT (and beyond), none is more pervasive and powerful than that of the exodus. What originated as a salvific and redemp-tive event in which YHWH delivered a weak and undeserving people called Israel from Egyptian bondage became a paradigmatic prototype of hope for subsequent generations of Israel, Judaism, and the Christian Church. In Israel's history, the original replayed itself over and over again in times of peril, sometimes only implicitly, but it became transmuted—especially in the prophetic and poetic texts—into an eschatological prism through which both Israel and the Church could clearly discern an ultimate salvation and restoration of God's people and his creation purposes. Both traditions focus on a messianic age built around a messianic figure who, in the last and most glorious exodus of all, will be a second Moses and, above all, a second Da-vid whose reign will be forever and forever. In the Christian faith, this was fulfilled in Jesus Christ, whose atoning death and triumphant resurrection became the exodus *par excellence* and the grounding of an eschatological expectation of the fullness of the Kingdom of God yet to come.

38. *NIDOTTE* 4:313–14.

2

Joshua and Israel's Exodus from the Desert Wilderness

HÉLÈNE DALLAIRE AND DENISE MORRIS

Introduction

THE EXODUS IS MENTIONED and reenacted over one hundred times in the HB—in narrative, poetry and prophecy. The event is supremely significant in Israel's story, both on historical and religious levels. "The experiences connected with it—the slavery of the Israelites, their liberation from Egypt, the covenant between God and His people at Sinai, and the journey in the wilderness toward the Promised Land—all constitute the dominant motif of the Scriptures in one form or another."[1]

As a paradigmatic event, the exodus is linked both to freedom from the past and hope for the future. It represents the prime event at the western threshold of the "wilderness tradition"[2] while the Jordan crossing, on the eastern outer limit of the wilderness wandering, completes the journey.[3] The wilderness experience and the giving of the Torah at Sinai provide the nexus

1. Nahum M. Sarna, *Exploring Exodus: The Heritage of Biblical Israel* (New York: Schocken, 1986) 1–2.

2. Discussed in detail by James Hoffmeier in *Ancient Israel and Sinai: The Evidence for the Authenticity of the Wilderness Traditions* (Oxford: Oxford University Press, 2005) the "wilderness tradition" is central to the Torah and represents an important formative period for Israel.

3. G. W. Coats, "The Traditio-Historical Character of the Reed Sea Motif," *VT* 17 (1967) 260n2.

between the two miraculous crossings. In addition, the exodus finds itself at the center of the *Canaan-Egypt-Canaan* motif where the Israelites, who had once lived in Canaan before entering Egypt, return after the Exodus out of Egypt. Walter Vogels highlights the *"aller-retour"* to and from Canaan with these words: "Le passage d'Égypte à Canaan n'est pas une simple migration d'un peuple vers un nouveau pays, mais il constitue un retour vers le pays d'où les ancêtres étaient partis. . . . On est donc en présence d'un aller-retour: Canaan-Égypte-Canaan."[4]

According to Vogels, the giving of the Torah at Sinai serves as the climax for the rite of passage between Egypt and the conquest of Canaan. Vogels proposes the following concentric chiastic structure for the narrative from the exodus to the entry into Canaan:[5]

A   Israel in Egypt (Exod 1–10)

    B   Passover and the Crossing (Exod 11:1—15:21)

        C   Journey in the Wilderness (Exod 15:22—18:27)

            X.   Sinai (Exod 19:1—Num 10:10)

        C'   Journey in the Wilderness (Num 10:11—Deut)

    B'   Crossing and Passover (Josh 1–5)

A'   Israel in Canaan (Josh 6–24)

First, both in Egypt (A) and in Canaan (A'), Israel lives for an extended period of time and finds life sustenance (fish, cucumbers, melons, leeks, onions, garlic in Egypt [Num 11:4–5]; produce, cakes, grain, fruit in Canaan [Josh 5:11]). The *manna* provided by the Lord in the wilderness serves as a link between the dietary descriptions of Egypt and Canaan. Second, according to the text, the Passover celebration and the Crossing occur in reverse order (B, B'). In Egypt, Israel celebrates the Passover before crossing the Sea of Reeds while the reverse is true in the book of Joshua. And third (C, C'), both wilderness journeys include similar events: complaints, hardships, and leader responses (Exod 16:3; 17:1–2; Num 12:1–2; 14:1–12). As with the exodus narrative, the crossing of the Jordan is associated with the national consciousness of Israel.

Numerous literary theories have been proposed to explain the relationship between the book of Joshua and the Pentateuch.[6] Due to space

4. Walter Vogels, "D'Égypte À Canaan: Un rite de passage," *Science et Esprit* 52, no. 1 (2000) 22.

5. Ibid., 24.

6. For a detailed discussion on Gerhard von Rad's *Hexateuchal* theory, Martin Noth's *Deuteronomistic History*, S. Mowinckel's *Tetrateuch-Pentateuch-Hexateuch* proposal, and other literary theories, see A. G. Auld, *Joshua, Moses and the Land* (Greenwood,

limitations in this paper, we will not address the literary theories presented by scholars, but rather, we will highlight the textual, thematic, and linguistic relationships that exist between the crossing of the Sea of Reeds[7] and the crossing of the Jordan. This paper will feature selected themes from both crossing narratives. These will include (1) the leadership connections —Moses and Joshua; (2) the crossings—before, during and after (mission, plagues, circumcision, Passover, children's questions, dry ground, aliens among them, promise-fulfillment and the land, and theophanies); and (3) literary features.

The crossing of the Jordan in the book of Joshua mirrors the events that surround the exodus out of Egypt in what Michael Fishbane calls "reflective historiography."[8] Some of the parallel features are presented as chiasms, *inclusios*, and a promise-fulfillment motif. For example, Moses initiates the journey to the Promised Land while Joshua completes it (*inclusio*). The promise of land made to Abraham and to his descendants centuries earlier (Gen 12:1–3; 13:15, 17; 17:8; 24:7; 26:3; 28:13; 35:12; 48:4) establishes a foundation for the parallels that exist between the two crossings (promise-fulfillment).[9] In Alberto Soggin's view, "From the time of the patriarchs until the Exodus from Egypt, and then in particular in the book of Deuteronomy, the promise of a land is one of the most characteristic elements in the relationship between the leading figures in the tradition and their God."[10]

For decades, scholars have discussed the various viewpoints related to an "early" cultic use of the crossing traditions celebrated at Gilgal.[11]

SC: Attic, 1980) 1–51; G. N. Knoppers and J. G. McConville, eds., *Reconsidering Israel and Judah: Recent Studies on the Deuteronomistic History* (Winona Lake, IN: Eisenbrauns, 2000).

7. T. B. Dozeman argues that the original meaning of *Yam Suf* (יַם סוּף) was "a mythological term devoid of geographical specificity." See Dozeman, "The *yam-sup* in the Exodus and the Crossing of the Jordan River," *CBQ* 58 (1996) 408. Modern translations for *Yam Suf* include the Red Sea, the Reed Sea, etc. For an additional discussion on the identification of the *Yam Suf*, see also L. S. Hay, "What Really Happened at the Sea of Reeds?" *JBL* 83, no. 4 (1964) 397–403; N. H. Snaith, "The Sea of Reeds: The Red Sea," *VT* 15, no. 3 (1965) 395–98.

8. Michael Fishbane, *Text and Texture: Close Readings of Selected Biblical Texts* (New York: Schocken, 1979), 122.

9. Both crossings are mentioned together in Ps 114:3, "*The sea [of Reeds] looked and fled, the Jordan turned back.*"

10. J. Alberto Soggin, *Joshua*, OTL (Philadelphia: Westminster, 1972) 19.

11. See H. J. Kraus, "Gilgal," *VT* 1 (1951) 181–83; Gerhard von Rad, *The Problem of the Hexateuch* (New York: ET, 1966) 3–5; Brevard S. Childs, "A Traditio-Historical Study of the Reed Sea Tradition," *VT* 20, no. 4 (1970) 406–18; John van Seters, *The Life of Moses: The Yahwist as Historian in Exodus–Numbers* (Louisville: Westminster John Knox, 1994) 139–47.

While Frank M. Cross supports this view,[12] Brevard S. Childs rejects it for the following reasons:

> The linking of the Reed Sea tradition with the Jordan crossing effected far more than simply the intermingling of vocabulary. The bringing together of the two traditions tended more and more to identify the Reed Sea with "going out of the land" and the Jordan crossing "with coming into the land." In other words, a definite force was exerted toward pulling the Reed Sea event away from its original prose setting in the wilderness tradition and attracting it within the cycle of the exodus tradition. However, it seems to me quite impossible to accept Cross' hypothesis that it was an early Passover ceremony at Gilgal which transmitted the traditions of the exodus and the conquest. On the one hand, in the early prose tradition of J which has the Passover tradition, the sea is not part of the exodus. On the other hand, in the poetic tradition of Ex. xv which has the sea within the framework of the exodus, there is not the slightest hint of the Passover. Therefore to assign the Passover ceremony the role of bearer of the exodus-conquest traditions at an early period is certainly to disregard the historical development of these traditions.[13]

On this issue, John van Seters concludes that since the sea tradition is rarely treated in Deuteronomistic History "or in the preexilic prophets and only comes to the fore in Second Isaiah and the exilic and postexilic psalms, . . . we must seriously consider the possibility that the sea event [in the prose narrative] is a late literary development of the exodus tradition."[14]

The Leadership Connections—Moses and Joshua

The HB identifies the connections that link Moses and Joshua explicitly. From his youth until his old age, Joshua is at Moses' side, assisting him (Exod 24:13), observing him (33:11), informing him (32:17), and doing his bidding (17:9). For decades, Moses models for Joshua what he would eventually need to lead the Israelites—a stiff-necked people—into the land of Canaan. His mentoring begins when Joshua is still young and continues until Moses' death in the Transjordan.

12. Frank M. Cross Jr., "The Song of the Sea and Canaanite Myth," *Journal for Theology and the Church: God and Christ: Existence and Province* 5 (1968) 1–25.

13. Childs, "A Traditio-Historical Study," 415.

14. Van Seters, *The Life of Moses*, 141.

Shortly after the crossing of the Sea of Reeds, while encamped at Rephidim, Israel encounters the Amalekites who are determined to stop the Israelites from journeying any further. It is at this point that Moses introduces his military leader Joshua, a young, faithful, and courageous man who leads the successful fight against Amalek (Exod 17:9–13). Following the victory, God instructs Moses to record the event "as a memorial in a book and recite it in the ears of Joshua" (17:14 RSV).[15] This recitation to Joshua may indicate that God was making a divine pledge to Joshua to fight Israel's enemies under his impending leadership.[16] The only individual—aside from Moses—who is mentioned in this oral recitation is Joshua. From this point on, the two leaders are seen together, with Moses as the senior and Joshua as the brave young apprentice (Num 11:28).

Joshua is the only individual invited to ascend Mt. Sinai with Moses during the giving of the law (Exod 24:12–14; 32:15–17). During one of Moses' visits to the Tent of Meeting, Joshua stands by outside the tent while Moses speaks with God face to face "as one speaks to a friend" (33:7–11). One is left to wonder what Joshua thought during these meetings since, following one of these divine encounters, Moses returns to the camp while Joshua remains at the tent (33:11). Joshua may have been mesmerized by the presence of God in the tent and hoping for a similar experience for himself in the future.

Shortly before his death, God commands Moses to lay hands on Joshua—a man in whom the spirit is (Num 27:18)—to invest his authority in him and to commission him as leader over Israel (Num 27:18–23; cf. Deut 31:7–8, 14, 23). Such an installation ceremony is common in the accession ceremony and the enthronement of a king.[17] This transition of power and authority from Moses to Joshua becomes official soon thereafter when Moses dies in Transjordan. At that point, Joshua begins to mediate between the Lord and Israel, with frequent reminders that "just as the Lord was with Moses, so He would be with him" (Josh 1:5; 3:7). This affirmation testifies that Joshua's leadership and relationship with Israel would certainly mirror that of Moses.[18]

---

15. This is the first explicit mention of literacy in Scripture. Moses' scribal abilities are also depicted in Exod 24:4; 34:7; Num 33:2; Deut 31:9. The addition of "reciting in the ears of" points to an oral tradition existing alongside a written tradition. Cf. Exod 24:7.

16. T. B. Dozeman, *Commentary on Exodus* ECC (Grand Rapids: Eerdmans, 2009) 396.

17. Roy Porter, "The Succession of Joshua," in *Reconsidering Israel and Judah: Recent Studies on the Deuteronomistic History*, eds. G. N. Knoppers and J. G. McConville, SBTS 8 (Winona Lake, IN: Eisenbrauns, 2000) 149.

18. Leadership transitions—successful and unsuccessful—are quite common in the Bible, e.g., Moses to Joshua (successful); Elijah to Elisha (successful); Eli to his sons (unsuccessful); Eli to Samuel (successful). See A. Kay Fountain, "An Investigation into Successful Leadership Transitions in the Old Testament," *AJPS* 7, no. 2 (2004) 187–204.

The following chart provides additional parallels between Moses and Joshua.

Moses	Joshua
Moses is chosen by God to lead Israel (Exod 3:1—7:6)	Joshua is chosen by God to take over the leadership from Moses after his death (Num 27:18, 23; Deut 31:14, 23)
Moses leads a mission divinely orchestrated by the Lord (Exod 3:13–15)	Joshua's mission is completely dependent on the Lord (Josh 1:5, 17; 10:11)
Moses encounters an angel of the Lord (Exod 3:1–3)	Joshua encounters the commander of the army of the Lord (Josh 5:13–15)
Moses unites the tribes for a major expedition with the help of the elders and officials (Exod 12:21)	Joshua calls the elders and officials to help him organize the people for the expedition (Josh 1:10–11; 3:2)
Moses receives divine approval as he pursues his mission (Exod 3:12, 14–15; 7:1–5)	Joshua is reminded that God is with him as he was with Moses (Josh 1:5–9; 3:7)
God promises to Moses that he will bring Israel to a land of milk and honey (Exod 3:8, 17; 13:5; 33:3; Deut 27:3)	Joshua remembers the Lord's promise of a land of milk and honey (Josh 5:6)
Moses learns that the Lord will drive out the Canaanites, Hittites, Amorites, Perizzites, Hivites, Jebusites[1] (Exod 3:8, 17; 13:5)	Joshua is reminded that the Lord will drive out the Canaanites, Hittites, Amorites, Perizzites, Hivites, Jebusites (Josh 3:10; 9:1)[2]

1. In some cases, the list is abbreviated or extended (e.g., Exod 13:5—Perizzites are not mentioned; Exod 23:23—Amorites are not mentioned; Exod 23:28—Perizzites, Amorites and Jebusites are not mentioned). From the group of seven nations mentioned in Josh 3:10, three are clearly identified in Ugaritic and Egyptian texts from the second millennium BCE. See Hélène Dallaire, "Joshua," in *Expositor's Bible Commentary*, eds. Tremper Longman III and David E. Garland, rev. ed. (Grand Rapids: Zondervan, 2012) 2:815–1042, esp. 822.

2. Girgashites are added in Josh 3:10. Joshua mentions that these nations have been driven out by Israel (Josh 24:11), but that the Canaainites remain their midst (e.g., Josh 16:10; 17:13).

Moses	Joshua
Moses sends spies to scout out the land (Num 13)	Joshua sends spies to Jericho (Josh 2)
Moses endures the challenges of commanding a rebellious people (Exod 17:4; 32:9; 33:3, 5; 34:9)	Joshua faces similar challenges as he leads Israel into Canaan (Josh 7:6–9)
Moses builds altars during covenant ceremonies (Exod 17:15; 24:4)	Joshua builds a stone altar immediately after crossing the Jordan (Josh 8:30)
Moses receives popular recognition and oral confirmation from the Israelites that they will obey the Lord their God (Exod 19:8; 24:3)	Joshua receives popular recognition and oral confirmation that the Israelites will serve the Lord their God (Josh 24:21–24)
Moses serves as an exceptional mediator between Israel and the Lord; Moses is given the epithet of "servant of the Lord" after his death (Deut 34:5; Josh 1:1, 13, 15; 8:31, 33; 11:12; 12:6; 13:8; 14:7; 18:7; 22:2, 4)	Joshua serves as an exceptional mediator between Israel; Joshua is also called by the honorific title "servant of the Lord" after his death (Josh 24:29; Judg 2:8)
Moses' old age and death is announced (Deut 31:2)	Joshua's old age and death is announced (Josh 13:1; 23:1–2)
Moses' age is revealed—120 (Deut 31:2; 34:7)	Joshua's age is revealed—110 (Josh 24:29; Judg 2:8; cf. Joseph—Gen 50:22, 26)[3]
Moses is instructed by the Lord to "stretch out your hand" before the crossing (Exod 9:22, 29, 33; 10:12, 21–22; 14:16, 21, 26–27; also the Lord in 7:5; Aaron in 7:19; 8:5, 17)	Joshua is instructed by the Lord to "stretch out your hand" before the conquest of Ai (Josh 8:18–26)

3. A number of parallels exist between Joseph who brought the children of Israel into Egypt (Gen 50:26; Exod 1:6–8) and Joshua who brought the children of Israel into Canaan (Judg 2:8–10): both died at age 110; in both cases, there is mention of burial preparation; in both accounts, there is mention of "that whole generation" passing away followed by information about the next generation that did not know Joseph/THE LORD. Joseph and Joshua both represent the end and the beginning of a new area for Israel.

The Crossings—Before, During, and After

In addition to the features listed above, the crossing narratives reveal numerous supplementary parallels.

The Mission

The calls to Moses and Joshua include a number of similarities. Moses was raised up by God precisely to deliver His people from Egypt, to bring them out of bondage, and to bring them "to a good and spacious land, a land flowing with milk and honey, the region of the Canaanites, the Hittites, the Amorites, the Perizzites, the Hivites, and the Jebusites" (Exod 3:8, 17; 13:4). Similar language is used to define Joshua's mission. Summoned by God to lead Israel into the Promised Land, Joshua reassures the Israelites that the Lord will indeed "drive out from before them the Canaanites, Hittites, Hivites, Perizzites, Girgashites, Amorites, and Jebusites" (Josh 3:10). It is clear that the charge given to Joshua—to lead Israel into Canaan—was the direct fulfillment of the charge given to Moses—to lead Israel out of Egypt and to bring them into the Promised Land.

Plagues

Before both crossings, God sends plagues that cause the death of a large number of individuals. In Exod 8–12, ten plagues afflict men, women, children, animals, water, etc.[19] The plagues (מגפה) inflicted on the Egyptians reflect God's judgment on sin, arrogance, and depravity. In the second crossing (the Jordan), God sends a plague on his own people as an act of judgment for their sinful and immoral deeds at Shittim. While encamped on the eastern shore of the Jordan, Israelite men had indulged in sexual behavior with Moabite women and had joined themselves to the Baal of Peor. As a result, a plague (מגפה) comes upon Israel and 24,000 perish because of their sexual union with foreigners (Num 25; Josh 22:17).[20] This event is retold by Phinehas decades later, shortly before Joshua's death, when the men of Gad, Reuben, and the half-tribe of Manasseh build an enormous memorial altar on the shore of the Jordan River (Josh 22). Fearing that God would send another plague to destroy his people, Phinehas and a delegation

19. Lists of plagues mentioned in Exodus also appear in Pss 78:42–51 and 105:28–36.

20. Because of its connection to rodents, this affliction has been identified with the bubonic plague. Ronald Hendel, "The Exodus in Biblical Memory," *JBL* 120, no. 4 (2001) 609n38.

from the western tribes confront the men of the eastern tribes to ensure that they are not acting unfaithfully towards the Lord. The plagues of Egypt are mentioned in Joshua's farewell speech (Josh 24:5), the historical prologue that introduces the final covenantal ceremony before his death.

Circumcision

Before Israel eats the Passover lamb in Egypt, God instructs Moses to circumcise all male foreigners/non-Israelites who reside in their midst (Exod 12:43–49). By this, we can assume that the Israelite males were already circumcised, since there is no mention of circumcising them and circumcision was a sign of the covenant performed by Israel since the days of Abraham (Gen 17). The instrument of choice to perform circumcision was probably a piece of flint from a rock (cf. Exod 4:25). In the Jordan crossing account, the Lord orders Joshua to "make flint knives and circumcise the Israelites again" soon after reaching the western shore (Josh 5:2–9). In this case, it is clear that those who were born in the wilderness had not yet been circumcised. The instrument used to perform the task (flint) is the same as that used by Zipporah on Moses' son in the wilderness before the Exodus out of Egypt (Exod 4:25). "Flint was readily available in Canaan at that time. Flint knives were used in the ancient Near East for ritual and non-ritual purposes."[21]

Passover

The first Passover account (Exod 12–13) mentions explicitly the celebration of the feast in the land of Canaan. To Moses the Lord commanded, "Obey these instructions as a lasting ordinance for you and your descendants. When you enter the land that the Lord will give you as he promised, observe this ceremony" (12:24–25). Both in Exodus and in Joshua, the Passover preparations begin on the tenth day of the first month (12:1–5; Josh 4:19) while the actual celebration takes place on the fourteenth day of the month (Exod 12:6–11; Josh 5:10). In the Exodus pericope, the Passover is celebrated *before* the crossing (Exod 12:1), while in Joshua it is celebrated at Gilgal *after* the crossing of the Jordan (Josh 4:19—5:11).

Some scholars have suggested that the Passover rituals performed at Gilgal after the crossing became a yearly event celebrated in the same location near the Jordan every Spring, especially since Gilgal is mentioned as an important sacred site until the end of the Northern Kingdom (e.g.,

---

21. Dallaire, "Joshua," 890.

1 Sam 10:8; 11:14–15; 13:4, 7–15; 15:12, 21, 33; Amos 4:4; 5:5; Hos 4:15; 9:15; 12:11; Micah 6:5).[22] According to A. J. Ehlen, who proposes that the celebration was liturgical in nature, "such recounting of God's past mighty deeds for Israel was surely intended to be done within the context of ritual worship."[23] Both in Exodus and Joshua (and elsewhere), the Passover celebration exhibits a corporate character in that it is celebrated in community, beyond the family unit, with neighbors, foreigners, and slaves (Exod 12:1–4, 43–49; Josh 5:10–12).

Children's Questions

After the Jordan crossing, Joshua erects a stone memorial for future generations who will be reminded of the Exodus out of Egypt, the crossing of the Sea of Reeds, and the entry of the Israelites into Canaan. During the Passover preparation at Gilgal, Joshua reflects on the questions children will surely ask when they see the stone structure erected on the western shore of the Jordan (Josh 4:21–24). "What do these stones mean?" (4:6, 21) is a significant question as it will provide Israel the opportunity to teach the next generations about the deliverance of Israel out of Egypt, the crossing of the Sea of Reeds, and the crossing of the Jordan into Canaan. In the Passover account (Exod 12–13), Moses introduces a similar question to be asked by curious children who will one day participate in the celebration. They will surely ask, "What does this ceremony mean?" (12:26) Again, the elders will have the opportunity to teach the younger generations about the mighty deeds of the Lord at the Sea of Reeds and at the Jordan River.

Dry Ground

In both crossing accounts, the Israelites march through a body of water on dry ground (Exod 14:16–18; 15:19; Josh 3:17; 4:18–22). According to Fishbane, the Israelites crossed the Jordan "in springtime, at harvest season, when the torrents of water piled up around them like a wall" (Josh 4:18–19).[24] Some have suggested that the parting of the waters of the Sea of Reeds and the Jordan River were due to natural causes and were void of supernatural intervention. This theory is based on the idea that the waters

22. See Cross Jr., "The Song of the Sea and Canaanite Myth," 11–13; A. J. Ehlen, "Deliverance at the Sea: Diversity and Unity in a Biblical Theme," *CTM* 44, no. 3 (1973) 168–91, esp. 172–74.

23. Ehlen, "Deliverance at the Sea," 173.

24. Fishbane, *Text and Texture*, 123.

of these two bodies of water could have gathered in one place by the natural force of the wind. Although this may be possible since an "east wind" is mentioned in Exod 14:21, the event was nonetheless orchestrated by God who controls the natural elements. In Thomas Soltis's view, "an abatement of the waters due to purely natural phenomena of winds and tides could hardly accomplish the feat of providing a bone-dry path through the sea in the short span of one night,"[25] and "scientific theologians . . . who strip Scripture of the miraculous . . . also strip God of His omnipotence in the eyes of mankind."[26]

Aliens among Them

During the exodus, a mixed multitude of non-Israelites joins Israel for the expedition (Exod 12:38). The social status of many of these non-Israelites was equal to that of the children of Israel while others remained on the margins of society (12:43–48). Vogels sees only minor distinctions in the social status of foreigners who joined Israel and those of Israelites. He fails to discuss the distinctions that exist between the circumcised and uncircumcised, the native and non-native, and the hired and non-hired worker who join the Israelites for the Passover celebration in Egypt (12:43–49).[27] According to Vogels,

> Dans cette période les personnes liminales, les néophytes ou les novices forment entre eux une vraie *communauté*, basée sur une parfaite égalité. Le groupe liminal constitue une communauté d'amis et non pas une société structurée avec des positions hiérarchiques. . . . Le sujet liminal a laissé derrière lui une structure sociale et il rentrera plus tard dans une nouvelle structure sociale, mais pendant la période liminale il vit la camaraderie sans distinction de classes ou de rangs. . . . par ailleurs, entre les néophytes et les instructeurs il y a *authorité et soumission absolues*.[28]

25. Thomas Soltis, "Scientific Theology and the Miracle at the Red Sea," *Springfielder* 38, no. 1 (1974) 55–59, esp. 58.

26. Ibid., 59.

27. For a discussion of this topic, see Matthew J. Hollomon, "The Place of the non-Israelite in Pre-exilic Israelite Society," MA thesis, Denver Seminary, 2013.

28. Translation: "During this period, liminal characters, proselytes and novices form among themselves a real community, based on a perfect egalitarian system. The liminal group is formed of a community of friends and not of an organized social group with a hierarchical system . . . The liminal character leaves behind a social structure, but in the future, he will reenter a new social structure. During this interim period, he lives among friends, without an organized class system . . . However, absolute authority and

In the second crossing narrative, Israel once again welcomes non-Israelites into her midst. To the two spies who are sent to survey Jericho, Rahab—a non-Israelite—reveals her knowledge of the exodus as she states, "We have heard how the Lord dried up the water of the Red Sea for you when you came out of Egypt" (Josh 2:10). Through successful negotiations with the two spies, Rahab and her family are permitted to join the community and to live in the midst of Israel permanently (6:22–25).

Promise-Fulfillment and the Land

The exodus and the acquisition of a homeland for Israel are mentioned frequently as unified themes throughout Scripture. The deliverance of Israel from the bondage of Egypt is directly linked to the acquisition of her territorial inheritance (Exod 3:8, 17; 6:4, 8; 12:25; 13:3–5). The Exodus represents a *going out* (יצא) of bondage while the entry into Canaan is defined as a *coming into* (בוא) the inheritance.[29] While the Exodus points back to the patriarchal age (when a territorial inheritance is promised to Abram and his seed, e.g., Gen 12:6; 13:15; 15:7, 18; 17:8; 24:7; 26:1–4; 28:4, 13, 15; 35:12; 40:15; 50:24), it also points forward to the fulfillment of the promise. The acquisition of a specific geographical area—a land filled with milk and honey—given to Israel as a territorial inheritance from God is mentioned numerous times in scripture (Exod 3:8, 17; 33:3; Lev 20:24; Num 13:27; 14:8; Judg 2:1).[30] In many cases, the procurement of the land is directly re-

---

submission exists between the proselyte and his [Israelite] leader" (Vogels, "D'Égypte À Canaan," 29–30).

29. This word pair functions as a merism, where יצא (*going out*) and בוא (*coming in*) indicate the completed work of promise/fulfillment (e.g., Exod 6:6–8,"I brought you out of Egypt . . . I will bring you to the land"). See also Gen 50:24; Exod 3:17; Lev 25:38; Num 16:13. Studies have shown that the word pair יצא/בוא often appears in military and political narratives where someone is identified as a successful military leader (e.g., Num 27:17; Deut 31:2; Josh 14:11; 1 Sam 18:6, 13, 16; 29:6; 2 Sam 3:25). See Anton van der Lingen, "*BW'-YS'* ("To Go Out and To Come In") as a Military Term, " *VT* 42, no. 1 (1992) 59–66. The word pair appears in other contexts, e.g., Deut 28:6, 19 (blessings and curses); 2 Kgs 11:8 // 2 Chr 23:7 (Joash entering and exiting the Temple); Jer 37:4 (Jeremiah coming in and out of the city); Ps 121:8 (THE LORD keeping one's going out and coming in).

30. The expression "land flowing with milk and honey" appears at least twenty times in the HB. It reflects language from the Egyptian talk of Sinuhe who lived during the twentieth century BCE and fled his native Egypt to find exile in Canaan. Sinuhe describes Canaan as "a good land . . . Figs were in it, and grapes. It had more wine than water. Plentiful was its honey, abundant its olives. Every [kind of] fruit was on its trees. Barley was there, and emmer. There was no limit to any [kind of] cattle" (ANET 80). A second Egyptian text that describes the fruitfulness of Canaan appears in a military campaign of Thutmoses III (ca. 1490–1436 BCE) in Karnak. The text mentions that the

lated to the purpose of the exodus out of Egypt (Judg 6:8–9; Amos 2:10). Without this promise of a physical, geographical location for Israel, the book of Joshua is incomprehensible and perplexing.

Theophanies

While shepherding his father-in-law's sheep deep into the wilderness (Exod 3:1), Moses encounters an "angel of the Lord" who identifies himself as "the God of Abraham, the God of Isaac, and the God of Jacob" (3:6).[31] Joshua has a similar encounter with a messenger near Jericho. Labeling himself as "commander of the army of the Lord," a mysterious visitor with a drawn sword in his hand meets Joshua. The messenger echoes the same command given by the angel of the Lord to Moses in the wilderness: "Put off your shoes from your feet, for the place where you stand is holy" (Exod 3:5; Josh 5:15).[32] This identical utterance confirms that the events of both crossing accounts are connected, though in reverse order. In the case of Moses, the encounter takes place before the crossing of the Sea of Reeds, while the theophany in Joshua occurs after the crossing of the Jordan.

In both cases, the encounter is unexpected. In both accounts, the recipient of the theophany and the location of the encounter are mentioned (Moses at Horeb and Joshua at Jericho). The response of both leaders is that of curiosity and involves the face. Recognizing the superiority of the messengers, Moses hides his face,[33] fearing the consequences of seeing God (Exod 3:6), while Joshua falls on his face to the ground and worships (Josh 5:14).[34] In the Exodus account, it is likely that Moses did not know how to approach "holy ground" since he had never encountered God before. For him, there was no sanctity to a burning bush in the wilderness in the heat of the day. As for Joshua, his encounters with the divine over decades

---

Phoenician coast had "various [kinds of] bread, with olive oil, incense, wine, honey, fruit . . . They were more abundant than anything" (ANET 237–38).

31. Such encounters also occur in Gen 16:7, 9, 11; 21:17 (Hagar); 22:11, 15 (Abraham); 31:11; 48:16 (Jacob); Judg 6:11 (Gideon); 13:3, 6, 9, 13, 15, 16 [2x] (Manoah and his wife).

32. Minor differences exist between the two passages: (1) Exod 3:5—"*your feet*" (רגליך); Josh 5:15—"*your foot*" (2) (רגליך); Exod 3:5—"*is holy ground*" (אדמת־קדש הוא); Josh 5:15—"*is holy* (קדש הוא)."

33. For additional examples of "hiding one's face," see Deut 31:17; 32:20; Job 13:24; 34:29; Pss 10:11; 13:1[2]; 22:24[25]; 27:9; 30:7[8]; 44:24[25]; 51:9[11]; 88:14[15]; 102:2[3]; 143:7; Isa 8:17; 54:8; 59:2; 64:7[6]; Jer 33:5; Ezek 39:23, 24, 29; Mic 3:4.

34. For additional examples of "falling on one's face," see Gen 17:3, 17; Lev 9:24; Num 14:5; 16:4, 22, 45; 20:6; 22:31; Josh 7:6; Judg 13:20; Ruth 2:10; 1 Sam 5:3; 17:49; 20:41; 25:23; 2 Sam 9:6; 14:4, 22; 1 Kgs 18:7; etc.

of service at Moses' side may have made him more attuned to such divine encounters. It is possible that, during their time together in the wilderness, Moses would have shared his burning bush story with Joshua.

Literary Features

As mentioned in the introduction to this chapter, additional features that contribute to the relationship between the exodus and the book of Joshua are listed in this concluding section of the chapter. The following list focuses primarily on the literary and linguistic parallels that exist between the crossing narratives. As shown in the chart, several *inclusios* support Vogels paradigm of a concentric chiastic structure for the narrative from the exodus to the entry into Canaan (see introduction to the chapter).[35]

Features	Exodus	Joshua
Inclusio: *Before—After*	Taking plunder from enemies before leaving Egypt (Exod 3:21–22)	Taking plunder from enemies after entering Canaan (Josh 8:2, 27; 11:14; 22:8)
Inclusio: *Before—After*	Circumcision of non-Israelite males before leaving Egypt (Exod 12:43–49)	Circumcision of Israelite males after entering Canaan (Josh 5:2–8)
Inclusio: *Before—After*	Passover celebration before leaving Egypt (Exod 12:1–28)	Passover celebration after entering Canaan (Josh 5:10–12)
Inclusio: *Before—After*	Divine use of natural elements before leaving Egypt (pillar of cloud and fire—Exod 13:21; 14:24)[1]	Divine use of natural elements after entering Canaan (hailstones—Josh 10:11)

1. For a discussion on the "pillar of cloud" as a symbol of the deity in the exodus narrative and in Ugaritic literature, see Thomas W. Mann, "The Pillar of Cloud in the Reed Sea Narrative," JBL 90, no. 1 (1971) 15–30. Mann proposes that both the "pillar of cloud" in the exodus narrative and the Ark of the Covenant in the crossing of the Jordan serve the same purposes. They indicate the presence of God in the midst of his people and the element that served to show them the way (Exod 13:21—ויהוה הלך לפניהם יומם בעמוד ענן הדרך לנחתם—*the Lord went before them during the day in a pillar of* cloud to lead them in the way; Josh 3:4—למען אשר תדעו את־הדרך אשר תלכו־בה—"[keep a distance between you and the Ark] so that you may know the way in which you should go") when crossing the Jordan.

35. Vogels, "D'Égypte À Canaan," 24.

Features	Exodus	Joshua
Inclusio: *Before—After*	Before leaving Egypt, the Israelites plundered the Egyptians and left with treasures of Egypt (Exod 3:21–22; 12:35–36; 14:23–28)	After entering Canaan, the Israelites plundered some of the Canaanite cities (Josh 6:24; 8:27; 11:14; 22:8)
Inclusio *Before—After*	Before the exodus, the Egyptian taskmasters burden the Israelites with hard labor (Exod 1:11; 2:11)	After entering Canaan, the Israelites burden the Canaanites with forced labor (Josh 16:10; 17:13)
Inclusio *Before—After*	Before leaving Egypt, Moses faces a foreign leader—Pharaoh (Exod 5:1–2; 6:11–13; 7:10)	After entering Canaan, Joshua faces Canaanite kings (Josh 6:2; 8:1; 9:1–2; 10:1–5; 11:1–5)
Before—Before	Trouble at the edge of the water before leaving Egypt (Exod 14:10–15)[2]	Trouble at the edge of the water before entering Canaan (Shittim, Peor—Num 15; Josh 22:15–17)
During—During	Pillar of cloud and fire as a symbol of the presence of the Lord during the crossing (Exod 13:21–22)	Ark of the Covenant as a symbol of the presence of the Lord during the crossing (Josh 3:4, 14; 4:10, 18)
After—After	Manna begins after leaving Egypt (Exod 16)	Manna ends after entering Canaan (Josh 5:10–12)
Repetition of expression	"Three days" (Exod 3:18; 5:3; 8:27; 10:22–23; 15:22)	"Three days" (Josh 2:16, 22; 3:2; 9:16)
Repetition of expression	"Hearts of enemies melting in fear after hearing about the Sea of Reeds event" (Josh 2:9–10)	"Hearts of enemies melting in fear after hearing about Jordan crossing" (Josh 5:1)
Repetition of expression	"Dry land" יבשה (Exod 14:6, 22, 29; 15:19)	"Dry land" יבשה (Josh 4:22)

2. After both crossings, trouble in the camp of Israel occurs on a number of occasions. After the crossing the Sea of Reeds, there are complaints over bitter water (Exod 15:22), over fear of starvation (16:1), and over a drought (17:1). After crossing the Jordan, we read about Achan's sin and the destruction of his family (Josh 7).

Features	Exodus	Joshua
Repetition of expression	"Pass over—cross over" עבר (Exod 12:12, 23; 13:12; 15:16; 17:5)	"Pass over—cross over" עבר (Josh 1:11, 14–15; 2:23; 3:1, 4, 6, 11, 14, 16–17; 4:1, 3, 5, 7, 10–13; 4:22–23)
Repetition of expression	"Prepared for battle" חמושים (Exod 13:18)[3]	"Prepared for battle" חמושים (Josh 1:14; 4:12)[4]

3. According to van Seters, "it would also seem that the detail in Ex. 13:18 about the people being 'armed' (*hamushim*) when they left Egypt is directly dependent upon the statement that the eastern tribes also crossed the Jordan 'armed' (*hamushim*), Josh 4:12 (cf. 1:14)." Van Seters, *The Life of Moses*, 144.

4. This word occurs only four times in the HB, once in the exodus account (Exod 13:18), twice in the Jordan crossing account (Josh 1:14; 4:12), and once in the book of Judges (Judg 7:11).

Conclusion

In conclusion, the crossing of the Jordan in the book of Joshua completes the wilderness journey that begins with the exodus out of Egypt. As God never intended for His people to live permanently under the oppression of foreign rulers (e.g., Egypt), He also

> never intended for his people Israel to be without a homeland. From the beginning of Israel's history, the plan was disclosed. To Abraham, God promised a growing family and a place where this family would thrive and flourish (Gen 12:1–3). . . . The patriarchs (Abraham, Isaac, and Jacob) settled in Canaan—the Promised Land. Living elsewhere always meant living in a foreign land (Gen 15:13//Acts 7:6; Ex 2:22; 3:18; Ps 137:4). The purpose of the exodus was to free Israel from slavery in Egypt and to bring her to the land promised to her centuries earlier (Ex 3:8, 17; 6:8; 13:5; 20:12; 23:23). The journey in the wilderness always pointed toward the land (Num 14:7–9; 15:1–2; 26:52–55; Dt 11:10–15), and the rest of Israel's history takes place primarily in the land.[36]

The book of Joshua is structured in such a way that the exodus is remembered, paralleled, alluded to, or mentioned in nearly every chapter. It is impossible to escape its influence on the book. "Joshua builds on the theology of the exodus deliverance."[37] The sacred act of leaving Egypt through di-

36. Dallaire, "Joshua," 837.
37. Adolph L. Harstad, *Joshua* (Saint Louis: Concordia, 2004) 29.

vine intervention is completed by the sacred act of entering Canaan through a second miraculous event. Joined together by leaders, divine encounters, journeys on dry ground, Passover celebrations, and focus on a homeland, the exodus out of Egypt and the book of Joshua are forever knit together into the fabric of Israel's history.

3

The Psalms, the Exodus, and Israel's Worship

Daniel J. Estes

Introduction

In the book of Psalms, the exodus of Israel from Egyptian bondage plays a prominent role in Israel's recollection of its national history and in its worship of YHWH. As Erik Haglund notes, the exodus, together with its associated events, "is the most common historical motif in the Book of Psalms,"[1] and Clark Hyde observes, "The deliverance from Egypt established Israel's corporate identity and served throughout her history as the paradigm of the relationship of Yahweh with the people."[2] Nevertheless, the scholarly literature on the exodus in the Psalms is relatively scant, with a notable exception of the recent article by Susan Gillingham,[3] which is a helpful impetus to the investigation of this important subject.

---

1. Erik Haglund, *Historical Motifs in the Psalms*, ConBOT 23 (Uppsala: CWK Glerup, 1984) 102.

2. Clark Hyde, "The Remembrance of the Exodus in the Psalms," *Worship* 62 (1988) 404. Cf. also the discussion in Aarre Lauha, *Die Geschichtsmotive in den alttestamentlichen Psalmen*, AASF 56 (Helsinki: Finnische Literaturgesellschaft, 1945) 45–91, 128–44.

3. Susan Gillingham, "The Exodus and Israelite Psalmody," *SJT* 52 (1999) 19–46, and esp. 19n3, in which she cites five prior relevant articles. She remarks that it is surprising that so few scholars have attempted to answer why the psalmists use the exodus narratives as they do: "Commentaries on the Psalms make little of it. Introductions to the Psalter have minimal discussion of it; and only a handful of articles are relevant in this respect."

A broad understanding of the exodus could conceivably span all of the events beginning with the cries of Israel for relief from their Egyptian bondage (Exod 2:23–25) up through the settlement in the land of Canaan (Joshua), but the scope of this paper is limited to three major episodes in the narrative in Exod 14–15: the deliverance of Israel at the ים סוף (Exod 14:19–22), the destruction of Pharaoh and his army and the rescue of Israel (Exod 14:23–31), and the subsequent rejoicing by Israel (Exod 15:1–21). It examines how the Psalms make reference to these episodes, and how these historical scenes function within the worship of Israel.[4] Other antecedent and subsequent events in Israel's history, including the Egyptian bondage, the call of Moses, the plagues in Egypt, the Sinai theophany, the wilderness wanderings, and the conquest, although mentioned in the Psalms, lie beyond the purview of the present study.

In considering how the Psalms make use of the exodus experience, this paper employs approaches drawn from the extensive scholarly literature on intertextuality. Although precursors of what is now called intertextuality can be traced back to ancient times, over the past fifty years it has become an increasingly important dimension of the study of biblical texts.[5] At the same time, appropriate cautions about the potential abuses of intertextuality have been raised by David Penchansky,[6] who warns against mere cross-referencing rather than genuine interaction with the ideological climate of the text, and Ellen van Wolde,[7] who insists that intertextuality must regard the later text as digesting and rearranging the earlier text.

As the collection of essays edited by Dennis MacDonald demonstrates, the modern approach of intertextuality was anticipated by the model of mimesis in the literature of classical Greece, second temple Judaism, and early

---

4. As Jörg Jeremias observes, "It was this act of God that became the reference point for any subsequent praise, and in the reiterations of salvation experiences in later hymns, this deed very often stands at the beginning." See Jeremias, "Worship and Theology in the Psalms," in *Psalms and Liturgy*, eds. Dirk J. Human and Cas J. A. Vos, JSOTSup 410 (London: T. & T. Clark, 2004) 91.

5. Recent surveys of intertextuality include Jeffrey M. Leonard, "Identifying Inner-Biblical Allusions: Psalm 78 as a Test Case," *JBL* 127 (2008) 241–65; Cynthia Edenburg, "Intertextuality, Literary Competence and the Question of Readership: Some Preliminary Observations," *JSOT* 35 (2010) 131–48; and Will Kynes, *My Psalm Has Turned into Weeping: Job's Dialogue with the Psalms*, BZAW 437 (Berlin: de Gruyter, 2012).

6. David Penchansky, "Staying the Night: Intertextuality in Genesis and Judges," in *Reading Between Texts: Intertextuality and the Hebrew Bible*, ed. Danna Nolan Fewell, LCBI (Louisville, KY: Westminster John Knox, 1992) 77–88.

7. Ellen van Wolde, "Trendy Intertexuality?" in *Intertextuality in Biblical Writings: Essays in honour of Bas van Iersel*, ed. Sipke Draisma (Kampel: Uitgeversmaatschappij J. H. Kok, 1989) 46.

Christianity.[8] This common ancient approach was given fresh impetus in the 1960s by literary theorists, prominently Julia Kristeva, who rejected the prevailing notion of the autonomy of a literary text, and instead emphasized how the study of the reuse of prior texts enriches the understanding of the text under consideration.[9]

In his notable study of ancient Jewish biblical interpretation, Michael Fishbane employed what he called inner-biblical exegesis as he explored connections within the biblical texts.[10] Beth LaNeel Tanner notes that Fishbane, although employing somewhat different terminology, was describing in the biblical texts and Jewish midrashim "exactly what Kristeva and others have described in theory; the transformation of pieces of law, story, and poetry via another reader-writer's ideology and historical circumstance."[11]

At nearly the same time, NT scholar Richard Hays in his examination of Paul's use of OT texts expanded upon the insights of Fishbane, but he also made explicit use of the language of the literary theorists as well. Hays argued that later biblical texts quoted and alluded to earlier texts in a fashion that he, following John Hollander, called metalepsis. In his thinking, "when a literary echo links the text in which it occurs to an earlier text, the figurative effect of the echo can lie in the unstated or suppressed (transumed) points of resonance between the two texts."[12]

With intertextuality now appropriated by biblical scholars, it was only a matter of time until the Psalms would be scrutinized in this way. In 2001, Beth LaNeel Tanner devoted her doctoral dissertation[13] to the study of the Psalms through the lens of intertextuality, in particular making use of the historical superscriptions and discussing how the Psalms were appropriated in a variety of NT texts.

8. Dennis R. MacDonald, ed., *Mimesis and Intertextuality in Antiquity and Christianity*, StAC (Harrisburg, PA: Trinity, 2001).

9. This point is made by Beth LaNeel Tanner, *The Book of Psalms Through the Lens of Intertextuality*, StBL 26 (New York: Lang, 2001) 5–47, in the succinct but comprehensive survey of six prominent paradigms of intertextuality by new literary critics (Julia Kristeva, Harold Bloom, Roland Barthes, Michael Rifaterre, Jonathan Culler, and Gérard Genette).

10. Michael Fishbane, *Biblical Interpretation in Ancient Israel*, 2nd ed. (Oxford: Clarendon, 1988). Note also the useful bibliography on inner-biblical exegesis in Leonard, "Identifying Inner Biblical Allusions," 241n1.

11. Tanner, *The Book of Psalms*, 29.

12. Richard B. Hays, *Echoes of Scripture in the Letters of Paul* (New Haven: Yale University Press, 1989) 20.

13. Tanner, *The Book of Psalms*. Her first two chapters provide a strong methodological foundation for the final four chapters, in which she applies the intertextual method to Pss 90, 112, 88, and kingship psalms.

In his recent groundbreaking study of textuality and education in the ancient world,[14] David Carr demonstrates that texts were not primarily transmitted in written form, but far more frequently they were memorized and recited in oral form. Consequently, it is important to be alert to the sounds of the text and their potential for intertextual significance. Because the biblical texts were committed to memory and passed on in this fashion, it is not surprising that later biblical texts, such as the Psalms, would use and adapt prior texts, such as the exodus narratives.

It must be acknowledged at the outset that intertextuality has been used by various scholars to describe a broad range of literary phenomena, only some of which are germane to the present study. As Peter Miscall observes in his discussion of the book of Isaiah, intertextuality "is a covering term for all the possible relations that can be established between texts. The relation can be based on anything from quotes and direct references to indirect allusions to common words and even letters to dependence on language itself. The effect of the relations can extend from support and agreement to one text's rejection and attempted destruction of the other."[15] Before purported intertextual links are analyzed, there must be a standard for evaluating them. Several scholars have formulated useful guidelines, chief among them Hays, whose criteria for identifying and interpreting intertextual references in *Echoes of Scripture in the Letters of Paul* (1989) were later expanded and illustrated in *The Conversion of the Imagination* (2005).[16] This paper proceeds on the basis of the standards proposed by Hays.

Intertextuality spans a range of textual links from quotations, which are explicitly stated references to a prior text, all the way to echoes, which are subtle, implicit references.[17] Between these endpoints lie allusions, in which prior texts are indirectly invoked and yet without direct quotation textual markers are given to alert the reader to the reference.[18] Hays notes

14. David M. Carr, *Writing on the Tablet of the Heart: Origins of Scripture and Literature* (Oxford: Oxford University Press, 2005).

15. Peter D. Miscall, "Isaiah: New Heavens, New Earth, New Book," in *Reading Between Texts*, 44.

16. Other helpful sets of guidelines have been formulated by MacDonald, "Introduction," 2–3 from his study of mimesis in ancient texts, and in Leonard, "Identifying Inner-Biblical Allusions," 246–57, and Paul R. Noble, "Esau, Tamar, and Joseph: Criteria for Identifying Inner-Biblical Allusions," *VT* 52 (2002) 219–52, from their analyses of biblical texts.

17. John Hollander, *The Figure of Echo: A Mode of Allusion in Milton and After* (Berkely, CA: University of California Press, 1981), provides an extensive explanation of echo drawn from his analysis of Milton.

18. Edenburg, "Intertextuality," 144; Andrew H. Wakefield, "When Scripture Meets Scripture," *RevExp* 106 (2009) 553; and esp. the important theoretical discussion in

well: "Quotation, allusion and echo may be seen as points along a spectrum of intertextual reference, moving from the explicit to the subliminal. As we move farther away from overt citation, the source recedes into the discursive distance, the intertextual relations become less determinate, and the demand placed on the reader's listening powers grows greater."[19] Consequently, the study of intertextual references requires as much the aesthetic sensitivity of the artist as the technical prowess of the scientist.[20]

In this paper, three episodes in the narrative of Exod 14–15 are examined. For each episode, intertextual links in Psalms will be identified, including quotations, allusions, and echoes, to demonstrate how the language of the exodus reverberates in the Psalter. The summary section will discuss how the lament and praise psalms function in part as liturgical reverberations of the exodus narrative.

Deliverance of Israel at the יָם סוּף

The deliverance of Israel at the יָם סוּף is presented in narrative form in Exod 14:19–22. YHWH, working by the agency of the angel of God, initiated the action by moving his accompanying pillar of cloud (cf. Exod 13:21–22) so that it served as a barrier between the Israelites and the Egyptian army that pursued them (Exod 14:19–20). Just when there seemed no way for the Israelites to escape calamity, YHWH intervened on their behalf. Throughout the night, the pillar of cloud kept the Egyptians in darkness, but it provided light for the Israelites, facilitating their flight from their previous masters.

When Moses stretched his hand over the sea (Exod 14:21), YHWH employed the natural force of the east wind in a supernatural way[21] to divide the waters, replicating the divine action on the third day of creation (Gen 1:9–10). The Israelites walked through the sea on dry ground framed by towering walls of water on either side of them. As Terrence Fretheim notes, this constituted an act of faith by the Israelites, as they appropriated YHWH's gracious provision for their deliverance.[22]

Ziva Ben-Porat, "The Poetics of Literary Allusion," *PTL: A Journal for Descriptive Poetics and Theory of Literature* 1 (1976) 105–28.

19. Hays, *Echoes*, 23.

20. Richard B. Hays, *The Conversion of the Imagination: Paul as Interpreter of Israel's Scripture* (Grand Rapids: Eerdmans, 2005) 30.

21. Victor P. Hamilton, *Exodus: An Exegetical Commentary* (Grand Rapids: Baker Academic, 2011) 217.

22. Terrence E. Fretheim, *Exodus*, Int (Louisville: John Knox, 1991) 159.

Quotations

Four passages in the Psalms quote in part the language of Exod 14:19–22.
The historical referent in Ps 66:6 is debated, with numerous scholars taking only line "a" to refer to the crossing of the ים סוף and line "b" to the
crossing of the Jordan River in Josh 3:14–17 (e.g., Erhard Gerstenberger;
Artur Weiser), but others make stronger arguments in support of viewing
the whole verse as recalling the deliverance of Israel from Egypt. Marvin
Tate observes that "river" (נהר) is not used elsewhere for the Jordan, but
in verses such as Jonah 2:4 and Ps 93:3–4 it is used for the sea.[23] To this,
John Goldingay adds evidence from Ugaritic texts "where both words can
refer to waters that embody threatening and assertive cosmic forces such as
were indeed embodied in the Red Sea."[24] In Ps 66:6, "sea" (ים) directly cites
the language of Exod 14:21 (cf. Exod 14:16, 21–23, 27–29 in the immediate context), and "dry land" (יבשה) repeats the term found in Exod 14:22,
as well as in Exod 14:16, 29; 15:19. In addition, the verb "passed through"
(עבר) recalls the poetic description of Israel's deliverance in Exod 15:16, and
"waters" (מים) hearkens back to the motif in Exod 14:21–22.

Psalm 78:13 employs several of the same textual citations as are evident in Ps 66:6, including "sea" (ים), "led through" (עבר), and "water" (מים).
The psalmist also speaks of how God divided the sea, using the same verb
(בקע) as was used with Moses as subject in Exod 14:16 and with YHWH
as subject in Exod 14:21; 15:18. As a result of this tangible demonstration
of God's power on behalf of his people, the waters stood up like a wall, a
description using the same language (נצב נד) as is found in Exod 15:8, although somewhat different from what is stated in Exod 14:22.[25]

The third passage in the Psalms directly citing the language in Exod
14:19–22 is Ps 106:9. Weiser argues that the textual differences between
these two passages indicate that there is no direct literary dependence between them, but that both texts originated in a common liturgical tradition.[26] It is true that Ps 106 does employ many terms that diverge from the

23. Marvin E. Tate, *Psalms 51–100*, WBC 20 (Dallas: Word, 1990) 149. His position
is supported by Frank-Lothar Hossfeld and Erich Zenger, *Psalms 2: A Commentary on
Psalms 51–100*, trans. Linda M. Maloney (Minneapolis: Fortress, 2005) 145.

24. John Goldingay, *Psalms Volume 2: Psalms 42–89*, Baker Commentary on the
Old Testament Wisdom and Psalms (Grand Rapids: Baker Academic, 2007) 290.

25. Leonard, "Identifying Inner-Biblical Allusions," 251–52, notes that the similarity of expression in Ps 78:13 and Exod 15:8 indicates that they are likely directly connected, particularly when it is considered that the term for "heap" (נד) is used only six
times in the HB.

26. Artur Weiser, *The Psalms: A Commentary*, trans. Herbert Hartwell, OTL (Philadelphia: Westminster, 1962) 681. A similar position is taken by Neil H. Richardson,
"Psalm 106: Yahweh's Succoring Love Saves from the Death of a Broken Covenant," in

narrative in Exodus, but there are also some repeated terms that suggest a degree of explicit quotation. Once again, "sea" (ים) recalls the language of Exod 14:21–22. In addition, the verb חרב ("dried up") is from the same root as the noun חרבה used for "dry ground" in Exod 14:21.

Psalm 136:13–14 provides the fourth example of direct quotation of the language of Exod 14:19–22 in the Psalter. Once again, "sea" (ים) occurs in Ps 136:13, and it is linked in verse 14 with "the midst of it" (בתוכו), closely matching "through the sea" (בתוך הים) in Exod 14:22. The same verse recalls that YHWH brought Israel through the sea, just as Exod 14:22 narrates that the Israelites went through the sea. Moreover, as in Pss 66:6 and 78:13, the verb "brought" (עבר) suggests a verbal link with Exod 15:16. This recollection of the exodus experience is part of the historical remembrance of YHWH's enduring love (חסד), which in Ps 136 is the cause for the worshiping community of Israel to give thanks to him. An experience that seemed so traumatic at the time became a touchstone for Israel's faith and worship.

Allusion

In addition to the direct quotations of the narrative in Exod 14:19–22, an allusion to the deliverance of Israel at the ים סוף can be detected in Ps 114:3, 5. This psalm employs highly poetic language that personifies the sea as it depicts the dividing of the waters from the perspective of the sea. Rather than forming a wall, as in the Exodus narrative, the sea instead flees as a defeated army before the Lord.[27] Psalm 114 also links the experience at the ים סוף with the later crossing of the Jordan, with both incidents serving as the impetus for the psalmist's expectation of the Lord's future intervention on behalf of Israel in 114:7–8. David Kennedy notes well,

> The psalm is not content merely to recount the exodus as an event. It certainly does not deny the historicity of the exodus, but instead returns to the exodus as a starting point in order to understand its significance. The same God who redeemed and covenanted with Israel in the past is called upon to do it again with his people in a new day. Because he was present in the past, he is expected to make his presence known again to a new generation.[28]

Love & Death in the Ancient Near East: Essays in Honor of Marvin H. Pope, eds. John H. Marks and Robert M. Good (Guilford, CT: Four Quarters, 1987) 194, who regards this psalm as a free retelling of the exodus experience without specific verbal quotations.

27. Frank-Lothar Hossfeld and Erich Zenger, *Psalms 3: A Commentary on Psalms 101–50*, trans. Linda M. Maloney (Minneapolis: Fortress, 2011) 195.

28. David B. Kennedy, "Hermeneutics and Psalm 114: The Meaning and Significance of the Exodus," paper presented at Midwestern ETS, March 25, 1989, p. 11.

Echoes

There also appear to be some subtle, implicit echoes to Exod 14:19–22 in psalmic passages in which there are no textual markers to the exodus experience. For example, the angel of God who accompanied Israel in Exod 14:19 may be compared to the angel of YHWH in Ps 34:7[8] who encamps around and delivers those who fear YHWH, as well as the angels who are commanded by YHWH to guard the psalmist in all his ways (Ps 91:11).

The strong east wind that YHWH used to divide the waters of the ים סוף (Exod 14:21) recurs in Ps 48:7[8], when YHWH destroyed kings "like ships of Tarshish shattered by an east wind." Even fainter echoes may possibly be detected in Pss 147:18 and 148:8, when the winds are depicted as doing YHWH's bidding.

In Ps 74:13–17, the language in the exodus narrative that speaks of YHWH dividing the waters of the sea (Exod 14:21) is adapted to describe in poetical terms his triumph over the forces of chaos, likely making use of Canaanite mythological language with a polemical intent. As Grisanti notes well, "What Baal could only claim in mythology, Yahweh actually performed in history"[29] as he created the world.

Destruction of Pharaoh's Army and the Rescue of Israel

The narrative in Exodus continues to describe how YHWH destroyed the army of Pharaoh as at the same time he rescued Israel (Exod 14:23–31). When the Egyptians recognized that the Israelites had gone through the sea on dry ground, their pursuit led to their undoing. Tactically, the Egyptians took the highly risky step of following the Israelites along the sea bed with chariots and horses that were much heavier than the Israelites, who walked along it (14:23). Mentally, the Egyptians were thrown into confusion by YHWH (14:24). The chariots experienced mechanical difficulties (14:25), perhaps as suggested by the LXX because the wheels became jammed with seaweed or reeds.[30] Stricken by terror, the Egyptians turned to flee from the Israelites and back to the shore, acknowledging that YHWH was fighting for the Israelites. As YHWH had predicted in Exod 14:4, 18, they had come to know that he was YHWH, in contrast to the arrogant dismissal of YHWH made previously by Pharaoh (Exod 5:2).

29. *NIDOTTE* 2:931.

30. John H. Stek, "What Happened to the Chariot Wheels of Exod 14:25?" *JBL* 105 (1986) 293–94.

as you are rescuing me, you are destroying my enemies

Their attempted evasive action, however, was too late, because when Moses at YHWH's command again stretched out his hand over the sea, the waters returned to their place and the entire army of Pharaoh was destroyed (Exod 14:26–28). By contrast, the Israelites had gone through the sea on dry ground (14:29). As YHWH saved Israel from the hands of the Egyptians (14:30), the Israelites saw the mighty hand of YHWH (14:31). In contrast to 14:10, where the sight of the approaching Egyptian army prompted the Israelites to be terrified (ירא), in 14:31 witnessing the mighty hand of YHWH against the Egyptians caused the Israelites to fear (ירא) him.

Quotations

Three psalms explicitly quote the language of Exod 14:23–31 as they recall the destruction of Pharaoh's army and the concurrent deliverance of Israel. Psalm 78 focuses on remembering the praiseworthy deeds of YHWH by telling them to the next generation (78:1–8). As the psalm details some of the interventions by YHWH on behalf of Israel, in verse 53 it states that the sea (ים) engulfed (כסה) their enemies, citing the exact terms used in Exod 14:28.

In Ps 106:10–12, the phrase "he saved (ישע) them from the hand (מיד) of the foe" in verse 10 precisely duplicates terms in Exod 14:30. In verse 11, three words—waters (מים), covered (כסה), and one (אחד)—repeat the language in Exod 14:28. Verse 12 recalls that the Israelites believed (אמן) YHWH's promises (cf. Exod 14:31).

Psalm 136:15 employs the rare verb נער, a term found in the OT only twelve times, but significantly also in Exod 14:27, to describe how YHWH swept Pharaoh and his army into the ים סוף. This historical reference is located in Ps 136 in a liturgy that uses YHWH's deeds in creation and history to emphasize his sovereign control and care for his people. Dirk Human notes perceptively: "For Israel this deliverance did not remain a mere fact of the past. Time and again the Israelites have experienced God's power in consecutive situations of hopelessness."[31]

Allusions

In the ancient world, horses and chariots were state of the art military forces, so references to them can be found throughout the OT. When the psalmist in Ps 20:7[8] contrasts those who trust in chariots and horses with

---

31. Dirk J. Human, "Psalm 136: A Liturgy with Reference to Creation and History," in *Psalms and Liturgy*, 73–88, esp. 86.

the worshiping community that trusts in the name of YHWH their God, he does not make a direct reference to the exodus experience (although similar language is used in Exod 14:23, 26, 28). Nevertheless, the juxtaposed verse that follows, portraying the enemies as brought to their knees and fallen in contrast to the people of YHWH who rise up and stand firm, hints that the psalmist is alluding to the drowning of Pharaoh's army and Israel's passage through the sea on dry ground.

Similar language is used in Ps 76:6[7], where the references to the horse and chariot are not linked directly with the exodus. It should also be noted that YHWH's rebuke, which in this psalm defeats valiant warriors (76:5[6]), refers in Pss 18:15[16] and 104:7 to YHWH's subjugation of the waters in his battle with chaos, a motif that parallels the poetic language in Exod 15.[32]

Echoes

As the Israelites sang their psalms, it is plausible that the familiar text of the exodus experience of their ancestors sensitized them to possible echoes of that event. Even when the language of Exod 14–15 is not explicitly quoted or alluded to, faint reverberations of that occasion can be reasonably construed in Israel's later songs.

Just as the Egyptians pursued (רדף) Israel in Exod 14:23, the same verb describes aggression by the enemies of the psalmists in Pss 7:1[2]; 31:15[16]; 35:3; 69:26[27]; 109:16; 119:84, 86, 157, 161; and 143:3. In Ps 142:6[7], the plea of the psalmist could easily have been the words of the Israelites as they faced the prospect of imminent annihilation by the Egyptian army: "Listen to my cry, for I am in desperate need; rescue me from those who pursue me, for they are too strong for me."

YHWH's deliverance of Israel at the ים סוף occurred in the morning (בקר; Exod 14:24, 27), and in the Psalms morning is also featured as the time when divine intervention can be expected (Pss 5:3[4]; 30:5[6]; and 46:5[6]). The psalmist prays for YHWH to come to his aid against his pursuing enemy in Ps 143:8: "Let the morning bring me word of your unfailing love, for I have put my trust in you."

In Exod 14:30, the narrative relates that YHWH saved (ישע) Israel from the hands of the Egyptians. In the Psalms, the same verb is used 136 times and in virtually every psalmic genre, with particular frequency in the laments and the declarative praise psalms.[33] YHWH is typically the subject of this verb, either in a statement of his act of deliverance or in a prayer

32. Hossfeld and Zenger, *Psalms 2*, 268–69.
33. *NIDOTTE* 2:559–60.

invoking his rescue of the psalmist. By this means, the psalmists called upon YHWH to deliver them from their distresses, just as he had previously intervened for their ancestors. For instance, the psalmist in Ps 54:1[3] appeals for divine assistance against the ruthless enemies who were attempting to kill him: "Save me, O God, by your name; vindicate me by your might."

Rejoicing by Israel

The two songs recorded in Exod 15 form a poetic counterpart to the narrative in the previous chapter, just as the song of Deborah and Barak in Judg 5 complements the narrative in Judg 4. The prose genre narrates the action, but poetry celebrates the response to the action. The initial term in Exod 15:1, "then" (אז) closely links the song that Moses and the Israelites sang with the events detailed in Exod 14. It was typical in the ancient world for prominent historical occasions to be preserved through song,[34] a pattern evidenced as well in the historical psalms (e.g., Pss 78; 105; 106; 135; and 136).

The first and longer song in Exod 15:1-18 seems to fit best the pattern of the song of thanksgiving or declarative praise psalm.[35] It begins with a call to praise in 15:1-3, followed by an extended report of deliverance in 15:4-17, incorporating a backwards look to the exodus from Egypt in 15:4-13 and a forward anticipation of the conquest of Canaan in 15:14-17. The song concludes in 15:18 with praise for YHWH's everlasting rule, a theme that recurs throughout the Bible, and in particular in the Psalms. Although the first person singular is used in 15:1-2, Moses and the Israelites (most likely the men) sang it as their corporate praise of YHWH. The same use of the singular when multiple voices are employed is evidenced in Judg 5:1, 3 when Deborah and Barak sing together. The text of the song includes many parallels to language familiar from the Ugaritic mythological texts describing Baal's victory over Yamm, the god of chaos, a phenomenon found also in Pss 29, 74, and elsewhere.

After a brief narrative section that in Exod 15:19 summarizes the defeat of the Egyptians and the deliverance of the Israelites in Exod 14:23-31, the second song, in which the women of Israel are led by Miriam, is introduced in Exod 15:20. The women sing in response to the song by Moses and the men.

---

34. Douglas K. Stuart, *Exodus*, NAC 2 (Nashville: Broadman & Holman, 2006) 363 points to biblical examples in Judg 5:1, 11; Num 21:17; 1 Sam 21:11; 2 Sam 1:17-27; 3:33; and 22:1.

35. Thomas B. Dozeman, *Commentary on Exodus*, ECC (Grand Rapids: Eerdmans, 2009) 327-33, presents a succinct discussion of the various form-critical alternatives for Exod 15:1-18.

The only change from 15:1 to 15:21 is from the first person cohortative "I will sing" to the second person imperative "sing." It is plausible that the quotation of the first line of the previous song suggests that the whole song was sung, rather than a truncated version of it. Stuart reasons well: "Verse 21 contains the incipit title of the song—the first few words or the first couplet of the song. Citing the incipit apparently was the most common method of titling songs in ancient Israel, as also in most of history until modern times. Moses had authored this great victory song; Miriam now popularized it among all the women so that it would be known and sung in every family, every home."[36] If the lyric in Exod 15:21 comprised the entire song, it would provide an example of the nucleus of the hymn or descriptive praise form, with the call to praise followed by the cause for praise, introduced by the conjunction "for" (כי).[37] However, it seems more likely that the women of Israel sang in responsive form and with instruments the entire song contained in 15:1–18.

Quotations

Two psalms directly quote the language of Exod 15:1–21 as they reflect specifically upon Israel's exodus experience. In Ps 77, the psalmist remembers the past deeds of YHWH (77:11–12[12–13]) to answer his questions about whether YHWH will continue to be faithful to Israel (77:7–9[10–12]). Terms such as "waters" (מים) and "sea" (ים) evoke the language of Exod 15:1, 4, 10, 19, 21. In Ps 77:20[21], the psalmist says, "You led your people" (נחה עם), which echoes the language in Exod 15:13. In an interesting transposition of meaning, he may well use the term (שנות) as an infinitive construct of the verb שנה (cf. BDB 1039) to speak of the *changing* of the right hand of YHWH in Ps 77:10[11], rather than the NIV reading, "the *years* [plural of the noun שנה] when the Most High stretched out his right hand."[38] If this is indeed the case, then he is contrasting YHWH's lack of intervention in his own predicament with his previous deliverance of Israel at the exodus with his right hand (Exod 15:6, 12). The psalm goes beyond the language of Exod 14–15 to depict YHWH as the warrior God coming to deliver his people, using the language of divine theophany familiar from passages such as Exod

---

36. Stuart, *Exodus*, 364.

37. Hermann Gunkel, *An Introduction to the Psalms: The Genres of the Religious Lyric of Israel*, completed by Joachim Begrich, trans. James D. Nogalski, MLBS (Macon, GA: Mercer University Press, 1998) 29, regards this verse as the oldest example of the causal sentence in a hymn.

38. John S. Kselman, "Psalm 77 and the Book of Exodus," *JANESCU* 15 (1983) 52 makes a good argument for this reading of the verse.

19:16–19 and Hab 3:3–15, but even in this it parallels תהמת in Exod 15:5, 8. Gregory Stevenson observes well:

> The function of the hymn in Exodus 15 is to praise God for his *past* deliverance in the exodus. The function of Psalm 77, by contrast, is to instill hope and trust for the *present* in what God can and will do in the *future*. This contrast between the past, present, and future provides the foundation for comprehending the importance of the exodus for Israelite faith. Since one knows who God is by what God does, the recitation and re-presentation of God's past acts serve to provide hope and faith for the present.[39]

In Ps 106:12, the psalmist recalls that when YHWH delivered the Israelites from their Egyptian adversaries, his ancestors believed his promises (cf. Exod 14:31) and they sang his praise. In the final phrase of the verse, "sang" (שיר) repeats the language in Exod 15:1, 21, and "praise" (תהלה) the term in Exod 15:12.

Allusion

Although the final line of Ps 66:6 contains no explicit lexical link to Exod 15, it clearly reflects the jubilant spirit in the Song of the Sea, as the Israelites joyfully recognized God at work on their behalf. Although many commentators have taken the cohortative נשמחה־בו as the confessional affirmation of the worshiping community,[40] it may well be better to read the term as a pseudo-cohortative selected for euphony, but indicating past time, with the sense "there we rejoiced in him."[41] This note of cultic joy is found frequently in the Psalms (e.g., 33:21; 34:2[3]; 67:4[5]; 90:14; 97:12; and 118:24).

Echoes

The Psalms are replete with echoes of the language of Israel's song of rejoicing in Exod 15:1–21, even when the exodus experience is not specifically in view. The range and frequency of these echoes suggests that the psalmists were familiar with the text of the Song of the Sea as they addressed YHWH in their own predicaments.

---

39. Gregory M. Stevenson, "Communal Imagery and the Individual Lament: Exodus Typology in Psalm 77," *ResQ* 39 (1997) 229.

40. Tate, *Psalms 51–100*, 149.

41. This is the rendering of WO'C 34.5.3b; cf. also GKC 108g.

The "horse" (סוס) which YHWH hurled into the sea in Exod 15:1, 21 is also seen to be an ineffectual military resource against him in Pss 20:7[8]; 33:17; 76:6[7]; and 147:10.

The language of Exod 15:2 reverberates frequently in the Psalter: "The LORD is my strength and my defense; he has become my salvation. He is my God, and I will praise him, my father's God, and I will exalt him." The strength (עז) of YHWH recurs at least twenty-seven times in the Psalms, and the salvation (ישועה) of YHWH with thirty-seven occurrences is a virtual *Leitmotif*. Moreover, the polel form of the verb רום in the sense of "exalt" is used in calls to praise YHWH in Pss 30:1[2]; 34:3[4]; 107:32; 118:28; and 145:1.

In Exod 15:3 YHWH is described as a warrior, or literally a man of war (מלחמה). This specific term is repeated in Pss 18:34[35]; 24:8; and 144:1. Even when the precise language is not used in the Psalms, in many places YHWH is portrayed as the champion of his people, so that when others rely in vain on military resources such as horses and chariots, those who worship YHWH trust in him (cf. Ps 20:7[8]).[42]

Twice in Exod 15:6 Moses and the Israelites extol the majestic right hand of YHWH that shattered the enemy. This figure of YHWH's enabling power on behalf of his people recurs extensively in the Psalms. As a petition, the psalmist cries in Ps 17:7, "Show me the wonders of your great love, you who save by your right hand those who take refuge in you from their foes." In 74:11, the community complains, "Why do you hold back your hand, your right hand?" The metaphor also occurs as part of a confession of trust in 63:8[9]: "I cling to you; your right hand upholds me." It is the ground for praise in 98:1: "Sing to the LORD a new song, for he has done marvelous things; his right hand and his holy arm have worked salvation for him." Additional examples of the right hand of YHWH are found in Pss 18:35[36]; 20:6[7]; 44:3[4]; 48:10[11]; 60:5[7]; 73:23; 77:10[11]; 108:6[7]; 118:15–16; 138:7; and 139:10.

Exodus 15:11 poses the rhetorical question—"Who among the gods is like you, LORD?"—and then describes three qualities that apply to YHWH alone: "majestic in holiness, awesome in glory, working wonders." The adjective translated "awesome" is נורא, and it is used several times in the Psalms to describe YHWH's preeminent status and extraordinary deeds (Pss 47:2[3]; 66:3, 5; 68:35[36]; 76:7[8]; 76:12[13]; 89:7[8]; 96:4; 99:3; 106:22; 111:9; and 145:6). YHWH's wonders (פלא) are his notable deeds that demonstrate his power and sovereignty over all,[43] as also seen in Pss 77:11,14[12,15] and 89:5[6].

42. For a broader discussion of the theme of YHWH as a warrior, see Tremper Longman and Daniel G. Reid, *God is a Warrior* (Grand Rapids: Zondervan, 1995).

43. Kruger, *NIDOTTE* 3:615–16 observes: "The root *plʾ* primarily signifies something

There is in Exod 15:13 an unusual collocation of the unfailing love (חסד) and the strength (עז) of YHWH. This rare juxtaposition echoes in Pss 59:16[17] and 62:11–12[12–13], as the psalmists express their confidence in him.

The final verse of the lyric sung by Moses and the Israelites in Exod 15:18 states jubilantly, "The LORD reigns for ever and ever." The verb (מלך) is featured in Pss 47:8[9]; 93:1; 96:10; 97:1; and 99:1, and similar terms referring to the kingship of YHWH permeate the Psalter. The final expression לעלם ועד is used only fifteen times in the OT, but twelve of the occurrences are in the Psalms: 9:6[7]; 10:16; 21:4[5]; 45:6[7],17[18]; 48:14[15]; 52:9[10]; 104:5; and 119:44.[44] Four of these examples refer explicitly to the everlasting reign of YHWH, echoing the words of the Israelites during the exodus experience.

The narrative in Exod 15:20 described how the Israelite women with timbrels and dancing joined with Miriam as she sang her response to Moses and the Israelite men, beginning with the words, "Sing to the Lord, for he is highly exalted. Both horse and driver he has hurled into the sea." In the Psalms, the timbrel is employed as musical accompaniment in the worship of YHWH in Pss 81:2[3]; 149:3 and 150:4, and celebratory religious dancing is enjoined in Pss 149:3 and 150:4, and is suggested as well in 30:11[12].

Conclusion

By appropriating the approaches of intertextuality, this paper has analyzed how the three episodes in Exod 14–15, encompassing the deliverance of Israel at the ים סוף, the destruction of Pharaoh and his army and the concurrent rescue of Israel, and the subsequent rejoicing of Israel in the Song of the Sea, are reflected in the Psalms. Each of these events reverberates in the Psalms in explicit quotations, allusions, and echoes. This extensive evidence in the Psalter demonstrates that the exodus experience was a crucial element in the content of the historical memory of Israel. As such, the exodus was an essential component of the faith of Israel in YHWH.

It is also evident that there are significant correlations between the structure of the language in Exodus and in the psalms of Israel. Although it lies outside the scope of this paper, the cry of the Israelites to YHWH and his response to their groaning in Exod 2:23–25 anticipate the lament

---

that, measured by the standards of what people are accustomed to or what they normally expect, appear to be extraordinary and wonderful. Such exceptional events or objects usually evoke a reaction of astonishment and praise from their beholders, which explains the exceptionally high incidence of this root in the hymnic literature."

44. Hamilton, *Exodus*, 227.

psalms, in which the psalmists appeal to YHWH to hear their cries and to intervene on their behalf. The song of Moses and the Israelite men in Exod 15:1–18 makes use of the same three-part pattern as found in the songs of thanksgiving[45] or declarative praise psalms,[46] including a call to praise, a report of deliverance, and concluding praise. Taken in isolation, the summary of the song of Miriam and the Israelite women in Exod 15:21 features the familiar structure of the hymn[47] or the descriptive praise psalm,[48] with a call to praise, the cause for praise, and a conclusion. This suggests that the exodus experience also may well have functioned in a paradigmatic fashion for the expression of Israel's communication to YHWH. Just as the exodus was a crucial part of Israel's faith, so it plausible that it played a major part in shaping the form of Israel's worship as well.

45. Gunkel, *Introduction to the Psalms*, 199–221.

46. Claus Westermann, *Praise and Lament in the Psalms*, trans. Keith R. Crim and Richard N. Soulen (Atlanta: John Knox, 1981) 81–90, 102–12.

47. Gunkel, *Introduction to the Psalms*, 22–65.

48. Westermann, *Praise and Lament in the Psalms*, 122–32.

4

Ezekiel as Moses—Israel as Pharaoh

Reverberations of the Exodus Narrative in Ezekiel

Nevada Levi DeLapp

Intertextual Narrative Parallels in Exodus and Ezekiel

Ellen van Wolde observes that the word "intertextual" is fraught with ambiguity.[1] Since the advent of the French post-structuralist movement, the relationship between *Text* and *Context* has been called into question. As a result, Michael Bakhtin's notion of author-directed dialogical intertextuality has been stretched to include reader-reception of intertexts. Thus, there tend to be two ways of thinking and speaking about intertextuality. On the one hand, scholars with diachronic concerns often think and speak about intertextuality in terms of text production. In biblical studies, the work of Richard B. Hays comes to mind.[2] On the other hand, scholars more interested in a text's final form have a marked tendency to refer to intertextuality in terms of text reception. Examples include van Wolde's work on Ruth and Tamar and David M. Gunn's work on the Samson narratives.[3] In between

---

1. Ellen van Wolde, "Texts in Dialogue with Texts: Intertextuality in the Ruth and Tamar Narratives," *BI* 5 (1997) 1–8.

2. Cf. Richard B. Hays, *Echoes of Scripture in the Letters of Paul* (New Haven: Yale University Press, 1989); Hays, *The Conversion of the Imagination: Paul as Interpreter of Israel's Scripture* (Grand Rapids: Eerdmans, 2005).

3. Cf. David M. Gunn, "Samson of Sorrows: An Isaianic Gloss on Judges 13–16," in *Reading Between Texts: Intertextuality and the Hebrew Bible*, ed. Danna Nolan Fewell (Louisville: Westminster John Knox, 1992) 225–53. See also Gunn, *The Story of King*

the two stances, one can observe a variety of points on the intertextual spectrum. The Canonical Criticism of Brevard Childs[4] and his disciples[5] represents one such point as does the work of Jewish scholar, Michael Fishbane.[6]
Though not all of these scholars have dealt specifically with the problem of
"intertextuality," their work touches on ways in which biblical texts relate to
each other.

In this essay I offer an intertextual reading of the books of Ezekiel and
Exodus from the standpoint of text reception. Though I do not consign
questions of text production to the realm of outer darkness, my main focus
will be on the "iconic" nature of the relationship between the two books.[7]
Consequently, I spend little time arguing over genotexts and phenotexts.[8]
Readers have long debated the Ezekiel date and authorship. Nonetheless,
despite disagreements over its redactional unity and exact chronological
provenance, scholars generally agree that there is a literary relationship between Ezekiel and the Pentateuchal sources, primarily P.[9] Naturally, with
differing opinions regarding date and purpose, the relationship is construed
by some to reflect a Pentateuchal dependence upon Ezekiel and by others to
reflect Ezekiel's dependence upon the Pentateuchal traditions.[10]

David: Genre and Interpretation, JSOTSup 6 (Sheffield: JSOT Press, 1978); Gunn, *The
Fate of King Saul: An Interpretation of a Biblical Story*, JSOTSup 14 (Sheffield: JSOT
Press, 1984). More recently, Gunn explores the possibilities of textual reception through
studies in reception history; cf. Gunn, "Bathsheba Goes Bathing in Hollywood: Words,
Images, and Social Locations," *Semeia* 74 (1996) 75–102; Gunn, "Cultural Criticism:
Viewing the Sacrifice of Jephthah's Daughter," in *Judges & Method: New Approaches in
Biblical Studies*, ed. Gale E. Yee, 2nd ed. (Minneapolis: Fortress, 2007) 202–36; Gunn,
Judges, Blackwell Bible Commentaries (Malden, MA: Blackwell, 2005).

4. Cf. Brevard S. Childs, *Introduction to the Old Testament as Scripture* (Philadelphia: Fortress, 1979); Childs, *The Struggle to Understand Isaiah as Christian Scripture*
(Grand Rapids: Eerdmans, 2004).

5. E.g., Christopher R. Seitz, *Prophecy and Hermeneutics: Toward a New Introduction to the Prophets* (Grand Rapids: Baker, 2007).

6. Cf. Michael Fishbane, *Biblical Interpretation in Ancient Israel* (New York: Oxford University Press, 1988).

7. Van Wolde defines "Iconicity" as denoting "the principle that phenomena are
analogous or isomorphic." See van Wolde, "Texts in Dialogue," 6.

8. Ibid., 5.

9. For a helpful summary of the literature, see Risa Levitt Kohn, "A Prophet Like Moses? Rethinking Ezekiel's Relationship to the Torah," *ZAW* 114 (2002) 236nn2–3.

10. John F. Evans offers a concise overview of current scholarly opinion as to the
relationship. See Evans, "An Inner-Biblical Interpretation and Intertextual Reading of
Ezekiel's Recognition Formulae with the Book of Exodus," ThD diss., University of Stel-
lenbosch, 2006, 43–49.

My own perspective is that the Wellhausian assumption of a late date for the majority of the Torah is inherently flawed and that the Pentateuchal sources predate the book of Ezekiel. As a result, I am convinced that Ezekiel's final redactors were well aware of some form of the Pentateuch (especially the Priestly Source).[11] Nevertheless, while diachronic concerns like these are not to be overlooked, in this essay I generally keep to a synchronic reading of the text's final canonical form, for it is at the level of the final form that the question of reading comes to prominence: given the textual parameters, how can a given text be read in relation to others?

This chapter explores the canonical and theological connections between the books of Ezekiel and Exodus as the two are read together.[12] It accomplishes this by reading them in terms of their narrative (or plotted) iconic parallels. In each book there is a protagonist who makes himself known to both recalcitrant and willing listeners through a mediate character. This mediate character functions in both stories as a conduit of prophetic pronouncements and actions delivering judgments and blessings. The end goal in the narratives is always a revealed knowledge of the protagonist.

The following diagram illustrates this narrative arc:

Protagonist
(Knowledge Revealer)   →   Mediate Character   →   Knowledge Receivers

For those familiar with Exodus and Ezekiel, it should not be difficult to fill in the narrative roles with their respective characters. In both books, God is the key knowledge revealer. This is especially clear from the repetition of the so-called "recognition formula" in the both texts (i.e., "then you/they will know that I am YHWH").[13] Though Exodus does not use

11. Here I find Risa Levitt Kohn's arguments compelling: "Without the benefit of additional information or clues to guide us, determining the literary dependence of one text upon another remains difficult. Notwithstanding, the preponderance of evidence calls into question the scholarly contention that P is literarily dependent upon Ezekiel. Ezekiel seems to be familiar with at least some of the material that now comprises the Priestly Source, but, clearly, his writing is more than just a product of its influence or tradition. The prophet appropriates P's terminology but feels comfortable situating it in new, different and even contradictory contexts. P language is not simply imitated in Ezekiel. It is skewed, poeticized, disarticulated and reconstituted. Ezekiel knows P, quotes P, but also modifies it at will, adding and deleting material as suits his personal agenda and the circumstances of his audience" (245). Kohn also notes Ezekiel's literary dependence upon D. See Kohn, "A Prophet Like Moses?," 246–48.

12. Since this chapter focuses on Ezekiel and the reverberations of the Exodus narrative in Ezekiel, my reading will tend to flow in a linear direction following the canonical order (i.e., from Exodus to Ezekiel rather than from Ezekiel to Exodus).

13. The term comes from the seminal essay by Walther Zimmerli, "Knowledge of

the formula with near the frequency of Ezekiel (ten in Exodus, seventy-two in Ezekiel), its use in Exodus is highly significant and revolves around Exod 3, the *locus classicus* for discussions of Divine self-revelation in the HB. Likewise, many of the instances of the formula in Exodus play off of Pharaoh and (implicitly) Israel's lack of knowledge of the one true God. In the end, God reveals himself to Israel through mighty acts of salvation and the people come to know that YHWH truly is the God of their ancestors, Abraham, Isaac, and Jacob. Conversely, God reveals himself to Pharaoh and Egypt through mighty acts of judgment, which bring the knowledge of the true God to the self-proclaimed god, Pharaoh.

In Ezekiel, as will become clear in what follows, the concept of Divine self-revelation through mighty deeds of judgment and salvation permeates the entire book. In fact, given the overwhelming repetition of the recognition formula in Ezekiel, one would be hard pressed to argue for any other "knowledge revealer" in the text. All of YHWH's actions are calculated to make YHWH known to Israel and the nations. In the end, YHWH will cause all to know that YHWH is God.

At this level, the parallel between the two books is apparent. Both are concerned with God's self-revelation in deeds of mercy and judgment. With this in mind, one can argue that, despite the various important characters contained in the stories of both books, it is ultimately God who is the protagonist.[14]

The Mediate Character—Moses and Ezekiel

The Prophetic Mediator

This moves us to the question of the mediate characters. It is not surprising that prophets are the mediate characters in both books. By definition, Hebrew prophets are mediators. They are liminal figures who stand on the border between the Divine and human realms. Canonically,[15] all prophets share

---

God According to the Book of Ezekiel," trans. Douglas W. Stott, in *I Am Yahweh*, ed. Walter Brueggemann (Atlanta: John Knox, 1982) 29–98.

14. On this note, it is interesting that both books introduce God early on as the key protagonist in the drama of redemption. Exodus presages what is to come not only in Exod 3 but also in 2:23–25 where God hears the people's groaning and remembers God's covenant with Abraham, Isaac, and Jacob. At the outset, the narrative makes clear who will act to save Israel. Similarly, Ezekiel's celebrated chariot vision (Ezek 1–3) introduces the Most High as the one who will judge and save Israel.

15. When I speak of "canon," I am referring to the HB as Jews and Protestant Christians define it.

similar vocational paths: mere Israelites who were once content minding their own business, they are swept up into holy service. It is not unusual that the stories surrounding their calls are filled with images of fire and cloud. They have come into contact with the Divine Presence (כבוד) and have been irrevocably changed.[16] Abraham Heschel's comment is helpful:

> The prophet's eye is directed to the contemporary scene; the society and its conduct are the main theme of his speeches. Yet his ear is inclined to God. He is a person struck by the glory and presence of God, overpowered by the hand of God. Yet his true greatness is his ability to hold God and man in a single thought.[17]

Moreover, the prophet is a "participant . . . in the council of God, not a bearer of dispatches whose function is limited to being sent on errands. He is a counselor as well as a messenger."[18] As a mediate person, the prophet functions chiefly as the bearer of revelation. When God speaks, the prophet utters the divine message to the people. From the Pentateuch's perspective, this dynamic stemmed from the chosen people's inability to stand before YHWH's glory. Exodus sets the pattern with Moses ascending and descending Mt. Sinai to bring God's Torah to the people while they look on in fear at the storm-covered mountain (Exod 19–24). Deuteronomy offers its own take on the situation with the people refusing to stand in the presence of God after an initial encounter at Horeb. The terror of YHWH fills the people, and they beg Moses to function as a mediator: "Go near, and hear all that the LORD our God will say; and speak to us all that the LORD our God will speak to you; and we will hear and do it" (Deut 5:27, RSV).[19]

In terms of the canon, it is clear why Moses functions as a prophetic archetype. His story precedes those of the court prophets and writing prophets. He is the first to see God (Exod 33). He is the first to encounter the Divine Presence in its fiery, cloud-wrapped form (Exod 3, 19, etc.). Most importantly, Moses receives the revelation of God's name, YHWH (Exod 3). At the burning bush, he enters liminal space (אדמת־קדש הוא) and YHWH commissions him to lead Israel out of Egypt. In a headstrong, fearful moment, Moses asks for proof that this Being speaking from the fire really is the God of Abraham, Isaac, and Jacob. In response, God gives God's name

---

16. For an excellent discussion of Divine Presence in the HB, see Benjamin D. Sommer, *The Bodies of God and the World of Ancient Israel* (New York: Cambridge University Press, 2009). Cf. Frank Moore Cross, *Canaanite Myth and Hebrew Epic: Essays in the History of the Religion of Israel* (Cambridge, MA: Harvard University Press, 1997) 163–77.

17. Abraham J. Heschel, *The Prophets* (New York: Perennial Classics, 2001) 25.

18. Ibid., 25–26.

19. Unless otherwise noted (as in this example), all translations are the author's own.

as a sign. When Moses speaks to the Israelites in Egypt, he is to reveal that this God, YHWH, is the God of their forefathers. Throughout the rest of Exodus, Moses functions as a mediator between YHWH and the people. At times he speaks for YHWH, and at times he speaks for the people. In each word on behalf of YHWH, Moses makes known this God. In the case of Pharaoh and Egypt, the knowledge comes with signs of Divine wrath. In the case of the slave people, Israel, the knowledge comes with signs of providential salvation and deliverance.

This basic story-pattern or plot becomes within the HB a type-scene[20] which plays out repeatedly in the stories of prophets. Some like Deborah, Samuel, and Nathan lack the element of explicit exposure in the narrative world to the fire and cloud of the Divine Presence. Nevertheless, they share with Moses the functional role of mediator. They make known YHWH and YHWH's will. At times their words enact comfort, and at times their words are catalysts for judgment. Other prophets like Elijah, Elisha, Isaiah, and (of course) Ezekiel follow Moses in encountering YHWH's storm-cloud presence. This commonality only heightens their function as mediate characters that make known the ineffable YHWH. They are the ones who stand at the boundary between mortals and the Immortal.

Ezekiel as Moses

With such a prophetic type-scene operant in the canon, it is understandable that scholars observe similarities between Moses and Ezekiel. The similarities, however, go beyond those typical of the prophetic office. There is something about the portrayal of Ezekiel in his literary namesake that aligns the two men's lives. As Rebecca G. S. Idestrom puts it, "When one compares Ezekiel with Isaiah, Jeremiah, and the prophets of the Book of the Twelve, more than any other prophet, Ezekiel is a prophet *like* Moses."[21] To speak in dramatic terms, it is as if Ezekiel has been cast in the role of a new Moses for a new generation facing a new turning point in redemptive-history.

Jon D. Levenson picks up on this language of a Mosaic "role" for Ezekiel. Arguing for a typological relationship between the two, he observes:

> Whoever the authors of chs. 40–48 be, the role of Moses falls
> upon the prophet Ezekiel. Ezek. 40–48 is the only corpus of

20. Robert Alter's seminal work on type-scenes in the HB remains the standard treatment. See Alter, *The Art of Biblical Narrative* (New York: Basic, 1981), esp. chapter 3.

21. Rebecca G. S. Idestrom, "Echoes of the Book of Exodus in Ezekiel," *JSOT* 33, no. 4 (2009) 509.

legislation of the Hebrew Bible which is not placed in the mouth of Moses. The similarity of Ezekiel's transport to the Sinaitic experience is fundamental to those chapters and not a reflection of later priestly insertion which, according to nearly all critics, make up some of them. In fact, the earliest stratum, the great Temple vision of 40–42, finds its only close biblical parallel in Moses' vision of the Tabernacle.[22]

In other words, Ezekiel plays the part of Moses in a manner analogous to the Deuteronomic hope for a "new Moses."[23]

Similarly, Henry McKeating posits that the figure of Ezekiel bears a strong resemblance to Moses.[24] Building on Levenson's work, he argues that the final redactors purposely organized the material to highlight similarities between the two prophets. Central to McKeating's thesis is the recognition that Ezekiel's three key visions mirror Moses's three-fold career. Like Moses, Ezekiel begins his prophetic vocation with an overwhelming experience of the holiness of God (Ezek 1–3). Also, like Moses on Mt. Sinai, Ezekiel responds with horror at the idolatry of his fellow Israelites in his second vision (Ezek 8; cf. Exod 32) and receives instructions for proper cultic procedure and the right function of the priesthood in his third vision. Finally, like Moses on Mt. Nebo, Ezekiel in his third key vision (Ezek 40–48) surveys the boundaries of the promised land and allocates a portion to each of the twelve tribes. While the final two elements of Moses' prophetic career do not neatly coincide with Ezekiel's second and third visions, the repeated similarities between the two prophets makes it difficult to discount McKeating's argument.

One could understand some level of scepticism if the only narrative connection between the two was their shared experience of the divine "glory" (כבוד) at their initial callings to service. After all, experiencing YHWH's כבוד was typical of the prophetic experience.[25] One cannot dismiss, however, their common pronouncements of Torah legislation and land division. Furthermore, McKeating observes that the third key vision sequence (Ezek 40–48) offers five specific points of overlap with the Moses story. To begin with, it offers a parallel narrative core. That is, Ezekiel finds himself on a mountain from which he can view the new temple (40:2). This connection with Moses and mountains needs no defense. In addition, McKeating observes that, during this vision, Ezekiel also receives instructions for cultic

---

22. Jon D. Levenson, *Theology of the Program of Restoration of Ezekiel 40–48*, HSM 10 (Missoula, MT: Scholars, 1976), 39–40.

23. Ibid., 38.

24. Henry McKeating, "Ezekiel the 'Prophet Like Moses'?" *JSOT* 61 (1994) 97–109.

25. I am indebted to Benjamin D. Sommer for this point.

activity, sacerdotal behavior, and land allotment as well as stipulations concerning the "prince" (45:7–17, 46:16–18), which echoes the Deuteronomic template for an ideal king (Deut 17:14–20). In light of these thematic connections between the two prophets' messages, it is hard to avoid the conclusion that those who shaped the final form of Ezekiel believed Ezekiel to be "one who repeats Moses' work in a new setting, and, be it noted, *repeats it with more success than Moses himself.*"[26]

Corrine Patton argues in an analogous manner.[27] Her basic position is that the final redactor of Ezekiel was aware of some form of the Exodus traditions and used them to put forward an idealistic restoration program in Ezek 40–48. In the process, the redactor places the prophet Ezekiel in the role of Moses: "He is led alone to a high mountain where he is given a written law and a sanctuary plan that he will take back to the people."[28] However, the role is not simply one of recapitulation. Ezekiel's New Torah surpasses that of Moses, which at best demanded the impossible (including child sacrifice). Thus, "if Ezekiel knew of Moses, Moses was not just irrelevant; he mirrored the deceived prophet of 14.9 who gave laws that led to violation, separation, death."[29] Ultimately, the role of Moses lacks any positive connotations for Patton. Her article's implicit assumption is that Ezekiel assumes the role in standard prophetic fashion to gain authority for his legal pronouncements.

Returning to McKeating's analysis, it is intriguing that he does not press the implications of his thesis beyond arguing for general similarities between Moses and Ezekiel. In fact, McKeating believes that the parallels exist only on the level of "broad content" and "not of detail." He even goes so far as to say, "there are practically no echoes of the Pentateuch's language, and the parallel themes are often developed and filled out in quite different ways."[30] His point is well taken. The Torah instruction that the two characters proffer differ in the details. Nonetheless, I think it is premature to suggest that the parallels between the two prophets tend to only occur in terms of broad content. There is, in fact, one key echo of the Pentateuch's language that occurs repeatedly in Ezekiel: the recognition formula. I will return to this in due course, but for now let it suffice to say that the incessant repetition of what Zimmerli calls the

---

26. McKeating, "Prophet Like Moses?," 104.

27. Corrine Patton, "'I Myself Gave them Laws that Were Not Good': Ezekiel 20 and the Exodus Traditions," *JSOT* 69 (1996) 73–90.

28. Ibid., 85.

29. Ibid., 89.

30. McKeating, "Prophet Like Moses?," 108.

"strict" recognition formula points to specific, detailed literary connections between Ezekiel and the Pentateuchal sources.

In stark contrast to McKeating's contention stands Risa Levitt Kohn's contribution. Analyzing strong literary and linguistic connections between Ezekiel and the Pentateuch, Kohn posits that the depiction of the prophet Ezekiel in the book of Ezekiel displays "a confluence of Priestly and Deuteronomic traditions."[31] For Kohn, in addition to receiving temple blueprints, Ezekiel mimics the Priestly Source's Moses in functioning as a priest and prophet who is warned by God ahead of time that "his mission will fail due to the strong resolves and hardened hearts of others."[32] Ezekiel is also similar, however, to the Deuteronomic Moses in that God places God's words in his mouth. The confluence of Pentateuchal sources in Ezekiel extends also to Ezekiel's own prophecies. In this way, Kohn believes that the prophet Ezekiel anticipates the final priestly Redactor of Torah who synthesizes JE, D, and P in the light of the exile.[33]

John F. Evans subsequently moved the discussion forward with his dissertation on the inner-biblical connections between the "recognition formulae" in Exodus and Ezekiel. Building on McKeating's work, Evans observes a number of other parallels between the two prophets. Both were Levites and took part in priestly activities.[34] Both "are commissioned by God to go to a people steeped in idolatry and held captive in a foreign land, and they reintroduce Yahweh to his chastened people."[35] In terms of narrative parallels, both Moses and Ezekiel meet with Israel's elders and intercede with YHWH on the people's behalf.[36]

Finally, Rebecca Idestrom surveys the literature on this topic while proffering conclusions similar to those of Evans (though reached independently). Her work is interesting for two reasons. First, Idestrom proposes that Ezekiel's so-called "revisionist history" makes sense if "Ezekiel is perceived as a second Moses figure." If so, "then Ezekiel has the 'authority' to

---

31. Kohn, "A Prophet Like Moses?" 249.

32. Ibid., 249.

33. Ibid., 254: "Ezekiel's dream of a unified national theology would attain ultimate realization with the promulgation of the Torah. As we have seen, Ezekiel modeled himself on the ancient lawgiver Moses, issuing laws in anticipation of the »Second Exodus« and resettlement of the Land. The anonymous Pentateuchal Redactor, no less than his precursor Ezekiel, was a »prophet like Moses«; his work was almost immediately adapted as the charter for all Judaism."

34. Evans, "An Inner-Biblical Interpretation," 191–92.

35. Ibid., 192.

36. Ibid., 193.

re-interpret Israel's history."[37] Second, she offers the tantalizing suggestion that the inhabitants of Qumran may have conceived of Ezekiel as a Second Moses,[38] which further suggests that, from its earliest reception, the book of Ezekiel generated intertextual readings that the prophet Ezekiel understood as fulfilling a Mosaic role in relation to Israel.

It should be clear that, when read in synchronic dialogue with the Exodus, the figure of Ezekiel is cast as a New Moses. Indeed, he is more of a Moses than other prophets who share the prophetic type-scene and mediatorial vocation. However, this raises a question. If the book of Ezekiel conceives of the prophet Ezekiel as assuming Moses' role, what roles do the other characters in the book of Ezekiel assume? Specifically, what role does Israel play? To answer this question, we must turn to Ezekiel's Mosaic message, which is designed to inculcate the knowledge of YHWH. Only after analyzing this message does Israel's role become clear.

The Divine Self-Revelation

Introduction

If one picks up an English edition of Ezekiel and reads several chapters in one sitting, a certain phrase begins to stand out. Time and again, the prophet—speaking on God's behalf—reiterates how, after divine activity, the people will come to know that "I am the LORD." Not only does the phrase become redundant, but it also seems to occur in multiple contexts. A careful reader cannot help but ask, why does Ezekiel use this phrase over and over? Is it merely a stylistic device, or is there more going on than meets the eye?

Turning to the Hebrew text of Ezekiel, it becomes clear that the phrase is formulaic. It always begins with some form of the verb ידע and is always followed within the immediate context by the same three words: כי אני יהוה (though, of course, the subject of the sentence can intervene). However, it is also clear that the formula is more than a stylistic device. Ezekiel is not the only place where it occurs. The formula and its variants are scattered throughout the prophetic corpus and the Pentateuch.

In what follows, I argue that the book of Ezekiel uses the formula to evoke images traditionally associated with the judgment and mercy of the exodus event. I first examine the three contexts in Ezekiel in which the formula appears.[39] Next, I briefly analyze the use of the formula in Exodus

37. Idestrom, "Echoes of the Book," 500n46.

38. Ibid., 508.

39. As will become clear, my categorization of the contexts of the recognition

before concluding with a discussion of Ezekiel's appropriation of the phrase. Given the status of Israel within the various contexts of occurrences, I propose that Israel fulfills a dual role in the text. On the one hand, Israel plays the role of its ancestors as it is both chastised and offered the hope of a New Exodus. On the other hand, Israel also plays the role of the recalcitrant Pharaoh/Egypt. This duality in Ezekiel highlights Israel's ambiguous nature as a chosen people from its national inception to the exilic present.

Contexts of Judgment in Ezekiel

The recognition formula mostly occurs in the context of judgment or divine wrath in Ezekiel.[40] Indeed, of the seventy-two[41] occurrences of the phrases וידעתם כי אני יהוה and וידעו כי אני יהוה,[42] fifty-two are located in this context.[43] Ezekiel 6:1–14 is a good example of this phenomenon. Containing four of these occurrences (two of each variant), the passage is set in the context of a prophecy of divine judgment. In Ezek 5, God commands Eze-

formula differs from Zimmerli's. Cf. Zimmerli, *I Am Yahweh*, 32.

40. Note again that when I speak of the book of Ezekiel, I am speaking of the final canonical form. As James M. Ward puts it, "it is much more difficult to distinguish the various strata in the book of Ezekiel than in that of [for example] Jeremiah. An interpreter of Ezekiel must deal with the message of the book largely in its canonical form." See Ward, *Thus Says the Lord: The Message of the Prophets* (Nashville: Abingdon, 1991) 173.

41. Some contention exists regarding the exact number of occurrences. Here I am limiting myself to the so-called "strict" recognition formulae outlined above. My numbering agrees with Evans and the early Zimmerli. See Evans's discussion of the problem, "An Inner-Biblical Interpretation," 144–48; and Walther Zimmerli, *A Commentary on the Book of the Prophet Ezekiel: Chapters 1–24*, trans. R. E. Clements, Hermeneia (Philadelphia: Fortress, 1979) 38.

42. These two phrases are the most common. However, there are a few instances included in the seventy-two occurrences where the parsing of the verb ידע is different. So, e.g., in Ezek 13:21–23, the phrase shifts to וידעתן כי אני יהוה to account for the recipients of the prophetic word (i.e., in this instance the "daughters" of the people). However, despite these differences in parsing, the formula remains the same.

43. There are fifty-one unambiguous times where the context is wrath (Ezek 5:13; 6:7, 10, 13, 14; 7:4, 9, 27; 11:10, 12; 12:15, 16, 20; 13:9, 14, 21, 23; 14:8; 15:7; 17:21, 24; 20:26, 38; 21:10; 22:16, 22; 23:49; 24:24, 27; 25:5, 7, 11, 17; 26:6; 28: 22, 23; 29:6, 9, 16; 30:8, 19, 25, 26; 32:15; 33:29; 35:4, 9, 12, 15; 38:23; 39:6) and once where the context is wrath towards the nations and covenant mercy towards the house of Israel (39:22). Thus, there are fifty-two total instances of judgment associated with the formulaic phrase and nineteen total instances associated with covenantal mercy (16:62; 20:42, 44; 28:24, 26; 29:21; 34:27, 30; 36:11, 23, 36, 38; 37:6, 13, 14, 28; 39:7, 28). In addition, there are three instances where the formula occurs in a context of historical recitation (20:12, 20, 26). However, one of these also doubles as a context of divine wrath (20:26). Because of the two doublings, the total number of times the formula is used is seventy-two.

kiel to perform a prophetic-symbolic action illustrating the destruction of Jerusalem. Afterwards, the word of the LORD comes to Ezekiel again. This time God commands him to prophesy against the mountains of Israel (5:2). Symbolizing Judah's religious idolatry, the mountains will see the desolation of their cults. God will come in judgment, throwing the bodies of the Israelites before their idols and scattering their bones around the forbidden altars (5:5). Verse 7 rounds out the first paragraph with its dim conclusion: "When the slain fall in your midst, then you shall know that I am YHWH" (ונפל חלל בתוככם וידעתם כי אני יהוה). The next paragraph offers a sparse hope: God will leave some of the people alive, but even in life, God will scatter them throughout the known world. Among the nations, they will finally remember their God and how their unfaithful hearts and roving eyes broke God's heart (5:9). With this knowledge, the people will loathe themselves, "and then they will know that I am YHWH" (וידעו כי אני יהוה).

The final paragraph of the chapter returns to the predicted destruction of Judah with a reiteration of the introductory prophetic expression found in Ezek 5:3: "Thus says the LORD God" (כה אמר אדני יהוה). Sword, famine, and pestilence will descend upon the idolatrous people through the fury of God. If they manage to escape one form of death, another will find them (5:12). A third time, the formulaic phrase sings out, this time again to the mountains: "You will know that I am YHWH when their slain are in the midst of their idols" (ידעתם כי אני יהוה בהיות חלליהם בתוך גלוליהם). God will stretch out God's hand against the people desolating their land. Once all this has taken place, "then they will know that I am YHWH" (וידעו כי אני יהוה).

Another example of the formula occurring in a wrathful context appears in Ezek 22:1–16. There the focus is on Jerusalem, the "bloody city" (עיר הדמים). In Jerusalem's midst, the princes shed blood, the children curse their parents, and the inhabitants oppress the foreigner and wrong widows and orphans (22:7). In addition, the people have profaned God's Sabbaths and despised God's holy things (22:8). Thus, not only is the city crooked in its horizontal relationships (i.e., person to person); it is also deformed in its vertical relationship (i.e., people to God). The problem is that the people have forgotten the Lord YHWH. God will therefore lash out at the bloody city. The people will find themselves thrown out among the nations and scattered throughout the lands. Just as they profaned the Sabbaths, they will be profaned in the eyes of the nations. All of this will produce one result: "then you (i.e., Jerusalem) will know that I am YHWH" (וידעת כי אני יהוה).

These two examples are only a sampling of the contexts of divine judgment that surround the formula and its variants. Given the preponderance of the formula for contexts of wrath, what becomes interesting about these fifty-two occurrences is how they differ. While the majority spell out wrath for the people of God, there are approximately twenty-one instances[44] where the formula is directed toward other nations. The Ammonites (25:5–11), the Philistines (25:17), the cities of Tyre (26:6) and Sidon (28:22–23), Egypt (29:6—32:15), Mt. Seir and Edom (35:4–15), and Gog and Magog (38:23; 39:6) all receive a word of judgment that culminates in their coming to know God as YHWH. Furthermore, it is intriguing that out of all the other nations receiving a rebuke or judgment that results in knowledge of God, Egypt receives the lion's share. Roughly eight times[45] (29:6, 9, 16; 30:8, 19, 25, 26; 32:15) wrath towards Egypt culminates with the phrase: "then they will know that I am YHWH" (וידעו כי אני יהוה). Mt. Seir and Edom only receive four,[46] the Ammonites three, Sidon and Gog/Magog two, and the Philistines and Tyre only one apiece, thus Egypt doubles its top competitor. While it is likely that the writer of Ezekiel was "incensed over the role played by Egypt in the fall of Judah,"[47] the significance of this set of proportions may also be the result of the strong intertextual relationship between the books of Ezekiel and Exodus already discussed.

Contexts of Covenantal Mercy in Ezekiel

While the majority of the recognition formula's occurrences appear in judgment contexts, a significant minority (nineteen of the seventy-two) appear in contexts of covenantal mercy. What is most intriguing about these instances is where they occur in the book in comparison with the wrath contexts. In Ezek 1–33, contexts of covenantal mercy appear six times (Ezek 16:62; 20:42, 44; 28:24, 26; 29:21) compared to forty-five in contexts of wrath. However, in Ezek 34–39,[48] contexts of covenantal mercy occur thirteen times compared to seven in contexts of divine judgment. So, contexts

---

44. I say "approximately" because some of these depend on how one reads them.

45. I say "roughly" because the number could be nine if one takes 29:21 as explicating wrath towards Egypt through the exultation of the horn of Israel. I am inclined to say, however, that this instance is referring to the knowledge of God that the house of Israel will gain when it observes Egypt's destruction.

46. If one added 25:14, one could perhaps argue that Edom has five occurrences of the formula. However, 25:14 states that Edom will come to know God's judgment, not God as YHWH (i.e.,וידעו את נקמתי נאם אדני יהוה).

47. Ward, *Thus Says the Lord*, 199. Cf. John T. Strong, "Ezekiel's Use of the Recognition Formula in His Oracles against the Nations," *Perspectives in Religious Studies: Journal of the National Association of Baptist Professors of Religion* 22 (1995) 129.

48. Ezekiel 39:28 is the final time that the formula appears in the book. It is interesting to speculate on why the remaining nine chapters lack the phrase.

of wrath dominate earlier portions of the book, while contexts of covenantal mercy take precedence later on.

Also, the ratio of wrath contexts in Ezek 25–33 is skewed towards the other nations. Indeed, sixteen of the wrath contexts are associated with other nations and only one with the desolation of Judah (33:29). Likewise, of the seven wrath contexts found in Ezek 34–39, six address surrounding nations while only one addresses the people of God. Intriguingly, Ezek 39:22 is the lone exception; and, it also happens to be the one context that doubles as a context of covenantal mercy. Thus, beginning already in Ezek 25, the pendulum begins swinging towards mercy. In addition, prior to Ezek 25 there are only three appearances of covenantal mercy contexts, and in each one the tone is still decidedly sober. For example, in Ezek 20:40–44, which contains two of the three covenantal mercy contexts found prior to chapter 25, God tells Ezekiel that all the house of Israel shall serve God on God's holy mountain. God will bring the people out of exile to be priests in the land, and "then you shall know that I am YHWH" (וידעתם כי אני יהוה). However, though the people are back in the land, they will still "loathe" (קוט) themselves for all the evil that they have done (20:43). In addition, God makes it clear that they will know that God is YHWH when God saves them for God's name's sake not because of anything that they have done (20:44).

In contrast to the soberness found in these three mercy contexts, those after Ezek 25 display more enthusiasm at the prospect of divine mercy (though, of course, the sober theme of "for my name's sake" also occurs (see, e.g., 36:23). For example, Ezek 36:8–15 celebrates the reversal of 6:1–14. Whereas earlier the mountains of Israel would witness desolation of the land and slaughter of the people, here Ezekiel prophesies (with almost Deutero-Isaianic fervor) that the mountains will produce branches filled with fruit for the Israelites returning from exile. Similarly, God will work the soil of the mountains by planting seeds of new life everywhere. As a result, people and animals will multiply, and God will treat the mountains (Israel) better than before. Furthermore, the mountains (Israel) will know that God is YHWH (וידעתם כי אני יהוה, 36:11b).

Perhaps the most telling example of the shift in tone lies in the formula's final occurrence in the book, Ezek 39:28. Like its neighbor in 39:22, 39:28 falls within a context of covenantal mercy; but, what is distinct about 39:28 and its context is how it revises the tone of texts like Ezek 20:40–44 and 36:23. God's name is still important, and the defense of that name comes in connection with the restoration of Jacob and compassion upon all the house of Israel (39:25). Yet Ezek 39:26 outlines how the house of Israel will "forget" (נשא) their disgrace and every deed that they did against God (contra 20:40–44). Instead, they will dwell securely in the land, and God will be sanctified in or through them in the eyes of many nations. At this point, they will know that YHWH is their God (וידעו כי אני יהוה אלהיהם) after sending them into exile and then re-gathering them into their own land (39:28). In addition, God promises to never again hide God's face from them, but instead to pour out God's spirit upon the house of Israel (a direct allusion to 37:1–14, which contains three occurrences of the formula within a context of covenantal mercy). Again, while there is undoubtedly a solemn undertone (Ezekiel, after all, is *not* Deutero-Isaiah), the promise of forgetting shame is played in a major key unlike the promise of 20:40–44, which reverberates in a minor one.

In summary then, there are generally two distinct kinds of contexts in which the formula "then you/they will know that I am YHWH" appears. The first is that of divine judgment or wrath. In this sort of context, the knowledge of God comes to the addressees after they have felt the sting of God's anger. The people of God mostly receive this kind of knowledge, but the surrounding nations also come to know YHWH in this way. The second kind of context is that of covenantal mercy. In some ways it both contrasts yet complements the first kind of context. It contrasts in that mercy towards the house of Israel becomes the dominant theme. No longer will judgment have the final word. On the other hand, it complements the first kind of context in that covenantal mercy is the other side of covenantal judgment. However, while these two contexts make up the vast majority of the passages which use the formula, there is a third context, which notwithstanding its small size, is extremely important.

Context of Historical Recitation in Ezekiel

The third and final context of the formula deserves its own elaboration. Despite the fact that it only contains three occurrences of the formulaic phrase, it is perhaps the most important in drawing connections between the Exodus traditions and the book of Ezekiel. In this regard, it will offer a perfect segue to a discussion of the use of the formula in Exodus.

The three instances occur close together and in same context: Ezek 20:12, 20:20, and 20:26,[49] which also doubles as a wrath context for reasons that will become clear. The context for each is historical recital. The chapter begins with the elders of Israel approaching the prophet to inquire of the

---

49. I am not entirely convinced that Ezek 20:26 is a secondary insertion and so have included it in my analysis. It is true that the substitution of אשר for כי is odd, and that the preface למען אשר is unusual. However, I am not inclined to excise it on such grounds. Authors are always free to vary their word choice.

YHWH. However, God is angry with them and commands Ezekiel to cause them to know the abominations of their fathers (את תועבת אבותם הודיעם, 20:4b). From this command emerges a recitation of all that God did for Israel during the time of the exodus.

At the outset, God made himself known to the people as YHWH (20:5). After this gracious self-revelation, God commanded the people to put away the idols of Egypt because they now had a new God (20:7). However, they were unwilling, and God almost destroyed them in the land of Egypt (20:8) but held back for the sake of God's name so that the nations might know the Most High (ואעש למען שמי לבלתי החל לעיני הגוים, 20:9a). So God brought the people out of Egypt and gave them statutes and rules for life. In addition, God graciously gave them Sabbaths as a sign between God and the people so that (and here is the first use of the formula) they might know God as YHWH, the one making them holy (לדעת כי אני יהוה מקדשם, 20:12b). Despite all of this kindness, Israel rebelled in the wilderness, and once again God's hand was stayed only for the sake of God's name (20:14). As a result, only that generation died in the wilderness. To the second generation God offered the same self-revelation and stipulations: "I am YHWH your God. Walk in my statutes and be sure to carefully keep my rules. In addition, make my Sabbaths holy, and they will be a sign between me and you to know that I am YHWH your God" (the second occurrence of the formula, לדעת כי אני יהוה אלהיכם, 20:19–20). However, the children turned out to be just as disobedient as the parents, and a third time God held back on account of God's name (20:22). Nonetheless, God swore to scatter the people in foreign lands and gave them impossible statutes and rules to eventually desolate them. All of this God did "so that they might know that I am YHWH" (אשר ידעו אשר אני יהוה, 20:26b).

At this point the recitation turns back into an indictment (20:27–29), and it is instructive to note how the ambiguity surrounding "they" in 20:26 enables this. The embedded pronoun could refer to either the people of Israel in the wilderness or the people of Israel in Ezekiel's day. In all likelihood it refers to both since they share the same story and thus the same judgment.

It should be clear by now why Ezek 20:26 functions as a contextual double and why these three instances require their own commentary. One could, of course, argue that they represent a subset of the initial category of contexts of divine judgment; but, while the larger context is one of judgment, the local context does not fit neatly into either category (judgment or mercy) and displays something of both in a retelling of the exodus story.

Truly the memory of the exodus tradition shaped the book of Ezekiel in its final form. Indeed, the recognition formula itself provides one tangible literary connection between the texts of Exodus and Ezekiel. In what follows, I examine Exodus's use of the formula. With this analysis complete, the question of Israel's role in Ezekiel becomes clear. Whether in contexts of mercy or judgment, the two books' use of the recognition formula displays a high degree of interdependence, and it is in that interdependence that Israel will take the stage.

The Formula in Exodus

Given the scope and emphasis of this chapter, questions of textual dependency are bracketed. It is sufficient to observe that the formula occurs canonically first in Exodus. In addition, diachronically the phrase is spread across P and non-P sources, suggesting that Ezekiel perhaps knew of Exodus in the form of a redacted Pentateuch.[50] Likewise, Ezekiel's special dislike of Egypt seems to hint at his textual sources. Regardless, from a canonical, synchronic perspective, the reading movement from Torah to Nevi'im encourages readers to hear the intertextual resonances as (at least initially) moving from Exodus to Ezekiel. Thus even if there is disagreement about the diachronic relationship between the two, the reading experience proffers Exodus as the base text with which Ezekiel interacts.

The formula occurs ten times in Exodus (Exod 6:7; 7:5, 17; 8:18 [ET 8:22]; 10:2; 14:4, 18; 16:12; 29:46; 31:33) with an additional seven similar uses of the verb "know" (5:2; 6:3; 8:6 [ET 8:10]; 9:14, 29; 11:7; 16:6). As in Ezekiel, there appear to be general contexts of judgment and mercy: five contexts of judgment (7:5, 17; 8:18; 14:4, 18) and four contexts of covenantal mercy (6:7; 16:2; 29:46; 31:13) with one context that contains both elements (10:2). Furthermore, in each case the formula occurs in contexts of divine *signs* intended to reveal the knowledge of YHWH to Israel and Egypt either through judgment or grace. For example, in Exod 7:17 the formula appears in a context of judgment as a result of Pharaoh's hardness of heart. Despite Moses' staff becoming a serpent, Pharaoh refuses to let Israel go, so God commands Moses to tell Pharaoh, "Thus says the LORD, in this you will know that I am YHWH. Behold, I am striking the water of the Nile with the staff in my hand, and it will turn to blood" (כה אמר יהוה בזאת תדע כי אני יהוה הנה אנכי מכה במטה אשר בידי על המים אשר ביאר ונהפכו לדם). Similarly, the phrase occurs twice in a context of covenantal mercy right before the

---

50. Cf. Brevard S. Childs' reconstruction of the sources of Exodus with the locations of the formula in Exodus. See Childs, *The Book of Exodus*, OTL (Louisville: Westminster Press, 1974) 111, 131. Evans also offers a helpful comparison of Childs's and S. R. Driver's source analysis of Exodus in the passages containing the recognition formulae. See Evans, "An Inner-Biblical Interpretation," 203.

sign of manna and quail in the wilderness. The sign is done so that Israel might know that the God whom they are dealing with is YHWH (16:6, 12). A third example connects directly with the historical recitation in Ezek 20. In Exod 31:13, God tells Moses to speak to the people of Israel regarding the Sabbath: "Surely you shall keep my Sabbaths for this is a sign between me and you throughout your generations to know that I am YHWH the one making you holy" אך את שבתתי תשמרו כי אות הוא ביני וביניכם לדרתיכם לדעת (כי אני יהוה מקדשכם).

In each instance, the formula occurs because neither Pharaoh (Egypt) nor Israel know who YHWH is. In Exod 5:2, Pharaoh famously rebukes Moses: "Who is YHWH that I should listen to his voice and send Israel forth. I do not know (ידעתי) YHWH and neither will I send Israel forth." In Exod 6:3, God tells Moses that God revealed God's Self to Abraham, Isaac, and Jacob as El Shaddai but was not known to them by the name YHWH (ושמי יהוה לא נודעתי להם). Thus, this "knowing" is a form of divine self-revelation. Pharaoh primarily learns it through signs of wrath, but Israel through signs of covenantal mercy and faithfulness (cf. Exod 6:4). Indeed, each time the formula occurs in a wrath context, Egypt is the one learning to know YHWH. In contrast, each time the formula occurs in a context of covenantal mercy or faithfulness, Israel is the one learning to know YHWH.

The Dual Role of Israel in Ezekiel's Drama

All of this brings us back to the question: what role does Israel play in the book of Ezekiel? Put otherwise, if Ezekiel parallels Moses as a mediator of Divine self-revelation, who or what does Israel parallel in receiving this knowledge? The answer is two-fold. On the one hand, Israel plays its perennial role of the disobedient but ultimately redeemed child. Like its ancestors at Sinai, Israel has the tendency towards idolatry even within sight of the cosmic mountain or *axis mundi*.[51] Whereas in the past Israel melded a calf at the foot of the holy mount, in the exilic present, Israel sets up an "image of jealousy" (סמל הקנאה, Ezek 8:5) and idolatrous carvings within the very precincts of the holy temple mount (Zion).[52]

51. For a discussion of mountains as the sight of interaction between the human and divine worlds in the ANE, see Jon D. Levenson, *Sinai & Zion: An Entry into the Jewish Bible* (New York: HarperOne, 1985) 111–37. Cf. Othmar Keel, *The Symbolism of the Biblical World: Ancient Near Eastern Iconography and the Book of Psalms*, trans. Timothy J. Hallett (Winona Lake, IN: Eisenbrauns, 1997) 113–20.

52. Evans also points out that Ezek 16:10–17 and 7:20 may be "an indirect reference to the Golden Calf episode in Exodus." See Evans, "An Inner-Biblical Interpretation," 194.

On the other hand, a comparison of the recognition formula in various contexts of judgment and mercy suggests another role. In Ezekiel, Israel also plays the part of Pharaoh or Egypt. To begin with, it is instructive that in Exodus the recognition formula only appears in contexts of judgment in relation to Egypt. In contrast, thirty-one of the fifty-two judgment context occurrences in Ezekiel relate solely to God's people. Juxtaposing the texts synchronically and canonically, this observation suggests that, in the book of Ezekiel, the house of Israel has become like Egypt. Those who once knew YHWH now live as though Pharaoh's angry statement is their creed: "Who is YHWH that I should listen to YHWH's voice? I do not know YHWH."

Ezekiel also describes the people as "hard of heart" (חזקי לב, Ezek 2:4; and קשי לב, 3:7). Intriguingly, Exodus repeatedly uses the Hebrew verb form of these adjectives to describe God's "hardening" of Pharaoh's heart (ואני אחזק ת־לבו, Exod 4:21; ואני אקשה את־לב פרעה, 7:3).[53] Furthermore, like Pharaoh, the house of Israel must come to know YHWH through signs or plagues of judgment.[54] Israel has become Egypt in its own land. It oppresses

---

53. Risa Levitt Kohn has also noted these linguistic parallels (among many others). See Kohn, "A Prophet Like Moses?," 241.

54. Evans observes these parallels but never formally identifies Israel as a Pharaoh/Egypt-like figure in Ezekiel. He writes, "In an ironic twist, clearly reminiscent of the Exodus story, Ezekiel warns that Yahweh will visit upon Israel—other nations, too—many of the same judgments Egypt experienced. Israel will hand over its jewelry as plunder to foreigners (7:21; cf. Exod. 12:36 [E]). Yahweh will turn the tables by leaving the women of Israel childless (5:17), even as Egypt bewailed the death of its firstborn (Exod. 12:29–30 [J]). The nation will experience "plagues"—in the general sense of "afflictions"—and they are of great variety. Plagues similar to those which struck Egypt mentioned by Ezekiel are: the land being drenched with flowing blood (32:6; cf. Exod. 7:17–21 [J/P]); darkness (30:18; 32:7–8; cf. Exod. 10:21–23 [E]; hailstones (13:11; 38:22; cf. Exod. 9:13–26 [J/E]); pestilence (דבר, bubonic plague?); and the destruction of cattle (32:13; cf. Exod. 9:1–7 [J]). Some of these plagues prophesied in Ezekiel strike Israel and some will be revisited upon Egypt. The general references to 'plague' may also be connected with God's judgment by plague after the Golden Calf incident (Exod. 32:35 [E])." See Evans, "An Inner-Biblical Interpretation," 195. Strong also is aware of connections between the plague narratives of Exodus and the book of Ezekiel, in Strong, "Ezekiel's Use of the Recognition Formula," 123. Levitt Kohn is the only scholar I have found who actually makes the formal step of identifying Pharaoh with Israel. Commenting on the relationship between P and Ezekiel, Levitt Kohn observes, "Numerous terms and expressions with positive connotations in P exhibit negative overtones in Ezekiel. It is as if Ezekiel parodies P language by using terms antithetically. This is especially true of language describing P's Exodus. Alternately, one would have to imagine the Priestly Writer composing Israelite history by transforming images of Israel's apostasy and subsequent downfall into images conveying her exceptional covenant and unique relationship with Yahweh. It is difficult to conceive that the Priestly Writer could have turned Ezekiel's land of exile into Israel's land of promise and Israel's abundant sin into a sign of Yahweh's covenant. It is, however, plausible that Ezekiel, writing in exile, re-evaluated P's portrayal of Israel's uniqueness, cynically inverting these images such that

the foreigner (לגר עשו בעשק בתוכך, Ezek 22:7) like Egypt oppressed the "foreigner" Israel (e.g., Exod 22:20 and 23:9, את וגר לא תלחץ ואתם ידעתם נפש הגר כי גרים הייתם בארץ מצרים). For these reasons, the house of Israel must have an exodus of judgment from its own "Egyptian" land.

Likewise, Israel must suffer a reverse Passover in which an angel clothed in linen receives a commission from YHWH to pass through Jerusalem and mark those who sigh[55] and groan at the idolatry of the city (Ezek 9:1–4). Following this angel are five others armed with war clubs. YHWH's instructions to them are eerily reminiscent of the Passover scene: "Pass over (עברו)[56] into the city behind him, and strike. Your eyes shall not pity nor shall you spare. You shall kill the elder, the young man, the virgin, the child, and the women for destruction. But every person who has the mark, you shall not approach" (9:5–6). Ezekiel is stunned at this Divine brutality and cries out (ואזעק) in a manner analogous to Egypt's cry at the death of the firstborn (צעקה גדלה במצרים, Exod 12:30). He also wonders aloud at YHWH's "destruction" (המשחית) of the remnant of Israel (Ezek 9:7–11).[57]

Ezekiel only goes so far with the analogy before turning it on its head. For the sake of God's name and the covenant (cf. Ezek 16:59–62), God will turn back towards Israel with covenant mercy. Whereas God hardened Pharaoh's heart, God will give Israel a heart of flesh (והסרתי לב האבן מבשרם ונתתי להם לב בשר, cf. 11:19b and its slight variant 36:26).[58] In the end, the

---

what was once a »pleasing odor to Yahweh« now symbolizes impiety and irreverence, *or such that Pharaoh's recalcitrance now characterizes that of Israel.*" See Kohn, "A Prophet Like Moses?," 244; emphasis mine.

55. The word used for "sigh" (אנח) is the same word found in Exod 2:23 for Israel's "groaning" or "sighing" in Egypt.

56. There appears to be a word play here echoing Moses' description of YHWH's "passing over" (עבר) to strike the Egyptians in Exod 12:23.

57. The word echoes YHWH's "destruction" (המשחית) of the Egyptians in Exod 12:23. Evans is aware of the intertextual possibilities resonant between Ezek 9 and Exod 12, but also suggests a resonance with the story of the avenging Levites putting to death idolaters after the golden calf incident in Exod 32. See Evans, "An Inner-Biblical Interpretation," 195. Given the verbal links, I am inclined to favor the former resonance though the dual nature of Israel's role in Ezekiel would be favorable to both.

58. Contra Ward's strange suggestion that Ezekiel is "rationalistic," conveying "no sense of the ambiguity of life, the inevitable conflict of values in human relations, or the nonrational [sic] factors in human behavior." See Ward, *Thus Says the Lord*, 171, 174. One wonders if Ward is still laboring under the shadow of certain strains of Protestantism that hold Priestly material in contempt. In contrast, Childs notes that Zimmerli has effectively challenged such a reading: "Frequently in the history of Ezekiel research, scholars have attempted to draw important theological implications directly from these peculiar stylistic features which were usually of a derogatory nature, e.g., Ezekiel was an unfeeling priest, a rigid legalist, or an individualist who repudiated corporate responsibility. Zimmerli has gone a long way in destroying the foundation of this basic

house of Israel will come to know that God is YHWH not only through judgment but also through signs of covenantal mercy (i.e., return from exile, the removal of shame, the rebuilt temple, etc.). In addition, while God raised up Pharaoh to show God's power and proclaim God's name in all the earth (Exod 9:16), God will use Israel to vindicate the divine name among the nations through a display of judgment but also (and especially) through a display of sweeping mercy (Ezek 36:22–38). In this way, both Israel and the nations will come to know who YHWH is.

At this point an apparent problem surfaces with the narrative analogy. One may object that Egypt's lengthy appearance in Ezek 29–32 voids the intertextual analogy. With such a large amount of prophetic verve spent denouncing Egypt, it may seem like the height of folly to suggest that Israel plays the role of Egypt/Pharaoh in Ezekiel. After all, would it not make better sense to view Egypt as reprising its old role? While at first glance the objection appears to have merit, further consideration proves problematic. The objection assumes a zero sum game in terms of dramatic, intertextual identities and analogies. Just because one character assumes an analogical role does not logically preclude another from sharing it or holding it in a different way. In the complicated web of intertextual discourse, a single book can contain multiple intertextual resonances reverberating in multiple ways. Likewise, multiple characters can share similar characteristics and can even merge at times in terms of dramatic identity.[59]

Such merging is evident in Ezek 29–32. In many ways, Ezekiel's sixth century BCE Egypt bears an uncanny resemblance to Israel in both its exodus and exilic forms. Like Israel, Egypt will receive exile as punishment for its sins (e.g., Ezek 29:12; 30:23, 26, etc.). Also like Israel of old, Egypt will return to its homeland after forty years of wandering (29:13–16). There is a strong sense that Israel and Egypt share a dramatic identity. Of course, they do not simply collapse into each other; but, they do merge to a certain

---

misunderstanding of the prophet's language. He has been able to show, particularly in the use of casuistic legal terminology, Ezekiel's effort to formulate a fresh and vigorous imperative which made use of the traditional language of the cult. When correctly interpreted, the prophet's message was highly existential!" (see Childs, *Introduction*, 363).

59. In literature this sort of thing is common. Characters routinely assume postures, roles, and positions once held (or simultaneously held) by other characters. Novels written around a "focalizing" character at times will shift the focalizing role between characters to explore the other characters' interiority. For more on "focalization," see Mieke Bal, *Narratology: Introduction to the Theory of Narrative*, 2nd ed. (Buffalo, NY: University of Toronto, 1997) 142–61. Similarly, in terms of narrative identity, different characters will share the role of protagonist, antagonist, etc. Such role-changing becomes especially apparent to a reader when the respective story is read in relation to other stories. Perceived intertextual relationships open up the possibilities for new character-understandings.

extent, and there is a play of ambiguity in discerning exactly how much Israel managed to actually separate itself from Egypt during the remembered exodus event. Ezekiel is blunt in maintaining that Israel became a prostitute in Egypt and never renounced her adulterous ways (23).

Part of what makes the contexts of judgment aimed at Israel in Ezekiel so pronounced is their intentional blurring of the boundary between the chosen people and the "unknowing" nations, which is especially the case in how Ezekiel juxtaposes Israel and Egypt. Israel's election almost seems in doubt (and is only reaffirmed later in the contexts of covenantal mercy and historical recitation). Rhetorically, when read as a canonical intertext with Exodus, Ezekiel conflates the dramatic identities of Israel and Egypt. Egypt, once the proud "unknowing" nation ruled by a prince hard of heart, gives way to Israel, the proud "unknowing" nation filled with people hard of heart. Just as Ezekiel is cast in the role of a New Moses who sees YHWH's glory, receives the Torah, and condemns Pharaoh/Israel, Israel is cast in the role of a New Egypt who refuses to know YHWH, practices idolatry, and receives plagues. Just as Ezekiel has merged with Moses in terms of dramatic role (this explains the lack of Moses' name in the book), Israel's fluid relationship with Egypt in Exodus merges into a coalesced dramatic identification that brings with it the possibility that Israel may not recover from judgment. Given the clustering of the contexts of judgment before the contexts of covenantal mercy, this makes good rhetorical sense. Israel can only hear a word of hope after losing all hope. Israel can only become a New Exodus people once it has finally been exercised of its Egyptian demons. Otherwise, Israel can at best only expect to mirror sixth century Egypt in its sober return to its homeland after desolation (Ezek 29:13–16).

Conclusion

When read together, Ezekiel and Exodus display a high degree of analogous material. Their intertextual relationship invites readers to view the prophet Ezekiel as a New Moses and to see the people of Israel as both a recapitulation of their rebellious ancestors and as a New Pharaoh/Egypt. In particular, the books' narrative parallels and similar uses of the recognition formula, along with verbal links and echoes, make it difficult not to read Ezekiel in this way. God as the protagonist reveals himself through acts of judgment and mercy. Ezekiel, as the mediate figure, bears an uncanny resemblance to Moses. Finally, Israel, as the receiver of the Divine self-revelation, plays the dual part of ancestors and national enemy.

Shifting momentarily to a diachronic angle, the point of Ezekiel's Exodus-laced rhetoric seems to be found in the perennial, prophetic call to repentance. It is only when Israel has seen itself in the mirror of Exodus and realized its own Egyptian culpability that new life can come forth. Once Israel has a true knowledge of self and God, the valley of dry bones will begin to rattle and snap as the Pharaonic people of God receive God's spirit in a resurrection return to the promised land (Ezek 37:1–14). Similarly, when read backwards with Ezekiel-eyes (i.e., from Ezekiel to Exodus), Exodus becomes its own prophetic warning, pleading with the covenant people not to emulate Pharaoh's exemplary standard of stubborn unknowing. The knowledge-revealer will reveal himself to the knowledge-receivers through a mediate figure. The only question is: will the revelation come in the context of judgment or of mercy?

5

Promise and Failure

Second Exodus in Ezra-Nehemiah

Joshua E. Williams

Introduction

Old Testament prophets knew well the devastation that God would bring on Israel as he judged them. For many of the prophets God's judgment culminated in Israel's exile. Despite the dark days of exile, the prophets envisioned better days in which Israel would return to the land that YHWH had given them. The prophets used a variety of images to characterize those better days; among them an image of a second exodus appears prominently.

Ezra-Nehemiah describes a period of time in which some from Israel returned to the land from exile. The question naturally arises how the period of return in Ezra-Nehemiah compares to the picture of the prophets, in particular the picture of a second exodus. I will argue that Ezra-Nehemiah presents the return from exile as an anticipated, but ultimately unsuccessful attempt to fulfill prophetic expectation of a second exodus. In order to demonstrate my claim, I will take the following course: (1) examine the explicit mention of the exodus in Neh 9, (2) examine how the exodus may have served as a model for the return alongside other models, (3) describe the role of prophecy in Ezra-Nehemiah, and (4) explore the role of Neh 13 in the message of Ezra-Nehemiah.

Before examining the possibility of a second exodus in Ezra-Nehemiah, there are some points of clarification. First, a second exodus refers to a way of portraying the return from exile analogous to the first exodus from Egypt. However, I am speaking of more than just the journey out of Egypt.

I am including the departure from Egypt, the time at Sinai, the way through the wilderness, and the conquest under Joshua. In other words, a second exodus is a description modeled on the journey of Israel from Egypt to the possession of the land.[1]

Second, I understand the returns of Ezra-Nehemiah (the return before Ezra, the return of Ezra, and the return of Nehemiah) to be presented as one complex event. The return to Jerusalem, construction of the temple, and building of the walls are organically connected together throughout the narrative by the overall logic of the book despite the fact that these events are described from different points of view.[2] Since the returns are presented as a single return, there will be no attempt to describe three separate instances of exodus; rather, the exodus will be compared to the narrative of Ezra-Nehemiah as a whole.

The Exodus in Nehemiah 9

One passage of Ezra-Nehemiah refers explicitly to the exodus from Egypt, the journey through the wilderness, and conquest of the land. The prayer of Neh 9 records important features of the exodus as described in the Pentateuch: the plagues, the crossing of the sea on dry ground, destruction of pursuers, leading through a pillar of cloud or fire, murmurings, and provision of water and food on the journey. Taking a close look at the prayer will help establish some expectations for the way Ezra-Nehemiah interprets the first exodus and how it relates to their present situation.

The prayer consists of two main sections. The first section highlights what YHWH has done (Neh 9:6–15). His activity includes making the sky, land, and sea, choosing Abraham and giving his descendants land, delivering them from Egyptian slavery, guiding them by a pillar of fire or cloud, bringing them to Sinai to give them good and upright laws, sustaining them with food from heaven and water from the rock, and finally commanding them to take the land that YHWH was ready to give them. The only human initiative addressed is that of the Egyptians who acted presumptuously (הזידו) against Israel. Even in the presumptuousness of Egypt, YHWH made a name for himself, presumably by sending the destruction of Egypt he brought about through signs and wonders (9:10). The only other

1. Cf. Michael Fishbane, *Text and Texture: Close Readings of Selected Biblical Texts* (New York: Schocken, 1979) 121–25, for the use of exodus as a "temporal-historical paradigm" and its connection to the conquest.

2. Cf. Tamara Eskenazi, *In an Age of Prose: A Literary Approach to Ezra-Nemehiah*, SBLMS 36 (Atlanta: Scholars, 1988) 38–42, 183. Her concern is not the notion of return, *per se*, but the unifying element of building the house of God.

person who receives an evaluation is Abraham. The prayer states that "You [YHWH] found his [Abraham's] heart faithful before you [YHWH]." The faithful heart of Abraham immediately leads to YHWH's making a covenant with him to give the land. In the first section of the prayer, Abraham's faithful heart is a contrast to the Egyptians' presumptuous treatment of Israel.

The second section highlights the sinfulness of Israel and the compassion of YHWH towards Israel (9:16–38 [HB 9:16—10:1]). Picking up on the presumptuousness of the Egyptians from 9:10, the prayer describes the response of that generation of Israel[3] in the same terms of acting presumptuously (הזידו). They stiffened their necks and refused to listen. However, despite their disobedience, YHWH did not forsake them because of his gracious and forgiving nature.[4] The prayer continues describing their disobedience, this time by describing their making of the golden calf. However, despite this disobedience YHWH does not forsake them, but he continues to sustain them through direction, instruction, food, water, and clothing through forty years in the wilderness. It describes YHWH's handing over Og and Sihon to Israel and then the conquest, including Israel's enjoyment of the land that YHWH gave them. Interestingly, the prayer does not interrupt the possession of the land (9:22–25) in order to describe any of Israel's failures; instead, it shows their victories: how they took possession of the land, captured cities, and enjoyed the fruit of the land.[5] After possessing the land, the prayer emphasizes the repeated disobedience of Israel and compassion of YHWH up to the day of the prayer. At 9:32 the situation shifts from the past to the present. The exile, which began under the Assyrians, continues to the day of the prayer. In all this YHWH acted righteously, but Israel acted wickedly. Even though Israel dwelled in the land that YHWH gave them, they did not heed his warnings or obey his laws.

Before addressing the final two verses of the prayer, let me make some observations regarding the prayer so far. One important observation is the way it relates promise and possession of the land. First, the covenant to possess the land is given to Abraham following YHWH's finding Abraham's heart

---

3. The text reads, "They, our fathers" (והם ואבתינו), following those who understand the *waw* as explicative; e.g., H. G. M. Williamson, *Ezra, Nehemiah*, WBC 16 (Waco, TX: Word, 1985) 304; Joseph Blenkinsopp, *Ezra-Nehemiah: A Commentary*, OTL (Philadelphia: Westminster, 1988) 300.

4. The prayer reflects the language of Exod 34:6 and other passages describing God's graciousness.

5. Blenkinsopp says the following regarding the fact that Joshua is absent from the prayer's portrayal of conquest: "The omission is probably deliberate, serving to emphasize the idea of the land as a divine gift rather than the outcome of human effort," Blenkinsopp, *Ezra-Nehemiah*, 306. Certainly it is a divine gift, but the prayer also appears to be making the point that receiving the land accompanied obedience rather than disobedience.

to be faithful to him (9:8). The implication seems clear enough: if the returning community wants to possess the land, YHWH will need to find in them a heart faithful to him. Connected to this observation is the fact that YHWH brought Abraham out of Ur of the Chaldeans, culminating in his possession of the land.[6] In other words, the prayer portrays God's choice and separation of Abraham from Ur as a means to fulfill his word to give his descendants the land. The same can be said for the exodus, that is, the prayer portrays the exodus as the means by which YHWH brought Israel into possession of the land.

Second, none of Israel's failures interrupt taking possession of the land from the defeat of Og and Sihon until the settling of the land of Canaan. Although the prayer emphasizes that YHWH cares for Israel despite their rebelliousness, the giving of the land itself accompanies obedience.[7] The implication is that YHWH will give the land when Israel faithfully obeys. However, upon their possession of the land, Israel again disobeyed (9:26). The warning rings clear to the generation then living in the land.

The exodus plays a significant role in the prayer. It serves as a means to God's fulfilling his promise regarding the land. The central element of the prayer is Israel's possession of the land. By alluding to the exodus, the prayer shows that God has dealt righteously and graciously with Israel on their way to possessing the land. He has held up his end of every promise. On the other hand, the exodus also shows that Israel has responded wickedly and ungratefully to God, threatening their possession of the land. Certainly, the prayer presents a pattern of behavior that serves as an encouragement to the generation then living in the land that YHWH has not left them and continues to work on their behalf. At the same time, it serves as a warning that the people should not turn away from YHWH as previous generations had done.

However, it may be more than a warning. It may be the model used to characterize those of the return. The final verses of the prayer read as follows:

> (36) Here we are, slaves to this day—slaves in the land that you gave to our ancestors to enjoy its fruit and its good gifts. (37) Its rich yield goes to the kings whom you have set over us because of our sins; they have power also over our bodies and over our livestock at their pleasure, and we are in great distress. (NRSV)

Although many terms of these verses are capable of positive or negative connotations,[8] it is more likely that these verses paint a negative picture

6. A rather obvious parallel to those returning to the land from exile.

7. One may note the same generally positive presentation of Israel's obedience, with some exceptions, in the book of Joshua.

8. Manfred Oeming, "'See, We Are Serving Today,' (Nehemiah 9:36): Nehemiah 9

of the return.[9] In fact, it appears that the prayer really makes no distinction between the period of exile and the present period of return to the land. The exile, which began with the Assyrians, continues on. Rather than experiencing freedom in the land given to their fathers, they are slaves. As a result they make an agreement to end their disobedience and follow God's law (9:38 [HB 10:1]). By looking at the role of the exodus in Neh 9, we have some indicators for how it may function in the rest of Ezra-Nehemiah.

The Return as a Second Exodus

Pilgrimage and Exodus

Although many scholars have characterized the narrative of Ezra-Nehemiah as a second exodus,[10] there are challenges to understanding certain features as depicting a second exodus theme. The first challenge regards the Ezra-Nehemiah narrative as describing a pilgrimage rather than an exodus. Melody Knowles has stated the case well that pilgrimage rather than exodus describes better what is taking place in Ezra-Nehemiah. She identifies several central features of an exodus: 1) it is a journey from a place of bondage to a place of freedom, 2) the oppressed group leaves as a single group, 3) it is primarily for political reasons, 4) and its destination is a general land rather than a specific cultic site.[11] On the other hand, a pilgrimage involves "those who (1) leave their daily sphere of activity, (2) to go to a place that the community has designated to be holy, (3) in order to worship or communicate with the divine."[12]

Although one may properly distinguish what type of journey is described in Ezra, the more important interpretive question is whether Ezra-Nehemiah purposefully employs imagery from other biblical material that involves the exodus from Egypt to describe the return during the Persian period. Furthermore, creating a dichotomy between exodus and pilgrimage

---

as a Theological Interpretation of the Persian Period," in *Judah and Judeans in the Persian Period*, eds. Oded Lipschits and Manfred Oeming (Winona Lake, IN: Eisenbrauns, 2006) 571–88.

9. Although the picture regarding Persian kings is generally positive, especially in comparison to those of other nations, it is still rather ambivalent; for a recent treatment of the subject, cf. Douglas J. E. Nykolaishen, "The Sway of the Persian Sceptre: The Narrative Characterisation of the Persian Kings in Ezra-Nehemiah," PhD diss., University of Edinburgh, 2006.

10. Many such scholars will be listed below when dealing with allusions to the exodus in Ezra-Nehemiah.

11. Melody Knowles, "Pilgrimage Imagery in the Returns of Ezra," *JBL* 123 (2004) 62.

12. Ibid., 63.

may separate what was originally held in common by these biblical authors.[13] This point may be demonstrated in two ways: 1) from the Pentateuch's account of the exodus and 2) from the prophets' description of future restoration from exile.

The Pentateuch's portrait of the exodus employs both exodus and pilgrimage language.[14] During God's calling Moses, he shows that the departure from Egypt has two destinations: the land flowing with milk and honey (Exod 3:8, 17) and the mountain where Israel will worship God (3:12, 18).[15] Moses' request to Pharaoh hits upon the pilgrimage theme: he requests that the sons of Israel be allowed to leave in order to hold a feast for YHWH in the wilderness (5:1). Moses repeats the request, but this time he speaks of going a three days' journey and sacrificing to YHWH (5:3//3:18). The request to leave is repeatedly put in terms of leaving to worship YHWH in the wilderness (7:16; 8:1, 20; 9:1, 13; 10:3, 7). Pharaoh's responses highlight how significant is the pilgrimage itself, not just the activity of worship. Pharaoh offers that they worship in Egypt (8:25), or worship very close to Egypt (8:28), or worship with only the men (10:11), or worship without their livestock (10:24), and then finally to leave with everyone to worship their God (12:31). It is not enough for Moses that the people worship YHWH; they must do it in the wilderness as a feast with all the people. Moses' words confirm this significant point: "we must journey three days in the wilderness and sacrifice to YHWH our God as he has instructed us" (8:27); "we will go with our sons and daughters and with our flocks and herds because ours is YHWH's feast" (10:9); and, "you must let us have sacrifices and burnt offerings so that we may perform them for YHWH our God" (10:25).

This pilgrimage image is overshadowed by exodus once Pharaoh allows the people to go to worship YHWH (12:31). The emphasis moves from the mountain of worship to the land flowing with milk and honey. On the surface these two images appear to be unrelated. However, the text itself may offer a clue that ties the exodus from Egypt to both the promise of land and the place of worship. The Song of the Sea reflects on YHWH's activity in bringing the people out of Egypt, but also describes the future work that YHWH will perform for the sake of the people. In this future work, the promise of land and place of worship merge. The song declares that YHWH will guide Israel to his holy habitation (15:13), plant them on the mountain of his possession

13. Ibid., 62, acknowledges that exodus and pilgrimage imagery intertwine in biblical accounts, pointing out Isaiah 51:9–11 specifically; her point is to demonstrate that pilgrimage explains more features of the descriptions of the returns in Ezra.

14. Cf. Mark S. Smith, *Pilgrimage Pattern in Exodus*, JSOTSup 239 (Sheffield: Sheffield Academic, 1997) 180–261.

15. Knowles, "Pilgrimage," 63, only mentions the former and not the latter, in distinction to Smith, *Pilgrimage Pattern*, 16.

(15:17), and establish his sanctuary (15:17) where YHWH will reign forever (15:18).[16] The obvious reference to a place of worship, his sanctuary, and to a place where the people will be planted, that is, settled permanently,[17] combines the images of exodus with the images of pilgrimage.

Noticing the pilgrimage pattern in the Pentateuch demonstrates that the two categories are not clearly delineated in the "exodus" account, much less other parts of the OT. What should be clear is that pilgrimage imagery alone does not rule out exodus or allusions to the exodus. In fact, in the prophetic material exodus and pilgrimage imagery are used to describe the return to the land.[18] Some passages, such as Isa 51:10–11, include both elements within the same context:

> Was it not you who dried up the sea, the waters of the deep; who made the depths of the sea a way for the redeemed to cross over? So the ransomed of the Lord shall return, and come to Zion with singing; everlasting joy shall be upon their heads; they shall obtain joy and gladness, and sorrow and sighing shall flee away.

The obvious allusion to the exodus, signified by the drying up of the sea so that the redeemed may cross over on its way to Sinai and ultimately the land (cf. Exod 14:21–22; 15:12), accompanies the imagery of pilgrimage, that is, coming to Zion with singing, joy, and gladness.[19] The fact that allusions to the exodus intertwine with pilgrimage imagery demonstrates that they were not treated separately in the Pentateuch or in the prophets. Even though pilgrimage imagery exists in Ezra-Nehemiah, this imagery does not rule out the possibility that Ezra-Nehemiah also casts the return in terms of a second exodus on the basis of the Pentateuch and prophets. The question that remains is whether or not there is sufficient evidence to determine that descriptions of exodus in the Pentateuch and/or the prophets form a paradigm for Ezra-Nehemiah to describe the return to the land. A careful look at the possible allusions between Ezra-Nehemiah and exodus passages should answer the question.

16. The history of research on these verses shows the difficulty in assigning a specific referent because of the proposed contexts for the development of the song. Scholars have assigned various parts of the song from a very early period to a much later one; cf. Smith, *Pilgrimage Pattern*, 222–26. For our purposes, it is only necessary to show that both a promise of land and place of worship are in view.

17. Whenever a people are planted (נטע), it refers to their permanent settlement; cf. 2 Sam 7:10//1 Chr 17:9; Ps 44:3; Jer 18:9; 24:6; Amos 9:15.

18. Eugene H. Merrill, "Pilgrimage and Procession: Motifs of Israel's Return," in *Israel's Apostasy and Restoration: Essays in Honor of Roland K. Harrison*, ed. Avraham Gileadi (Grand Rapids: Baker, 1998) 262–70.

19. Although not all the elements of pilgrimage are present, the intended destination is a cultic site to which they proceed with joyful worship.

Ezra 1–6 and Building Inscriptions

Before looking at the possible allusions between Ezra-Nehemiah and exodus passages, I will look at another challenge to seeing a second exodus theme, especially in Ezra 1–6. This challenge pertains to a possible building inscription underlying the account of Ezra 1–6. Many scholars have argued that Ezra 1:4, 6 contain an allusion to the motif of "despoiling the Egyptians."[20] However, these supposed allusions may be explained as reflecting a common schema of building inscriptions.[21] Apparently, temple-building inscriptions from the Persian period, which reflect an underlying common schema of building, often contain descriptions of "free-will donations from foreigners."[22] Furthermore, the account of Ezra 1–6 closely follows the schema, so that one may infer that the account is based on a building inscription from the period.[23]

Regarding a temple-building paradigm underlying the picture of the return, the following should be kept in mind. First, even though a temple-building schema may lie behind certain features of the narrative presentation of Ezra 1–6, it is clear that Ezra 1–6 is not a building inscription. Other concerns besides temple-building are reflected in the text as it currently stands.[24] Therefore, a temple-building paradigm is only one component of Ezra-Nehemiah's presentation of the return.

Second, even if the temple-building schema accounts for the narrative inclusion of Gentiles bringing in materials for the construction of the temple, the similarities between Exod 12:31–36 and Ezra 1:1–6 still exist.[25] In fact, comparing Ezra 1:1–6 with two other temple-building accounts, one biblical and one extra-biblical, one can see how similar the Ezra account is to the exodus over the two other temple-building accounts. The temple-building account in 1 Kgs 5:15—9:25 describes the acquisition of building materials from foreign peoples in a way much different than Ezra. The most

---

20. See below for more detail.

21. Cf. Lisbeth S. Fried, "The Land Lay Desolate: Conquest and Restoration in the Ancient Near East," in *Judah and Judeans in the Neo-Babylonian Period*, 21–54; cf. Victor Hurowitz, *I Have Built You an Exalted House: Temple Building in the Bible in Light of Mesopotamian and Northwest Semitic Writings*, JSOTSup 115 (Sheffield: Sheffield Academic, 1992) 32–128.

22. Fried, "Land Lay Desolate," 38; cf. Hurowitz, *Exalted House*, 207–10.

23. In fact, Fried argues for an "authentic bilingual building inscription"; see Fried, "Land Lay Desolate," 34–52. It should also be noted that the temple-building account in 1 Kgs 5:15—9:25 corresponds to the schema; see Hurowitz, *Exalted House*, 129–321.

24. Cf. Fried, "Land Lay Desolate," 34–35; as an example, the list of returnees in Ezra 2 does not correspond to any building inscription.

25. Again, see below for more detail.

striking differences include the limited number of contributors (Hiram and Solomon) and the nature of the agreement in terms of trade rather than free-will donations.[26] Comparing Ezra 1:1–6 to the building inscription of Darius I in the Persian period reveals striking dissimilarities as well. Table 1 below lists these texts alongside one another in English translation.

Ezra 1:4–6	Foundation inscription of Darius I at Susa (DSf)[1]
4 And let each survivor, in whatever place he sojourns, be assisted by the men of his place with silver and gold, with goods and with beasts, besides free-will offerings for the house of God that is in Jerusalem." 5 Then rose up the heads of the fathers' houses of Judah and Benjamin, and the priests and the Levites, everyone whose spirit God had stirred to go up to rebuild the house of the LORD that is in Jerusalem. 6 And all who were about them aided them with vessels of silver, with gold, with goods, with beasts, and with costly wares, besides all that was freely offered.	3g. (30–35.) The cedar timber, this—a mountain named Lebanon—from there was brought. The Assyrian people, it brought it to Babylon; from Babylon the Carians and the Ionians brought it to Susa. The yakâ-timber was brought from Gandara and from Carmania. 3h. (35–40.) The gold was brought from Sardis and from Bactria, which here was wrought. The precious stone lapis lazuli and carnelian which was wrought here, this was brought from Sogdiana. The precious stone turquois, this was brought from Chorasmia, which was wrought here. 3i. (40–45.) The silver and the ebony were brought from Egypt. The ornamentation with which the wall was adorned, that from Ionia was brought. The ivory which was wrought here, was brought from Ethiopia and from Sind and from Arachosia. 3j. (45–49.) The stone columns which were here wrought, a village named Abiradu, in Elam—from there were brought. The stone-cutters who wrought the stone, those were Ionians and Sardians. 3k. (49–55.) The goldsmiths who wrought the gold, those were Medes and Egyptians. The men who wrought the wood, those were Sardians and Egyptians. The men who wrought the baked brick, those were Babylonians. The men who adorned the wall, those were Medes and Egyptians.

1. Roland G. Kent, Old *Persian,* 2nd ed. (AOS 33; New Haven, CT: American Oriental Society, 1953), 144.

26. The possible exception to this limited picture may be LXX 3 Kgdms 5:14 in which the kings of the earth bring gifts to Solomon. The problem with identifying this passage with temple building is that the text specifically describes the kings giving these gifts because of Solomon's wisdom rather than as providing materials for the construction of the temple; cf. Hurowitz, *Exalted House,* 221. The same would apply to 1 Kgs 10:24–25.

The expected similarities between the account of Ezra 1 and the building inscription of Darius I are not immediately clear. In fact, one of the most prominent features of the Ezra material is the emphasis on the voluntary nature of the gifts. Even though the Darius inscription may imply such voluntary offerings in distinction from Assyrian inscriptions, the voluntary nature of the offerings is ambiguous at best.[27] The clearest parallel to these sorts of free-will offerings are found in two places in the OT: offerings for the tabernacle construction (Exod 25:2; 35:21, 29) and offerings for the temple construction under David (1 Chr 29:5–9, 14, 17). Such a connection to the acquisition of materials for the construction of the tabernacle and first temple may be expected; however, in contrast to these passages, Ezra 1 seems to describe two kinds of gifts: voluntary gifts for the temple construction and gifts to support the people as they make the journey to rebuild the temple. The emphasis is not on the materials for the construction, but the provision provided for those who will return to Jerusalem so that they may build the temple.[28] The focus of the passage is not only the destination to rebuild the temple but also the journey. In this way, the author shapes his narrative around two models from Israel's past: 1) the construction of the tabernacle/first temple and 2) the journey from Egypt. Both of these elements align well with a second exodus.

Allusions to Exodus

Beginning with Koch, scholars have noted several thematic correspondences between the return in Ezra-Nehemiah and the exodus from Egypt. Koch focused on Ezra's return (Ezra 7–9). He described it as "a cultic procession which Ezra understood as a second Exodus and a partial fulfillment of prophetic expectations."[29] His connections between the return from Babylon and the exodus from Egypt proceeded from the following main points. First, he argued that Ezra set out in the first month from Babylon as a cultic procession because the exodus from Egypt took place in the first month (Exod 12:2; Num 33:3).[30] Second, Ezra required Levites in order to make the

27. Fried, "Land Lay Desolate," 38–39, and Hurowitz, *Exalted House*, 208–10, state that free-will offerings characterize building inscriptions of the Persian period; however, as one can see from the Darius inscription cited above, the voluntariness of these offerings in building inscriptions is not nearly as clear as it is in Ezra-Nehemiah. Hurowitz makes the claim on the basis of his comparing the inscriptions to those of the Assyrians; it is not clear if such an impression would exist for those in the Persian period itself.

28. Nykolaishen, "Persian Sceptre," 96.

29. Klaus Koch, "Ezra and the Origins of Judaism," *JSS* 19 (1974) 184.

30. Ibid., 186. Notice that part of Koch's argument requires viewing the original

journey because the Levites played an important role on the way through the wilderness. He also connected the proclamation of their holiness with Isa 52:11–12 as a way of explaining Ezra's refusal of a military escort (contrary to Nehemiah, cf. Neh 2:9).[31] Third, he noted that upon Ezra's arrival, his actions were similar to those of the conquest: Israel separated from the people of the nations (Ezra 9:1) and later celebrated the Feast of Booths as they did in Joshua's day (Neh 8:17).[32]

Even though Koch only addressed the theme of a second exodus in Ezra's return (Ezra 7–9), other scholars have identified the theme in other passages of Ezra-Nehemiah, especially Ezra 1–6. J. G. McConville provides three important connections between Ezra and the exodus: "(i) release by imperial decree . . . (ii) the aid received by the returned exiles from their Gentile neighbors . . . (iii) the purpose of establishing worship."[33] The most prominent connection of these three is the motif of the "despoiling of the Egyptians."[34] Ezra 1:6 mentions the materials freely given by the other nations as the exiles went on their way back to Jerusalem.[35] The connection to the exodus helps H. G. M. Williamson explain a couple of specific features of the text. First, he points out a "slight change between the wording of the decree [of Cyrus] and its fulfillment, namely the addition of the word כלי 'vessels'"[36] which are included in the Exodus passages that address the "despoiling of the Egyptians" (Exod 3:21–22; 11:2; 12:35–36). Second, this backdrop explains the title assigned to Sheshbazzar as "prince of Judah" since the book of Numbers records the many "princes of the tribes" (Num 2:3–31; 7:1–83; 34:18–28), especially

---

exodus from Egypt as a cultic procession, or at least like a cultic procession. Here again, the pictures of exodus and pilgrimage overlap. Cf. Knowles, "Pilgrimage Imagery," 60–61.

31. Koch, "Origins," 187–88. Since YHWH would protect them, Ezra had no need of a military escort.

32. Ibid., 188; Ralph W. Klein, "The Books of Ezra & Nehemiah," in *The New Interpreter's Bible* (Nashville: Abingdon, 1994–2002) 3:730, also points out that Ezra and those with him rested three days after crossing into the land just as Joshua and those with him rested three days after crossing the Jordan (Josh 3:1–2).

33. J. G. McConville, "Ezra-Nehemiah and the Fulfillment of Prophecy," VT 36 (1986) 208n12. These elements occur in Exod 12:31–36 and have their parallel in Ezra 1:2–6.

34. Peter Ackroyd, *I & II Chronicles, Ezra, Nehemiah: Introduction and Commentary*, TBC (London: SCM, 1973) 215. Cf. Sara Japhet, "The Temple in the Restoration Period: Reality and Ideology," USQR 44 (1991) 213–14; McConville, "Ezra-Nehemiah," 208n12; Williamson, *Ezra, Nehemiah*, 16.

35. Both Ezra 1:4 and 1:6 mention materials to be given to those who return. It seems likely that those giving materials in 1:4 are the Jews who remain behind among the nations rather than returning to Jerusalem, cf. Knowles, "Pilgrimage," 58; however, 1:6 more likely refers to Gentiles, cf. Williamson, *Ezra, Nehemiah*, 16.

36. Williamson, *Ezra, Nehemiah*, 16.

since Num 7:84–85 specifically mention these princes as bringing plates, bowls, and dishes of silver or gold.[37] Third, it explains the use of עלה (hifil "to bring up") rather than יצא (hifil "to bring out") in Ezra 1:11, that is, the people were brought up from Babylon to Jerusalem just as they were brought up from Egypt to the land (Exod 33:1).[38]

Other features of Ezra-Nehemiah may also relate to the return as a second exodus. Jewish tradition identified Ezra as a second Moses. Fourth Ezra 14 portrays Ezra in a manner similar to Moses[39] and the Babylonian Talmud argues that if Moses had not received the law, then Ezra would be worthy to do so.[40] Its argument is based on the following similarities in the portrayal of Moses and Ezra: 1) Moses went up to God (Exod 19:3) to receive the law while Ezra went up from Babylon (Ezra 7:6) in order to do the same, and 2) Moses was commanded to teach Israel statutes and judgments (Deut 4:14) and so Ezra prepared his heart to teach Israel statutes and judgments (Ezra 7:10). This tradition of Ezra as a second Moses continues into the medieval era, as evidenced in the masorah of Codex Leningradensis. It has included the catchwords משה ועזרא ("Moses and Ezra") to the phrase לחם לא אכל ("he did not eat food") at Ezra 10:6, showing that the phrase occurs only here and one other place in the HB: Exod 34:28.[41] Just as Moses fasted before receiving the Ten Commandments after Israel's failure at Sinai, so also Ezra fasted after learning of Israel's failure in their mixed marriages.[42] Identifying Ezra as a second Moses strengthens the case that the return is a second exodus.[43]

Furthermore, the larger plot of Ezra-Nehemiah shares other features with the exodus account: the departure from Egypt eventually leads to the

37. Ibid., 18.

38. Ibid., 19; however, also see the use of עלה pertaining to pilgrimages, Knowles, "Pilgrimage Imagery," 67–68.

39. Cf. Reinhard Kratz, "Ezra—Priest and Scribe," in *Scribes, Sages, and Seers: The Sage in the Eastern Mediterranean World*, ed. Leo G. Perdue (Göttingen: Vandenhoeck & Ruprecht, 2008) 164–69, for a full discussion of the identification and its possible motivations.

40. For instance, see b. Sanh. 21b–22a.

41. For an explanation of the catchwords, see David Marcus, "The Unpublished Doublet Catchwords in Ezra-Nehemiah," in *New Perspectives on Ezra-Nehemiah*, ed. Isaac Kalimi (Winona Lake, IN: Eisenbrauns, 2012) 185–86.

42. Ibid., 195.

43. For a contrary opinion, cf. Robert Piani, "Ezra and the Mediators of the Torah," paper submitted at the Annual Meeting of the Society of Biblical Literature, Chicago, Nov. 17, 2012; Piani rightly points out that Ezra belongs to a line of those who mediated Torah in distinction to Moses. Despite this observation the connections are sufficient to describe Ezra as a second Moses.

proclamation of the law and the establishment of a covenant;[44] the journey from Egypt includes non-Israelites who are often identified with some of its failings (Exod 12:38; Num 11:4);[45] and marriage with foreign women becomes a grave concern (Num 25). These features have parallels in Ezra-Nehemiah: proclamation of law (Neh 8), establishment of covenant (Neh 10), an exclusion of non-Israelites (Neh 13:3),[46] and concern with marrying foreign women (Ezra 9–10; Neh 13).[47]

Discontinuity Between Ezra-Nehemiah and Exodus

Despite the number of thematic connections adduced, admittedly, there are few clear verbal connections between the exodus and the return in Ezra-Nehemiah. Even analyzing the most prominent connection, the despoiling of the Egyptians, reveals little shared vocabulary. For instance, Knowles points out that the word used for "despoiling" in the exodus account (piel נצל) carries negative connotations and is absent from the Ezra account. Instead, Ezra speaks of assisting (piel נשא) and supporting (piel חזק), both words carrying positive connotations.[48] The only clear parallels between the exodus account and the return narrative is the phrase "vessels of silver and gold" (Exod 3:22; 12:35 // Ezra 1:4, 6); however, even this parallel is not complete. The Exodus account reads, "vessels of silver, vessels of gold, and clothing" whereas the Ezra account reads, "vessels of silver, gold, goods, animals, and gifts." As Knowles puts it, "one wonders why the 'clothing' was left out and why beasts and goods and valuable gifts were included."[49]

44. Cf. Mark Throntveit, *Ezra-Nehemiah*, Int (Louisville: John Knox, 1991) 100, where he connects the covenant renewal under Ezra and Nehemiah as reflecting the pattern of the first exodus; this connection accounts for the drastic shift from joy to sorrow.

45. Israel departs from Egypt with a mixed multitude, ערב (Exod 12:38). This group is often associated with the complaining crowd of Num 11:4; cf. Dennis T. Olson, *Numbers*, Int (Louisville: John Knox, 1996) 64; Baruch A. Levine, *Numbers 1–20*, AB 4a (New York: Doubleday, 1993) 321; George B. Gray, *Numbers*, ICC (Edinburgh: T. & T. Clark, 1903) 102; Martin Noth, *Numbers: A Commentary* (Philadelphia: Westminster, 1968) 85.

46. The mixed multitude, ערב (Exod 12:38), has a parallel at the end of Nehemiah (Neh 13:3) where, upon reading the law, Israel separates itself from those who are foreign, ערב.

47. Throntveit, *Ezra-Nehemiah*, 51, argues that the list of peoples in Ezra 9:1 represents a "flashback" to Israel's old enemies in the days of the conquest (and exodus).

48. Knowles, "Pilgrimage," 59.

49. Ibid., 60; also cf. similar observations from Piani, "Ezra."

Besides the distinct vocabulary of the accounts, there are also significant thematic differences as well. The portraits of the foreign kings are virtually opposite of one another. The pharaoh stands in direct opposition to the people leaving Egypt and going to the land; in contrast Cyrus (and his successors) instigates and supports the people going to the land.[50] Other thematic differences already addressed in the distinction between exodus and pilgrimage should also be mentioned. For instance, in Ezra-Nehemiah the people are gathering from all parts of the earth rather than one location as in the exodus and their journey has primarily religious purposes (building the temple) rather than political (establishing a state).

Summary

Looking at the evidence regarding the return of Ezra-Nehemiah as a second exodus leaves a complex picture: it appears that several points of comparison exist between the return and the exodus; however, many of these points are ambiguous, possibly pointing to other paradigms as well, such as pilgrimage and temple-building. Even though the return is portrayed on the basis of more than one model and even though there are incongruities between the exodus and the return, there is still sufficient evidence to argue for the presence of a second exodus theme in Ezra-Nehemiah, although its role may be more limited than sometimes supposed. Certainly the return as a second exodus does not provide explanatory power for all of Ezra-Nehemiah, yet despite its limited role in the book, it still helps uncover an important aim of the book. In order to articulate this aim clearly, a look at the role that prophecy plays in the book is needed.

The Role of Prophecy

Another important point to bear in mind is the relationship between Ezra-Nehemiah and the prophets, in particular Jeremiah. Ezra begins with a reference to the word of YHWH delivered by Jeremiah. Which prophecy or prophecies are in view is difficult to determine.[51] However, evidence in

50. Although see Nykolaishen, "Persian Sceptre," 100–101, for lines of similarity as well.

51. Generally, commentators relate the prophecy to Jer 25:11–12; 29:10 and the seventy years based on the connection to 2 Chr 36:21; Williamson assigns it to Jer 51 and the stirring up of Cyrus to destroy Babylon and rebuild the temple, Williamson, *Ezra, Nehemiah*, 9–10. More likely the reference should be left unspecified so that "the reader [may] ponder what precisely will be completed [of Jeremiah's prophecies]," Eskenazi,

the book suggests that Jeremiah's prophecies concerning the restoration of Israel from exile are in view. In particular, Ezra 7–9 adopts the language of Jer 31, the passage mentioning the new covenant.[52] The verbal similarities are matched by thematic similarities. Jeremiah predicts a return along a straight path and Ezra prays for one. Ezra "has gathered the exiles (viii 15); he is confident that it is God who is the real deliverer and that he (God) leads them for their good (viii 22) and will protect them from the enemy (viii 22, 31); the destination is the holy place."[53] Beyond Ezra 7–9, Neh 8–10 appears to be "in conversation" with Jer 30–33. Thematically, the two accounts are similar. Jeremiah imagines an Israel in which everyone will know the law and will be willing to obey it as God makes a new covenant with them.[54] In Nehemiah all the people of Israel invite the reading of the law, understand it, and are willing to pledge to keep it.[55] The introduction to Ezra-Nehemiah and the correspondences between Ezra 7–9 and Neh 8–10 to Jer 30–33 make it clear that Jeremiah's picture of restoration forms part of the backdrop to the book.[56] Furthermore, the fact that the word of YHWH through Jeremiah introduces the book provides a possible avenue for reading the book: it is a book about the realization of the restoration promises of the prophets, Jeremiah in particular.[57]

Age of Prose, 44; cf. A. Philip Brown II, *Hope Amidst Ruin: A Literary and Theological Analysis of Ezra* (Greenville, SC: Bob Jones University Press, 2009) 126–27.

52. McConville, "Ezra-Nehemiah," 214–18. The parallels that he produces are as follows: Jer 31:7 את שארית ישראל//Ezra 9:14 שארית; Jer 31:8, 10 וקבצתים, יקבצנו//Ezra 8:15 ואקבצם; Jer 31:12, 14 טוב, טובי//Ezra 8:22 לטובה; Jer 31:16 איב//Ezra 8:22, 31 (מ) איב; Jer 31:9 (cf. 21) דרך//Ezra 9:6 (cf. 8:22) בשתי ונבלמתי וגם נכלמתי בשתי; Jer 31:19 ישר//Ezra 8:21 ישר; Jer 31:40 קדש//Ezra 9:8 (קדשו) במקום (קדשו); Jer 31:6 (ציון) ונעלה//Ezra 7:9 (יסד) המעלה. One may also look at the parallels between Ezra 9:11 and Jer 2:7; 16:18 and especially Ezra 9:12 and Jer 29:6–7, Mark Leuchter, "Ezra's Mission and the Levites of Casiphia," in *Community Identity in Judean Historiography*, eds. Gary Knoppers and Kenneth Ristau (Winona Lake, IN: Eisenbrauns, 2009) 187–88. Christiane Karrer-Grube produces further comparisons especially for Neh 8–10 and Jer 30–33, Karrer-Grube, "Scrutinizing the Conceptual Unity of Ezra and Nehemiah," in *Unity and Disunity in Ezra-Nehemiah: Redaction, Rhetoric and Reader*, eds. Mark J. Boda and Paul L. Redditt, HBM 17 (Sheffield: Sheffield Phoenix Press, 2008) 150–54.

53. McConville, "Ezra-Nehemiah," 215.

54. Karrer-Grube, "Conceptual Unity," 152.

55. Ibid., 153: "The idea of all people being responsible to join the covenant and to keep Torah corresponds with the characterization of the new covenant in Jeremiah 31 and 32."

56. Ibid., 158, in fact concludes that "almost the whole text of Nehemiah can be read as a fulfillment of the promises of Jeremiah."

57. Generally, the language of Ezra 1:1a is considered straightforward: "In the first year of Cyrus king of Persia, so that the word of YHWH by the mouth of Jeremiah might be fulfilled." However, upon closer examination several questions concerning the

Despite a number of correspondences between Jeremiah's restoration promises and Ezra-Nehemiah, there is still some dissidence. Some of this dissidence is felt when looking at the role the exodus plays among Jeremiah's restoration promises. Two passages in particular contrast the future restoration after exile to the exodus from Egypt: Jer 16:14–15 and Jer 23:7–8. These verses indicate that the future restoration will be so great that there will no longer be a need to remember the exodus from Egypt. In Jer 31:31 the covenant of the exodus also serves as a contrast to the covenant God will make in the future restoration. The contrast between the two covenants is the contrast of disobedience and obedience. When YHWH makes this new covenant, Israel will no longer be characterized by their rebellion since he will place his law within them.

As mentioned above, Neh 8–10 appears to have Jer 30–33 in the background. Christiane Karrer-Grube argues that Ezra-Nehemiah alludes to Jeremiah in order to demonstrate how the word of YHWH through him was fulfilled in the days of Ezra and Nehemiah.[58] However, Jer 31 is not concerned with whether the people are willing to obey the law. Israel at Sinai was willing to obey the law, and even agreed to do so—they just failed. The picture of Jer 31 is one in which Israel will succeed in obeying where it previously failed.[59]

Prophecy serves an important function in Ezra-Nehemiah. In particular, YHWH's word through Jeremiah sets the narrative in motion (Ezra 1:1) and drives it forward. Several aspects of the prophecy appear to be fulfilled during the days of the return. There is a sense of hope and anticipation that accompanies the successes of the returnees and their attempts to deal with any shortcomings. At the same time there is a tension that arises because Jeremiah's promises set up readers to expect an ultimately obedient people

---

syntax and semantics of this phrase arise; cf. Serge Frolov, "The Prophecy of Jeremiah in Esra 1,1," *ZAW* 116 (2004) 595–601. Despite the ambiguities, I understand the verse in the traditional way, as a statement of purpose although not necessarily a purpose that is fulfilled.

58. Karrer-Grube, "Conceptual Unity," 152–54.

59. Eskenazi, "Unity and Disunity," 325, raises two problems with connecting Neh 8–10 with Jer 30–33. First, she argues that many of the points of similarity could be explained by other biblical passages besides Jer 30–33. Second, Ezra-Nehemiah portrays the relationship with YHWH as governed by one covenant, the covenant made with Abraham (Neh 9:7–8). Eskenazi states, "The unbroken nature of this covenant is crucial to Ezra-Nehemiah and may explain why the pact in Nehemiah 10 is not called a 'covenant' but an אמנה." Despite these problems Neh 8–10 still has Jer 30–33 in the background: the emphasis on everyone knowing the law and obeying it is sufficient to tie the two together. Furthermore, Ezra-Nehemiah's emphasis on one covenant governing the relationship between Israel and YHWH signifies lines of continuity that will be traced in the discussion below regarding Neh 13.

to carry out the return. A look at Neh 13 will help determine if the people returning fulfilled such an expectation.

The Role of Nehemiah 13

Nehemiah 13 holds a critical role in determining the book's portrayal of the post-exilic community and its relation to restoration promises of the prophets, especially Jeremiah. Its position at the end of the book gives it the opportunity to present the last word. However, one wonders whether it is an evaluation of what has led up to it or simply an appendix, somewhat detached from what immediately precedes it.[60] Its placement within the chronological framework of the book is important to answering the question. The initial phrase of Neh 13:4, "now before this" (ולפני מזה), is most often understood to refer to the time before the reading of the law recorded in Neh 13:1. Many scholars argue that the events of Neh 13 go back even further to the time preceding the oath to which the community agrees in Neh 10.[61] Although the chronological picture from Neh 12:44—13:31 is difficult to determine because the chronological notices are generally vague,[62] it appears that verses 4–31 have a common temporal point of departure: Nehemiah's return to Jerusalem. Nehemiah's absence is highlighted in Neh 13:6, and his return forms the backdrop for his discovering the evil of Eliashib and finding out the people's neglect of the Levites. Therefore, the phrase "now before this" sets the stage for the subsequent problems recorded in Neh 13 to be the results of Nehemiah's absence.[63] This backdrop is confirmed by the repetition of the chronologi-

---

60. In other words, is Neh 13 an attempt to characterize the entire book of Ezra-Nehemiah or is it an attempt to fill out the picture of Nehemiah's importance in the reforms? Cf. Williamson, *Ezra, Nehemiah*, 383–84. Blenkinsopp, *Ezra-Nehemiah*, 353, refers to the section as a "rather longer extract from the NM [Nehemiah Memoir] dealing with various problems encountered toward the end of his administration and how he solved them."

61. E.g. Williamson, *Ezra, Nehemiah*, 331; Throntveit, *Ezra-Nehemiah*, 124–25: "According to widespread scholarly opinion, the community's promise to abide by the covenantal stipulations in Nehemiah 10 *historically* took place following the events of Nehemiah 13 as a positive response to Nehemiah's reforms."

62. The notices are as follow: "in those days" (13:5, 23), "on that day" (12:44; 13:1), "now before this" (13:4), and "while this was happening" (13:6).

63. Cf. Greg Goswell, "Time in Ezra-Nehemiah," *TrinJ* 31 (2010) 200–201. One may also consider the suggestion of Throntveit, *Ezra-Nehemiah*, 122, that the phrase translated "Now before this" is circumstantial, meaning "in the face of this, despite this," rather than temporal. If such were the case, then the reference point in the chronology of the passage would still be Nehemiah's return to Jerusalem.

cal marker "in those days" (13:15, 23).[64] In other words, "those days" are the days in which Nehemiah returned to Jerusalem from his visit with the king. Before his return, while he was absent, Eliashib prepared a room for Tobiah, the people failed to support the Levites, the people violated the Sabbath, and some of the men had married foreign wives. Upon his return, he sought to deal with the evils of the people.

In light of the chronological picture that emerges in 13:4–31, the final episode is not just a flashback to a previous period in the book in order to bolster the picture of Nehemiah (i.e. before the taking of the oath recorded in Neh 10), but it constitutes a final look into the community of the return. This final look draws a point of comparison to the oath of the people recorded in Neh 10. The oath requires prohibition of intermarriage to foreign women (10:30 [HB 10:31]), observance of the Sabbath (10:31 [HB 10:32]), and support for the temple and its attendants (10:32–39 [HB 10:33–40]). Upon Nehemiah's return to Jerusalem, he discovers that the people have violated each of these provisions of their oath. Thus, despite the tremendous positive outlook towards the return to Jerusalem, the building of the temple, and the construction of the walls of the city, the book ends with an anticlimax: "The book ends (Neh 13:4–31) with the depressing picture of the re-emergence of the problems that earlier beset the community (Neh 10:28–39)."[65]

If the negative outlook were unique to Neh 13, one may doubt whether it should hold such an important role in the book. However, this type of anticlimax has been anticipated by other anticlimaxes in the book.[66] When the temple foundation is completed, the sound of rejoicing is mixed with the sound of weeping (Ezra 3:12–13). After the wall is finished, Neh 6:17–19 mentions Tobiah's attempts to intimidate Nehemiah, portraying Tobiah as a continual threat.[67] This anticlimax in particular is helpful for understanding the role of Neh 13 since Tobiah appears again at the end of the book so that "the narrator deliberately subverts the reader's perception that the returned community had successfully reached the goal for which it strove."[68]

---

64. One might object because Williamson has argued that Neh 12:44–13:14 forms a unit "drawn up on the basis of a chiastic structure," Williamson, *Ezra, Nehemiah*, 380. However, Goswell has demonstrated that 13:4–31 also constitutes a chiastic structure, Goswell, "Time," 202.

65. Goswell, "Time," 202.

66. Cf. McConville, "Ezra-Nehemiah," 207–13, for signs of disappointment reflected in the view of Persia, the relation to cultic institutions, and the issue of mixed marriages.

67. Regarding the genuineness of the location of these verses, cf. Goswell, "Time," 198–99.

68. Goswell, "Time," 199.

This negative outlook is furthered confirmed by taking another look at the prayer of Neh 9. As pointed out above, the prayer presents the exodus as a means for achieving the possession of the land promised to Abraham because of his faithful heart. At the same time the exodus generation acted presumptuously against YHWH, yet he was compassionate and did not abandon them. That generation clearly served as a warning for the generation of returnees; it is because of God's mercy and Israel's past disobedience that the community agrees to the oath (באלה ובשבועה) of Neh 10. At the same time the description of the exodus generation served as more than just a warning. It served as a paradigm for interpreting the returned community. They, just like the exodus generation, observed the mercy of YHWH but still struggled with disobedience.

The connection becomes clearer when comparing Ezra 9 to Neh 9. In Ezra 9:8–9, Ezra refers twice to the conditions of his day as slavery (עבדות). The same word occurs only one other time in the HB: Neh 9:17. In that passage the word describes the exodus generation's slavery in Egypt. A feature of the exodus generation's rebellion was their desire to return to slavery in Egypt. Yet, Ezra describes his own situation in the same terms because the returnees had failed to separate themselves from the nations living in the land.[69] The prayers of Ezra 9 and Neh 9 present a disobedient community still in bondage, in exile. The measures of Ezra 10 and Neh 10 were intended to head off the community's disobedience by following the Law of Moses (Neh 10:29). Despite the attempts to shape the returnees into an obedient community through oaths to keep God's law through Moses, Neh 13 demonstrates that such attempts ultimately failed.

Conclusion

Ezra-Nehemiah closes by highlighting the failure of those living in the land to keep their end of the covenant stipulations spelled out in Neh 10. YHWH had worked on their behalf, bringing them back to the land he had promised and restoring the temple in Jerusalem. God had worked to fulfill the promises of restoration declared by the prophets, especially Jeremiah; however, despite the best efforts of Ezra, Nehemiah, other leaders, and even the people themselves, they failed to hold up their end of the bargain. This failure on the part of the people casts a long shadow on Ezra-Nehemiah. It calls into question the fulfillment of Jeremiah's prophecies regarding restoration. In particular, it rules out the possibility that this return is the restoration

69. McConville, "Ezra-Nehemiah," 212, states "that mixed marriage is closely associated with the idea of slavery."

that is so great that no one will even mention the exodus from Egypt. It rules out the possibility that this return is the restoration in which a new covenant is made (although a covenant is made in Ezra-Nehemiah) and there is no longer any need to teach the law to one another. The returnees are like that generation that God brought out of Egypt and even though he was a husband to them, they broke the covenant he made with them.

YHWH is faithful, and his faithfulness is exhibited in the growing anticipation that the promises made by the prophets will be fulfilled in the days of the return. The signs of success throughout the narrative function to show the power and faithfulness of YHWH to accomplish what he has promised. However, disappointment settles in as Ezra-Nehemiah draws to a close. The people have failed, just as Israel of the past did. Israel after the exile is the same as Israel before the exile, and the promises of restoration linger on into future days.

The picture that emerges from Ezra-Nehemiah is as follows: the return is portrayed with increasing expectation that returned Israel will fulfill the restoration promises, in particular those of Jeremiah. These promises are based on a comparison to the exodus from Egypt and the taking of the land. Although there are setbacks, the community does rather well, heading off problems as they arise (much like Achan's sin in the days of Joshua). As the narrative reaches its highpoint in the reading of the law, the prayer of confession and repentance, the swearing of the oath, settling of Jerusalem, and construction of its walls, the community looks most like the picture of the restored community promised by the prophets. However, just as the expectation reaches its highest level, the book portrays the community's final failure and pushes the promises into the future. The book presents the signs of fulfillment as a way of exalting the faithfulness and power of YHWH. The signs of failure magnify the disappointment with the post-exilic community: post-exilic Israel is the same as pre-exilic Israel. God's promises are yea and amen, but the Israel of Ezra-Nehemiah is not the Israel of Jer 31.

6

The (New) Exodus in Luke and Acts

An Appeal for Moderation

Joshua L. Mann

Few books in the NT have received as much attention related to the use of Exodus traditions as Luke and Acts.[1] Scholars often argue that the Exodus story enters through one of two ways: Exodus/Moses typology or the use of Isaianic New Exodus themes and allusions. While not denying the presence of either, this essay especially questions the extent to which the Isaianic New Exodus is present in and controls the narrative(s) of Luke and Acts. In so doing, the essay will interact extensively with the most substantial and influential contribution to the topic, David W. Pao's *Acts and the Isaianic New Exodus*.[2] After discussing some preliminary matters, there is a brief

1. I will refer to the Third Gospel and the book of Acts together (i.e., Luke-Acts) on occasion when discussing a work that does the same, but most often I will refer to the two books as "Luke *and* Acts" so as to encompass the two common views of the unity of Luke and Acts: (1) The two comprise two-volumes of the same literary project and thus should be read together—a common view in recent decades, argued as early as Henry J. Cadbury, *The Making of Luke-Acts* (New York: Macmillan, 1927); and (2) Acts is perhaps composed as a sequel to Luke (or is similarly related), but the two do not represent a singular planned project—see discussions in Andrew F. Gregory and C. Kavin Rowe, eds., *Rethinking the Unity and Reception of Luke and Acts* (Columbia, SC: University of South Carolina Press, 2010); cf. Mikeal C. Parsons and Richard I. Pervo, *Rethinking the Unity of Luke and Acts* (Minneapolis: Fortress, 1993). Note a third view: Luke and Acts are written by different authors, therefore any unity between the two must be explained without reference to shared authorship; see Patricia Walters, *The Assumed Authorial Unity of Luke and Acts: A Reassessment of the Evidence*, SNTSMS 145 (Cambridge: Cambridge University Press, 2009).

2. I would like to thank David Pao for his willingness to read a draft of this essay. Pao's thesis was first published by Mohr Siebeck in 2000 and reprinted by Baker in 2002.

94

presentation of the relevant scholarly discussion to date. Next, there is a summary of Pao's argument followed by an extensive critique which shows that the case he makes for the extent of Lukan[3] usage of the Isaianic New Exodus is too fragile to stand without significant moderation.

Preliminary Matters: Exodus Traditions

When examining how the Exodus traditions may be employed in Luke and Acts, one should first clarify what constitutes an Exodus tradition in the first place. In using the term "Exodus" here, reference is made to the event(s) of the Exodus narrated within the canonical book by the same name, roughly including the events narrated in Exod 1–15. The climax of the Exodus story is, to risk stating the obvious, the parting of the Red Sea, Israel's successful crossing, and the destruction of Israel's pursuer, the Egyptian army, all of which demonstrates the power of YHWH wrought for the sake of Israel (Exod 14). But in speaking of the Exodus, one must also recall the events which precipitated the aforementioned climax, not only the oppression of Israel and escalating conflict between Israel (esp. Moses and YHWH) and Egypt (esp. Pharaoh and the Egyptian gods) (Exod 1–13), but God's covenant promises to Israel, originally made to Abraham (Gen 12:1–3; 15:13–21)—promises that appear to be in jeopardy in the early Exodus narrative. The book of Exodus mentions the Abrahamic covenant as early as Exod 2:24–25. It appears again in 6:2–9 and after the Exodus event in 32:13 and 33:1–3. The Song of Moses, appearing just after the climax and summary statement (14:30–31), alludes to the land promise of the covenant: "Lead and plant them in the mountain of your inheritance, to your prepared dwelling that you made, Lord, a sanctuary, Lord, that your hands prepared" (Exod 15:17 LXX).[4] Thus the Exodus story is roughly contained in Exod 1–15 and includes the backdrop of the covenant promises God made to

---

See David W. Pao, *Acts and the Isaianic New Exodus*, WUNT 2/130 (Tübingen: Mohr/Siebeck, 2000).

3. I will refer to the author of Luke and Acts as "Luke" out of convenience and without assuming his precise identity (e.g., Luke, the companion of Paul). I will similarly use the adjective "Lukan."

4. I here translate from the LXX since it is most likely the version of the material with which the author of Luke and Acts would be familiar. The LXX follows closely to the MT in this instance, most notably translating the two Hebrew imperfects that begin the verse with imperatives in Greek. The sense one has when reading the LXX is that verses 16–17 are an entreaty (note the optative in verse 16 and imperatives in verse 17) whereas in the MT the verses are statements about what God has done and will do.

Israel. Subsequent uses of the Exodus story in Scripture often invoke this theme of a promised inheritance.

For our purposes, an "Exodus tradition" is a text which cites, alludes to, or thematically utilizes the Exodus story as described above.[5] Examples of an Exodus tradition could include the recollection of the Exodus events in Deuteronomy (e.g., Deut 6:20–25), allusions to the Exodus in Psalms (e.g., Ps 65:6 LXX), or Moses/Exodus typology in Luke's travel narrative (roughly Luke 9–19). The Exodus tradition in which this essay is primarily interested is found in Isa 40–55. Isaiah's evocation of Exodus themes and language to describe Israel's future salvation is often described as the Isaianic New Exodus (e.g., Isa 40:3–5; 43:14–21). These New Exodus themes are applied to the stories of Jesus and the early Christian movement, and they are claimed to be present in Luke and Acts through Isaianic citations, quotations, allusions, and echoes.

Lukan Use of Scripture and the Exodus in Scholarship

The use of Scripture in Luke and Acts has received a healthy amount of attention in recent scholarship.[6] That Luke employed the LXX for citations and allusions has become a strong consensus view.[7] Paul Schubert's seminal essay, "Structure and Significance in Luke 24," articulates what has become a common description of Luke's use of the Scriptures—an apologetic "proof-from-prophecy" hermeneutic.[8] Darrell Bock notably rejects the apologetic intention of Luke, but similarly described Lukan use of Scripture as *proclamation* from prophecy and pattern, arguing that Luke predominately uses the Scriptures christologically to show how Jesus is the fulfillment of various promises in the Scriptures, most significantly that Jesus is the "Messiah-Servant" and "Lord of all."[9] Schubert, Bock, and others emphasize Luke's use

5. One could speak of an oral Exodus tradition, but the data for this study includes only textual data.

6. A full account of recent scholarship on the subject of Lukan use of Scripture lies outside the scope of this essay. For a recent summary, see Kenneth D. Litwak, "The Use of the Old Testament in Luke-Acts," in *Issues in Luke-Acts: Selected Essays*, eds. Sean A. Adams and Michael Pahl, Gorgias Handbooks 26 (Piscataway: Gorgias, 2012) 147–69; cf. François Bovon, *Luke the Theologian: Fifty-five Years of Research (1950–2005)*, 2nd ed. (Waco, TX: Baylor University Press, 2006) 87–121, 525–31.

7. Since Traugott Holtz, *Untersuchungen über die alttestamentlichen Zitate bei Lukas*, TU 104 (Berlin: Akademie, 1968).

8. Paul Schubert, "The Structure and Significance of Luke 24," in *Neutestamentliche Studien für Rudolf Bultmann*, ed. W. Eltester (Berlin: Alfred Töpelmann, 1954) 165–86.

9. Darrell L. Bock, *Proclamation from Prophecy and Pattern: Lucan Old Testament Christology*, JSNTSup 12 (Sheffield: JSOT Press, 1987) 270.

of a "promise-fulfillment" hermeneutic by which he seeks to demonstrate especially that Jesus fulfills messianic hopes spoken of in the Scriptures.[10]

Other scholars empasize that Luke's use of Scripture is as much (or more) ecclesiological as (than) christological, showing that the new Christian community is in some sense part of the people of God and heir of Israel's promises.[11] Many publications from the last two decades take an intertextual approach to examining Luke's use of Scripture, influenced especially by Richard Hays's book, *Echoes of Scripture in the Letters of Paul*.[12] Such an approach is especially sensitive to how texts relate to one another, paying careful attention to detect possible echoes of texts within texts, and examining how those texts inform one another.

In particular, the presence and influence of Exodus traditions in the Lukan narratives has been observed in various ways. Scholarship reflects two common views regarding the presence of Exodus traditions in Luke and Acts: (1) The Exodus is used to pattern Jesus after Moses, as a prophet who is leading a salvific exodus; and (2) The expectations of Isaiah's New Exodus are portrayed as fulfilled (or being fulfilled) by Jesus and the early Christian movement. Scholars often focus on just one of these or the other.[13] Jindrich Mánek argues that Luke extensively develops a New Exodus typology and structures his narrative around the framework of the Exodus story.[14] However, more modest Moses/Exodus typology proposals have been made for Luke and Acts.[15] David Moessner, for example, finds a Moses/Deutero-

10. E.g., Mark L. Strauss, *The Davidic Messiah in Luke-Acts: The Promise and Its Fulfillment in Lukan Christology*, JSNTSup 110 (Sheffield: Sheffield Academic, 1995); Rebecca I. Denova, *The Things Accomplished among Us: Prophetic Tradition in the Structural Pattern of Luke-Acts*, JSNTSup 141 (Sheffield: Sheffield Academic, 1997).

11. E.g., Pao, *Acts*; Kenneth Duncan Litwak, *Echoes of Scripture in Luke-Acts: Telling the History of God's People Intertextually*, JSNTSup 282 (London: T. & T. Clark, 2005).

12. E.g., Robert L. Brawley, *Text to Text Pours Forth Speech: Voices of Scripture in Luke-Acts* (Bloomington: Indiana University Press, 1995); Pao, *Acts*; Litwak, *Echoes*. Cf. Richard B. Hays, "The Liberation of Luke-Acts: Intertextual Narration as Countercultural Practice," in *Reading the Bible Intertextually*, eds. Hays et al. (Waco, TX: Baylor University Press, 2009); and Hays, "The Paulinism of Acts, Intertextually Reconsidered," in *Paul and the Heritage of Israel: Paul's Claim Upon Israel's Legacy in Luke and Acts in the Light of the Pauline Letters*, eds. David P. Moessner et al., LNTS 452 (London: T. & T. Clark, 2012) 35–48.

13. Though both are emphasized in Robin Ernest Nixon, *The Exodus in the New Testament* (London: Tyndale, 1963).

14. Jindrich Mánek, "The New Exodus in the Books of Luke," *NovT* 2 (1957) 8–23.

15. Note Edgar L. Allen's proposal, which predates Mánek's by about a decade, in Allen, "Jesus and Moses in the New Testament," *ExpTim* 67 (1955–1956) 104–6, as well as that of Félix Gils, *Jésus prophète d'après les Évangiles synoptiques* (Louvain: Publications Universitaires/Insituut voor Orientalisme, 1957); cf. Paul S. Minear, *To Heal*

nomic pattern present in Luke and Acts, especially in the travel narrative of
the Third Gospel:

> The consummated Exodus journey of the Prophet like but
> greater than Moses (Luke 9:51—19:44) forms the dynamic
> center of Luke's unfolding drama of the journeying history of
> Israel's salvation. . . . As that great work of the Deuteronomist
> historians consists of the deliverance wrought for Israel in the
> Exodus story of Moses (Deuteronomy) and is completed by the
> unfolding history of that salvation (Joshua—2 Kings), even as
> Moses foresaw and prophesied, so Luke's first volume presents
> the consummation of the first Exodus in the New Exodus story
> of Jesus and is completed in the unfolding history of that salva-
> tion, even as Jesus foresaw and prophesied.[16]

The other common way Exodus traditions are proposed to have found
their way into Luke and Acts is through Luke's use of the New Exodus found
in Isaiah (esp. Isa 40–55). This view stands on three legs: (1) Isaiah 40–55
presents Israel's future salvation in the language of the Exodus, and thus
presents an eschatological New Exodus for Israel;[17] (2) Luke and Acts utilize
Isaiah in significant ways and at key locations in the narrative showing that
the book of Isaiah is significant for understanding the narrative; and (3)

---

and to Reveal: The Prophetic Vocation according to Luke (New York: Seabury, 1976)
102–21. Also note the discussion of the possible influence of Deuteronomy (and Kings)
on Luke's structure in Craig A. Evans, "The Function of the Elijah/Elisha Narratives in
Luke's Ethic of Election," and Evans, "Luke 16:1–18 and the Deuteronomy Hypothesis,"
in Luke and Scripture: The Function of Sacred Tradition in Luke-Acts, eds. Evans and
James A. Sanders (Minneapolis: Fortress, 1993) 70–83, 121–39; cf. J. Severino Croatto,
"Jesus, Prophet like Elijah, and Prophet-Teacher like Moses in Luke-Acts," JBL 124,
no. 3 (2005) 451–65. Thomas L. Brodie has argued extensively for the influence of the
Elijah-Elisha narrative/Genesis–Kings on Luke-Acts in Brodie, "Luke-Acts as an Imita-
tion and Emulation of the Elijah-Elisha Narrative" in New Views on Luke and Acts,
ed. Earl Richard (Collegeville, MN: Liturgical, 1990) 78–85, and for its influence upon
the Gospels in Brodie, The Crucial Bridge: The Elijah-Elisha Narrative As an Interpretive Synthesis of Genesis-Kings and a Literary Model for the Gospels (Collegeville, MN:
Liturgical, 2000).

16. David P. Moessner, Lord of the Banquet: The Literary and Theological Significance of the Lukan Travel Narrative (Minneapolis: Fortress, 1989) 325.

17. See, e.g., Bernhard W. Anderson, "Exodus Typology in Second Isaiah," in Israel's
Prophetic Heritage: Essays in Honor of James Muilenburg, eds. Anderson and Walter
Harrelson (New York: Harper & Brothers, 1962) 177–95; Joseph Blenkinsopp, "Scope
and Depth of the Exodus Tradition in Deutero-Isaiah, 40–55," in The Dynamism of
Biblical Tradition, Concilium 20 (New York: Paulist, 1967) 41–50; Rikki E. Watts, "Consolation or Confrontation? Isaiah 40–55 and the Delay of the New Exodus," TynBul 41,
no. 1 (1990) 31–59.

The New Exodus found in Isaiah is detectable at textual, conceptual, and structural levels in Luke and Acts.

Four publications in the decade leading up to and including the year 2000 stand out for mention in regard to research on the Isaianic New Exodus, the first publication of which focuses on the concept in the Gospel of Mark but influences subsequent related studies in Luke and Acts. Rikki Watts's dissertation (subsequently published) argues that the narrative of Mark proceeds on the Isaianic New Exodus's three-fold framework—YHWH delivers his people as Warrior and Healer (cf. Jesus' Galilean healing/exorcism ministry), "leads the blind along the [New Exodus] way of deliverance" (cf. Jesus' "way" to Jerusalem), and finally arrives at Jerusalem (cf. Jesus' "enthronement" in Jerusalem, ironically *via* the cross).[18] Mark tips off his reader to the programmatic use of the Isaianic New Exodus in his prologue's citation of Isa 40:3 and Mal 3:1/Exod 23:20, highlighting the theme of not only New Exodus hope (Isa 40–55) but pending judgment (Mal 3).[19] Watts's broader claim of the influence of the Isaianic New Exodus on Mark is generally well-received; and, it is cited as support by Lukan scholars observing similar phenomena in Luke and Acts, including those in the discussion that follows.[20]

Mark Strauss's *The Davidic Messiah in Luke-Acts* devotes a chapter to the "Exodus of the Royal Messiah."[21] He argues that the New Exodus motif begins not with the transfiguration event (contra Moessner) or its apparent Moses-typology (though it includes these), but with the citation of Isa 40:3–5 in Luke 3:4–6; and, he argues that the motif is largely based on Isaiah (not, e.g., Deuteronomistic history).[22] Strauss makes no claim that the New Exodus *controls* the Lukan narrative (as Watts does for Mark or, as we will see, Pao does for Luke-Acts), though he affirms that Isaianic imagery permeates the Third Gospel.[23] According to Strauss, "[W]hen Isaiah is read as a unity, the eschatological deliverer may be viewed as a Davidic king who (like Moses) leads an eschatological new exodus of God's people through suffering as the servant of Yahweh."[24] As only a brief suggestion, he adds

18. Rikki E. Watts, *Isaiah's New Exodus and Mark*, WUNT 2/88 (Tübingen: Mohr/ Siebeck, 1997) 5; see also chapter 5.

19. Watts, *Isaiah's New Exodus*, esp. chapter 3.

20. Strauss, *The Davidic Messiah*, 304n2, while examining the Isaianic New Exodus for Luke, admits he is "indebted to [Watts] work for alerting [Strauss] to the possible influence of the Isaianic new exodus in the Gospels."

21. Strauss, *The Davidic Messiah*, 261–336.

22. Ibid., 303–5.

23. Ibid., 298–302.

24. Ibid., 304.

that Luke may understand the "way" as Jesus' exodus and that, "[F]or the church the new exodus probably continues in Acts . . . ," an idea similar to that which Pao subsequently argues.[25]

Before discussing Pao's view, however, one other important contribution should be noted, and it comes in the form of an excursus in Max Turner's monograph, *Power from on High*.[26] Aware of Watts's dissertation on Mark, and in agreement with Strauss's work on the topic for Luke (Turner oversaw Strauss's thesis), Turner argues that the Isaianic New Exodus appears as early as Luke 1–4 (and then beyond), and further that "Luke understands the mission of Jesus (as outlined in 4.18–21) not in messianic Jubilee terms but in New Exodus terms."[27] He claims that this background best explains Luke's "otherwise curious or 'promiscuous' fusion of prophet-like-Moses and Davidic Christologies."[28] Turner's conclusion helps him establish part of his broader argument, that "for Luke Jesus' baptismal reception of the Spirit . . . is an empowering by which to inaugurate Israel's New Exodus liberation."[29] Turner also argues that the restoration of Israel, which comes out especially in Acts 1–2, figures prominently into this New Exodus liberation.[30] Thus Turner—and Watts and Strauss before him—laid groundwork for a monograph-length study of the Isaianic New Exodus in Luke and Acts.

Pao's Acts and the Isaianic New Exodus

Pao sets out with an ambitious study of the influence of the Isaianic New Exodus on the structure and theology of Luke and Acts. Similar to Watts and Strauss, Pao sees an early citation from Isa 40 as a strong indicator of a paradigmatic usage of Isa 40–55 in the respective Gospel (Mark for Watts, Luke for Strauss, Luke-Acts for Pao) that can be traced from there throughout the narrative(s). Like Watts claims for Mark, Pao (contra Strauss) argues that the Isaianic New Exodus is paradigmatic for Luke-Acts, both in terms of theology and structure. Like Turner, Pao sees the New Exodus theme of restoration significantly present in Acts and significant for ecclesiology,

25. Ibid.

26. Max Turner, *Power from on High: The Spirit in Israel's Restoration and Witness in Luke-Acts*, JPTSup 9 (Sheffield: Sheffield Academic, 1996) 248–50.

27. Ibid., 266.

28. Ibid. With the word "promiscuous," Turner is alluding to Hans Conzelmann's description of this feature in Conzelmann, *The Theology of St. Luke*, trans. Geoffrey Buswell, 2nd ed. (New York: Harper & Row, 1961) 171.

29. Turner, *Power*, 266.

30. Ibid., esp. chapter 10.

not just Christology[31]; but Pao advances and refines these points and others in a study that remains the most recent and thorough examination of the Isaianic New Exodus in the Lukan corpus.[32]

While Pao focuses in large part on the book of Acts, he begins with the Gospel of Luke. He examines the quotation of Isa 40:3–5 in Luke 3:4–6 and concludes: "It functions as a hermeneutical lens without which the entire Lukan program cannot be properly understood."[33] Pao argues that, when Luke cites Isa 40:3–5, he evokes not only the larger context of Isa 40:1–11, but that of the Isaianic New Exodus in Isa 40–55 (for which Isa 40:1–11 is a prologue).[34] He gives examples of Second Temple literature handling Isa 40:3–5 similarly. Next, Pao argues that in the narrative of Acts, Isa 40:3–5 (and thus the major themes of Isa 40:1–11, and by extension, Isa 40–55) is evoked in two ways: through similar thematic emphases and through ὁδός ("way") terminology. The three major themes that Acts shares with Isa 40:1–11 are the restoration of the people of God (Isa 40:1–2, 9–11), universal revelation of the glory/salvation of God (Isa 40:3–5), and the power of the word of God and the fragility of the people (Isa 40:6–8). Isaiah has transformed the Exodus tradition to look forward to a future hope in which God will recreate through his agent (i.e., his "word"), and (Luke-)Acts applies this Isaianic New Exodus paradigm to the narrative of the early Christian community.[35] Acts uses the ὁδός terminology—alluding to Isa 40:3—in "polemical contexts where the identity of the 'true' people of God is at stake."[36] This fits with similar usage in the Qumran literature[37] and reveals that Luke

---

31. Note again Denova, *The Things* (recognized by Pao), which affirms the significance of Isaiah for Luke, as well as the importance of the restoration theme.

32. Articles, essays, and parts of monographs continue to touch on this and related themes, but I am aware of none that substantially engage or advance the discussion (though see note 59 below). E.g., in addition to works cited already, John R. Levison affirms the influence of Isa 40–55 and the restoration/consolation theme in the Gospel in Levison, "The Spirit, Simeon, and the Songs of the Servant," in *The Spirit and Christ in the New Testament and Christian Theology*, eds. I. Howard Marshall, Volker Rabens, and Cornelis Bennema (Grand Rapids: Eerdmans, 2012) 18–34. Also, Mark L. Strauss acknowledges that he and "recent commentators" (mentioning only Turner and Pao) share the view that the Isaianic New Exodus is "central for Luke's soteriological, Christological, and ecclesiological purposes." See Strauss, "Jesus and the Spirit in Biblical and Theological Perspective," in *The Spirit and Christ in the New Testament and Christian Theology*, 266–84.

33. Pao, *Acts*, 37.

34. Ibid., 41.

35. Ibid., 51–59.

36. Ibid., 60.

37. Ibid., 66–67.

is making an identity claim for his readers and thus evoking Isa 40(–55) for an ecclesiological purpose, a point that Pao argues throughout the book.[38]

In the next major section, Pao examines five "programmatic" passages in Luke-Acts and attempts to show that "the Isaianic New Exodus tradition is evoked in all five passages to depict the significance of the new movement in light of its claim of continuity with the past."[39] First, the citation of Isa 61:1–2 in Luke 4:16–30 emphasizes the Isaianic New Exodus themes of prophetic rejection and the reconstitution of the people of God (i.e., inclusion of the Gentiles) and introduces "the claim that the Christians are now the legitimate heirs of the ancient Israelite traditions."[40] Second, an allusion to Isa 49:6 is claimed for Luke 24:46–47 on the following basis: Since two parallel programmatic passages to Luke 24:46–47 (Acts 1:8 and 26:23) clearly allude to Isa 49:6, quoted in Acts 13:47, one can conclude that the scriptural reference behind Luke 24:47 is also Isa 49:6, a significant Isaianic New Exodus reference.[41] Pao further argues that Luke 24:44–49 anticipates the various themes that are developed in the narrative of Acts, especially Gentile inclusion. Third, various words and phrases in Acts 1:8 correspond to words and phrases in Isaiah, particularly ἐπελθόντος τοῦ ἁγίου πνεύματος ἐφ᾽ ὑμᾶς (cf. Isa 32:15), ἕως ἐσχάτου τῆς γῆς (cf. Isa 49:6), and ἔσεσθέ μου μάρτυρες (cf. Isa 43:10–12).[42] Pao also argues that terms in Acts 1:8 (i.e., "Jerusalem," "Judea and Samaria," "ends of the earth") that are usually thought of as geographical should rather be understood as "theopolitical" terms that reveal the three stages of the Isaianic New Exodus: "(1) the dawn of salvation upon Jerusalem; (2) the reconstitution and reunification of Israel; and finally (3) the inclusion of the Gentiles within the people of God."[43] Fourth, the quotation of Isa 49:6 in Acts 13:46–47 helps Luke show continuity between the ministry of Jesus and that of the apostles (cf. Luke 4:16–30) and,

---

38. Ibid., esp. 51–68. Note that claims that Luke is providing some sort of legitimation for his audience or community are not uncommon and certainly not without merit. Legitimation is variously related to Roman rule, Gentile inclusion, God's faithfulness to Israel, or a number of other issues. See, e.g., Gregory E. Sterling, *Historiography and Self-Definition: Josephos, Luke-Acts, and Apologetic Historiograph*, NovTSup 64 (Leiden: Brill, 1992); Jacob Jervell, *Luke and the People of God: A New Look at Luke-Acts* (Minneapolis: Augsburg, 1972); R. L. Brawley, *Luke-Acts and the Jews: Conflict, Apology, and Conciliation*, SBLMS 33 (Atlanta: Scholars, 1987); Philip F. Esler, *Community and Gospel in Luke-Acts: The Social and Political Motivations of Lucan Theology*, SNTSMS 57 (Cambridge: Cambridge University Press, 1987).

39. Pao, *Acts*, 70.

40. Ibid., 77–81, quoting from p. 77.

41. Ibid., 84–86.

42. Ibid., 91–93.

43. Ibid., 95.

in a transformation of the Isaianic New Exodus, that the "locus of salvation" has moved to the Gentiles.[44] The fifth and final programmatic passage Pao examines is Acts 28:25–28, in which Isa 6:9–10 is quoted, revealing a "dramatic reversal" of Isaiah—Whereas Isaiah begins with blindness and rejection in Isa 6:9–10 and ends with recovery of sight and salvation in Isa 61:1–2, Luke begins Jesus' ministry with recovery of sight and salvation (citing Isa 61:1–2 in Luke 4:18–19) and concludes the narrative of Acts with the blindness and rejection of the Jews (citing Isa 6:9–10 in Acts 28:25–28).[45] "Through such evocation of the Isaianic traditions . . . [t]he Isaianic program becomes, therefore, the hermeneutical framework in which isolated events can be interpreted."[46]

In the second half of the monograph, Pao unpacks further the major Isaianic New Exodus themes that he earlier argued were introduced in Luke and developed in Acts: the restoration of Israel, the word of God, the anti-idol polemic, and salvation to the Gentiles. The first theme, the restoration of Israel, serves as a foundation to the other three themes, and it is most evident in the first half of Acts. "It is upon such [a] foundation that the rest of the narrative is built."[47] Pao breaks down the Isaianic restoration of Israel into six subthemes that he argues appear in Acts in the following ways: (1) The "reconstitution of Israel" is seen in the reestablishment of the Twelve (Acts 1:15–26) and through the evangelistic activity in Judea and Samaria (symbolic, too, of a unification of the divided kingdom; cf. Acts 1:8); (2) The "ingathering of exiles" happens as Diaspora Jews return to Jerusalem in Acts 2; (3) The "community of the Spirit" is apparent in the outpouring of the Spirit on those who repent as part of the restorative process; (4) The "rebuilding of the Davidic Kingdom" is seen in Luke's emphasis on the Davidic dynasty; (5) "Repentance and the turn to the Lord" is emphasized in the apostolic proclamation, especially in Acts 2–3; and (6) "Inclusion of the outcasts" is demonstrated in the narrative of the conversion of an Ethiopian eunuch (Acts 8:25–40).[48]

The second of the four Isaianic themes Pao unpacks is the "word of God." He argues that the word of God in Acts "conquers in the midst of opposition and that the word never visits a geographical location twice during its journey even when the various Lukan characters in Acts may have visited

44. Ibid., 96–101.

45. Ibid., 101–9.

46. Ibid., 110.

47. Ibid., 111.

48. Ibid., 111–43.

a city more than once."[49] According to Pao, this "journey of the word" in Acts, which especially recalls Isa 2:2–4 and corresponds to concepts in Isa 40–55, depicts the word as an "independent being,"[50] a "powerful agent that parallels the figure of Jesus,"[51] and as "related to the speaker and yet attain[ing] its own existence as an active entity."[52] Luke's portrayal of the journey of the word, its growth, and its marking out of the true people of God, is best understood through the backdrop of Exodus traditions, especially those transformed in Isa 40–55, where the word is seen as a powerful, active agent (Isa 40:6–8; 55:10–11).[53]

The final two Isaianic themes examined are the anti-idol polemic and status of the nations/Gentiles. Pao argues that the Isaianic anti-idol polemic is used by Luke to emphasize the sovereignty of the risen Christ and the impotence of rivals, whether rival peoples or idols.[54] This serves also as an identity claim Luke makes for his community: "God's victory over the idols symbolizes the power of the true people of God over against other competitive claims to legitimacy and power."[55] Pao finally examines Luke's "transformation" of the Isaianic program in redefining the people of God in a way which elevates the status of the Gentiles to a level (nearly) equal to that of the Jews.[56] Luke does this especially through emphasizing the mission to the Gentiles in the face of Jewish rejection.

49. Pao includes in his search the following phrases in Greek: ὁ λόγος τοῦ θεοῦ, ὁ λόγος τοῦ κυρίοῦ, ὁ λόγος τῆς σωτηρίας, ὁ λόγος τῆς χάριτας αὐτοῦ, ὁ λόγος τοῦ εὐαγγελίου, and the absolute use of ὁ λόγος when it clearly refers to the word of God. Ibid., 150.

50. Ibid., 161.

51. Ibid., 164.

52. Ibid., 167.

53. Ibid., 176.

54. Ibid., 181–216.

55. Ibid., 212. Pao does not elaborate on what competitive claims are being made, but assumes throughout the book that Luke's community is in conflict.

56. Ibid., 217–48.

A Critique of Pao's Acts and the Isaianic New Exodus

Many scholars have warmly received Pao's work.[57] A sufficient critical engagement of the book has yet to appear.[58] Pao's argument is not without major problems. These do not necessarily invalidate the general claim that Isa 40–55 is important for understanding Luke and Acts, or even that the Isaianic New Exodus serves as a backdrop behind the narrative of Acts, if not also Luke, but the issues raised here need to be clarified and explained if Pao's argument is to bear the weight of its own claims. What follows shows that Pao fails to make a convincing argument that the Isaianic New Exodus pervades and controls the narrative(s) of Luke and Acts to the extent he claims.

The Citation of Isa 40:3–5 in Luke 3:4–6

The foundation of Pao's argument is the claim that Luke cites Isa 40:3–5 in Luke 3:4–6 to evoke the Isaianic New Exodus of Isa 40–55.[59] Pao supports this claim by arguing the following: (1) Allusions and echoes to Isa 40:3–5 in Luke and Acts suggest that the citation in Luke 3:4–6 is more than just an explanation of John the Baptist's ministry; (2) Certain Second Temple texts use Isa 40:3–5 to evoke the larger Isaianic context; (3) Themes from Isa 40:1–11 and the larger context of Isa 40–55 are present in Acts; and (4) "Way" terminology in Acts alludes to Isa 40:3–5.

57. Craig S. Keener, e.g., says of Pao's work: "Certainly, Isaiah proves to be the most critical grid of the narrative's movement to the Gentiles, making Pao's contribution one of the most helpful recent studies on Acts." He finds Pao's demonstration of the use of Isaiah in programmatic statements in Luke and Acts particularly decisive. See Keener, *Acts: An Exegetical Commentary: Introduction and 1:1—2:47* (Grand Rapids: Baker Academic, 2012) 482.

58. Peter Mallen perhaps comes closest but falls far short of a thorough engagement. Most of Mallen's citations of Pao are mutually supportive. He agrees to a large extent with Pao about the importance of the Isaianic New Exodus in Luke and Acts, though he argues that the servant motif (Isa 49:6) is a more important interpretive grid. As for critique, Mallen rightly notes some circularity in Pao's argument (though fails to see how he himself is guilty of the same) (18; cf. 116n58). Mallen interprets the "way" terminology more christologically than Pao (72) and quite unconvincingly criticizes Pao in a short excursus, "Unravelling of the New Exodus?" (187–89); See Mallen, *The Reading and Transformation of Isaiah in Luke-Acts*, LNTS 346 (New York: T. & T. Clark, 2008). Steve Moyise recently interacted with both Mallen and Pao briefly and suggests (as does this essay) that the use of Scripture in Acts is too diverse to claim that an Isaianic theme "controls" it; see Moyise, *The Later New Testament Writings and Scripture: The Old Testament in Acts, Hebrews, the Catholic Epistles, and Revelation* (Grand Rapids: Baker, 2012) 36–39.

59. Pao, *Acts*, 38–45.

First, Pao notes that the neuter noun σωτήριον in the citation of Isa 40:5 in Luke 3:6 is also found in Luke 2:30 and Acts 28:28 and nowhere else in Luke or Acts.[60] As Pao suggests, both passages quite plausibly allude to Isa 40:3–5, especially Luke 2:30.[61] This leads him to claim that "the constant recalling of the Isaianic context provides meaning for the development of the story."[62] Yet one citation and two possible allusions to Isa 40:3–5 hardly demonstrate *constant* recalling. Pao then notes echoes of Isa 40:3–5 in Luke 1:17, 1:76, and Acts 13:23–26, yet these passages do not support his claim since each refers to the ministry of John the Baptist just as Luke 3:4–6 does.

Second, Pao surveys Second Temple texts and finds evidence that some of them evoked Isaianic New Exodus themes through allusions to Isa 40:3–5. He persuasively shows that these texts assign connotative value to the Isaianic passage, thus providing precedent for Luke to do the same. However, this in itself provides no positive evidence that Luke is in fact doing the same thing, nor is Pao able to show that any of these texts evokes the Isaianic New Exodus in the programmatic way he claims for Luke and Acts.

Third, Pao examines themes introduced in Isa 40 which he later argues are developed in Acts. It is unclear, however, that the corresponding themes in Acts are as developed as Pao claims or that they are dependent only upon Isaiah. Indeed, similar themes can be found elsewhere in the Scriptures (as shown further below).

Fourth, Pao argues that the "way" terminology in Acts, likely derived from Isa 40, is used in polemical contexts and so represents an identity claim for Luke's community. This is an insightful observation but a moot point: Even assuming Luke employs the "way" terminology through creative use of Isaiah,[63] it is difficult to establish a firm connection between "way" terminology in Acts with the use of Isaiah in Luke 3:4–6.[64]

---

60. Ibid., 40. Pao notes that outside the Lukan writings, the neuter σωτήριον appears only in Eph 2:3, which he must mistake for Eph 6:17 (p. 40n9). Note that its use in the LXX outside of Isaiah is quite common, especially in the Psalms, though Luke's usage seems to reflect Isaianic influence.

61. Though one should also note the similarity of Ps 97:3 (LXX) in both passages.

62. Pao, *Acts*, 40.

63. Yet as Pao notes, some Qumran texts use "way" terminology as an identity marker (ibid., 66–67).

64. Pao's strongest case that Luke evokes the Isaianic New Exodus through the "way" terminology is that both Acts and Isaiah use it to redefine the people of God. But this ignores the dissonance between Isaiah's conception of God's people and Luke's, as Pao later observes, labeling it a "transformation" of an Isaianic theme. As Mallen (rightly) says, "One also wonders why key elements of the Isaianic New Exodus programme are either missing from the narrative (e.g. the reglorification of Jerusalem), reversed (e.g. return to Jerusalem becomes movement away from Jerusalem), or have

It in fact appears that the allusions and echoes of Isa 40:3–5 in Luke and Acts are not strong enough evidence to circularly reinforce Pao's argument for the evocation of the whole Isaianic New Exodus context in Luke 3. This neither discounts that scriptural citations and allusions might evoke a larger context from which they are drawn, nor that Isaiah was especially significant in early Christian literature, including Luke and Acts.[65] I am in agreement with Pao on both of these points. A more moderate claim would be that Luke, following Mark, simply included a fuller citation from Isa 40 describing John the Baptist's ministry in fitting with some purpose Luke had, even a theological purpose influenced by Isaiah.

Perhaps some of the problems raised here could be avoided if Pao's argument was less dependent on the Gospel of Luke (see further under "The Unity and Composition" below). Pao seems disproportionately and unnecessarily dependent on Luke 3:4–6 and its citation of Isa 40:3–5. It would be understandable if examining this passage in Luke simply served a starting point for the larger work, but the argument seems to put undue weight on the citation in Luke 3: "[The citation] functions as a hermeneutical lens without which the entire Lukan program cannot be properly understood."[66] The view here is that the cumulative argument Pao makes for the importance of Isa 40–55 in Acts is more able to handle the burden of the overall argument than what he places on the Luke 3 citation.

Source- and Redaction-critical Issues

One of the most significant redactional questions Pao raises and leaves unanswered is the relationship between Mark's use of Isaianic New Exodus themes with that of Luke. In view of the fact that Pao makes an argument for Luke-Acts very similar to that of Watts for Mark—i.e., the evangelist begins the narrative with an important citation from Isa 40, tipping off the

---

ironic fulfillment (God's chosen people, Israel, largely reject salvation while the enemies of God's people, the Gentiles, receive salvation)." See Mallen, *The Reading*, 18.

65. On the evocation of Scriptural contexts through citations and allusions, see C. H. Dodd, *According to the Scriptures: The Sub-Structure of New Testament Theology* (London: Nisbet, 1952). Pao uses "evocation" to highlight "the fact that the scriptural traditions recalled in the use of certain key words may be more profound than the content explicitly noted in the scriptural quotations and allusions" (Pao, *Acts*, 7n26). Citing James L. Kugel, he notes, too, that the Lukan material, like some midrashic literature, assumes the wider context of the source text. See Pao, *Acts*, 9n35; cf. Kugel, "Two Introductions to Midrash," in *Midrash and Literature*, eds. Geoffrey H. Hartman and Sanford Budick (New Haven: Yale University Press, 1985) 77–103. Pao also notes the influence of Isaiah in early Christian literature (Pao, *Acts*, 31–36; cf. 10–17).

66. Pao, *Acts*, 37.

informed reader to the Isaianic New Exodus programmatic for understanding the whole work—how might this similarity be explained, especially since Mark is a major source for Luke?[67] It could be that Pao is not persuaded by Watts and so ignores him.[68] Interaction with Watts is surprisingly rare and lacks detail.[69] It seems strange to imagine that Luke, whom Pao argues is very acquainted with the Isaianic New Exodus and had an incredible ability to paint his narrative with the New Exodus brush, would be unaware of how similar Isaianic themes are present in Mark. If Luke is aware of those themes, one should consider why and how he changes them or incorporates them in distinct ways. Pao assumes Markan priority and, at least implicitly, the two-source theory.[70] At various places he discusses Lukan redaction, even if briefly.[71] Pao acknowledges that behind the larger pericope (Luke 3) could be other traditions, including Mark and Q, but he does not elaborate.[72] Elsewhere, in suggesting a reason for dissimilarity between a theme in Isaiah and Luke-Acts, Pao allows that Luke could at times be "constrained by the traditions at his disposal."[73] Determining when this is or is not the case is extremely difficult, and such an argument cannot be invoked *only* to explain dissimilarities between Luke-Acts and the Isaianic New Exodus. It could serve Pao's argument to examine the possibility that Luke has in fact

67. In introducing his discussion to Luke's citation of Isa 40:3–5 in Luke 3:4–6, Pao pictures Luke as having "the text of Mark before him" (ibid., 38). It should be noted that one difference in Luke's citation of Isa 40:3–5 is that it in fact does not begin the Gospel.

68. Though note that Pao references Watts for support that Isaianic themes are utilized in the Gospels (ibid., 33).

69. Pao references Watts a handful of times for support, but never engages him to any extent. Pao notes that he was given an advanced copy of Watts' manuscript (ibid., 12n51). Watts's 1990 dissertation was published in 1997, one year prior to the completion of Pao's Harvard PhD, and three years prior to the publication of Pao's thesis.

70. Pao clearly states he assumes Markan priority (ibid., 28n146). He also assumes the two-source theory a number of times, e.g., he describes Luke 7:18–22 as "most likely taken from Q" (75) and includes a mention of Q as among "traditional material" Luke could use to present his story (39n5).

71. E.g., the ending of Luke 24 (ibid., 84, 86–87), the additional phrase in the Isa 40 citation compared with Mark (38–39), Q's possible influence on Luke's exclusion of Mark's use of Mal 3:1 in his prologue (40).

72. Ibid., 39n5, in which Pao notes in particular that Bovon has suggested this; cf. François Bovon, *Das Evangelium nach Lukas: 1. Teilband Lk 1,1–9,50*, EKKNT III/1 (Zürich: Benziger, 1989) 165–66.

73. This is a suggestion Pao makes to explain why Luke does not include a full-blown anti-idol polemic in Acts as found in Isaiah (Pao, *Acts*, 215). This argument from constraint of sources is dubious, however, because it fails to explain how, in Pao's view, Luke could be so free to rework source material in his gospel in fitting with the Isaianic framework.

taken over and reworked the Isaianic New Exodus which Mark (it is argued) introduces in his prologue through the Isa 40:3–5 citation.[74]

Another redactional question arises when Pao argues that Luke's addition to Mark's parable of the sower in Luke 8:4–15 (i.e., adding the line "the seed is the word God" in Luke 8:11) "prepares the way for the summary statement in Acts concerning the growth of the word."[75] His suggestion is intriguing but remains unproven as argued. Even if one assumes a strong view of the unity of Luke and Acts, the claim of a thematic connection is distinct from the claim that the author is preparing the reader to see that theme. Pao, citing Evans, supports his case further by noting that the background to the parable is Isa 55:10–11, a passage that influences Luke's portrayal of the word in Acts.[76] It is difficult to know how important this is for understanding Luke's theology or his use of Isaiah since the Isaianic background to the parable of the sower could be equally present in Mark's version. A more convincing argument from Luke's redaction of the parable might include a discussion of other telling differences with Mark or provide an explanation for Luke's placement of the parable in his narrative in comparison with that of his source.

While one should be hesitant to fault Pao for not covering more material in Luke since his focus is on Acts, another avenue for further research would include an investigation of how "L" material in the Gospel—material derived from sources other than Mark and Q—is utilized to possibly convey Isaianic themes. As mentioned above, Pao examines certain programmatic passages in the Gospel including passages with evidence of Lukan redaction, but much of the L material is left unexamined (with the exception of brief suggestions of allusions in keeping with the Isaianic New Exodus). In this way the infancy narratives are not examined on their own terms, yet these narratives are how Luke begins his story. One wonders, for example, about Mary's *Magnificat* or Zechariah's *Benedictus*, each rich with scriptural allusions from various sources, the possible connection between Luke 3:16–17 and Acts 2:2–4,[77] or the Lukan redaction of the transfiguration narrative (Luke 9:28–36; especially Jesus' ἔξοδος in 9:31). One wonders, too, about

---

74. While I remain skeptical of Watts's argument that the Isaianic New Exodus is paradigmatic for Mark, the fact that Mark begins his entire gospel with the Isa 40 passage is in Watts's favor.

75. Pao, *Acts*, 171.

76. Craig A. Evans, "On the Isaianic Background of the Sower Parable," *CBQ* 47 (1985) 464–68.

77. Particularly significant is Luke's addition of "fire" in verse 16; see Joshua L. Mann, "The Rhetorical Function of Chiasmus in Acts 2:2–4," *MJT* 8, no. 2 / 9, no. 1 (2010) 66–77.

the travel narrative with its alternating L and Q material and especially the argument of Moessner (and others) that Luke presents Jesus as a prophet like Moses leading a kind of exodus.[78] The uniquely Lukan features of these passages betray influence beyond the Isaianic New Exodus and raise serious doubts about whether Isa 40–55 can really be the hermeneutical lens through which Luke and Acts should be read.

The Unity and Composition of Luke and Acts

Closely related to important redaction- and source-critical questions is the issue of the unity and composition of Luke and Acts. Of the five (or six) programmatic statements of Luke and Acts which Pao examines, two (or three)[79] are found in the Gospel—the same Gospel in which surprisingly, "many of the Isaianic themes critical in the narrative of Acts are absent."[80] The argument seems to be, then, that Luke's Gospel, while not developing major Isaianic New Exodus themes critical to Acts, nevertheless contains two of the five (or three of six) programmatic passages in Luke and Acts which betray the Isaianic New Exodus program. This argument necessarily depends upon a strong view of the unity of Luke and Acts, which Pao in fact assumes without any significant elaboration.[81] Pao does suggest that the "common Isaianic story underlying both works" supports such an assumption, but this is problematic for two reasons: (1) As Pao admits, "While it seems that Isaianic influence is more evident in Acts, the presence of the common story behind both volumes of the Lukan writings cannot be ignored."[82] However, the disproportionate development of the Isaianic New Exodus in the Gospel and Acts might actually suggest a *lesser* amount of unity than what must be assumed for the argument.[83] (2) The argument

78. See discussion above. Pao does not interact with Moessner outside of the introduction, yet implies some level of agreement with him (*Acts*, 10).

79. It is three of six programmatic statements if one counts Luke 3:4–6, a crucial passage for Pao.

80. Pao, *Acts*, 13.

81. Pao devotes a small paragraph to the issue of the unity of Luke-Acts in his introduction, noting Cadbury's claim for unity (*Making of Luke-Acts*) on the one hand and the challenge to this view by Parson and Pervo (*Rethinking the Unity*) on the other. He says, "While the unity of Luke-Acts will not be the primary concern of this study, it will both be assumed and affirmed especially in light of the common Isaianic story underlying both works" (ibid., 19; cf. a similar statement regarding unity on p. 39).

82. Ibid., 19n93.

83. Pao returns to the issue of unity in his conclusion and seems to argue the opposite point I am making: The fact that the Isaianic theme is introduced yet undeveloped *until* Acts suggests unity. This is apparently because, in Pao's view, Acts depends on

becomes rather circular: It assumes unity to link the crucial citation of Isa 40:3–5 in Luke 3 with Acts; then it uses the parallels to support the assumption of unity. Granted, internal evidence for the unity of Luke and Acts is necessarily derived inductively, and some circularity is inevitable. The point, however, is to question whether such a strong view of unity can be assumed in this way and then circularly reinforced.

Pao's argument implies something about the composition of Luke and Acts, too. One must think of Luke as having carefully planned out how he would narrate the story of Jesus and the early church through the lens of the Isaianic New Exodus. That Luke planned a unified two-volume narrative is not implausible,[84] but neither is it so obviously true that it can be assumed.[85]

Even assuming the unity of Luke and Acts, one still questions whether Pao has successfully proven many of the Isaianic allusions, especially those that are dependent on links between Luke and Acts. For example, the argument he makes for an Isa 49:6 allusion in Luke 24:46–47—one of five programmatic passages for Pao—is unconvincing. He argues that, since two parallel programmatic passages to Luke 24:46–47 (Acts 1:8 and 26:23) clearly allude to Isa 49:6, quoted in another programmatic passage (Acts 13:47), the scriptural reference behind Luke 24:47 is Isa 49:6.[86] What if, however, Luke is not alluding to any particular passage at all? Perhaps Luke has multiple references "in mind"—such knowledge of Luke's thoughts eludes us. Further, what Luke may have had in mind is a different issue than whether or not he has alluded to a particular passage in the text.

Luke for the introduction of the theme. The problem of circularity is again detectable.

84. For example, I. Howard Marshall has argued that Luke-Acts exhibits characteristics of a pre-planned unified narrative in light of the prologues (Luke 1:1–4 and Acts 1:1), the ending of Luke (which seems to anticipate a sequel), and most significantly, evidence that the author has redacted the Gospel in view of traditions used in Acts. See Marshall, "Acts and the 'Former Treatise,'" in *The Book of Acts in Its First Century Setting*, eds. Bruce W. Winter and Andrew D. Gregory (Grand Rapids: Eerdmans, 1993) 1:163–82. For a recent helpful discussion of the issues of the unity of Luke-Acts, see Gregory and Rowe, eds., *Rethinking the Unity*.

85. Of course, even if Luke did in some sense write the Gospel with Acts in mind, the extent of planning is a question that seems nearly impossible to answer with any kind of precision, hence the ongoing unity debate. If Luke wrote his gospel without having precisely planned a second volume, one might still postulate that he had a theological framework—even one influenced especially by Isaiah—which influenced his writing of the gospel and then, later, his writing of Acts. In any case, it seems wise to exercise more caution when arguing for possible links between Luke and Acts than links within one or the other.

86. Pao, *Acts*, 84–86.

A straightforward reading of Luke 24:44–49 suggests that Luke's main point is that Jesus fulfills the whole of the Scriptures.[87] The citation formula in 24:46 (οὕτως γέγραπται) is not intended to recall a single passage but refers to the Scriptures broadly.[88] Luke 24:44–49 opens with Jesus reminding his disciples of his former instruction, that "all the things written concerning me in the Law of Moses and the Prophets and the Psalms must be fulfilled" (24:44). Having made reference to the trifold division of the Scriptures, Luke adds, "Then He opened their mind to understand the Scriptures" (24:45).[89] Thus when the following verse begins with an introductory citation and the summary statement which follows (with no obvious allusion), it seems Luke is continuing to refer to the whole of Scripture.[90] Pao agrees about the generic nature of the citation, but says, "Nevertheless, throughout the Lukan writings, Luke does have particular passages in mind when he discusses scriptural references to the suffering and resurrection of Jesus," citing five examples of this in Acts.[91] Pao's examples, however, are explicit citations or quotations, not allusions of the sort he is arguing for in Luke 24:47. Pao surprisingly offers no direct comparison between Luke 24:47 and Isa 49:6; rather, he depends on comparing Isa 49:6 to passages parallel with Luke 24:47, concluding, "Therefore, if one accepts the parallels between Acts 1:8 and Luke 24:47, one should also understand the scriptural reference behind Luke 24:47 as Isa 49:6."[92]

Using Pao's argumentation, why not also suggest that scriptural references regarding Jesus' death and resurrection in Acts 2 are "behind" Luke 24:46–47 (e.g., 2 Sam 7:12; Ps 15:8–11; 109:1 [LXX]; 132:11)? As Acts demonstrates (and Pao rightly notes), Luke was capable of alluding to and citing Scripture in support of Christ's suffering and resurrection, as well as

87. Pao seems to acknowledge this (ibid., 85).

88. This does not mean that Isa 49:6 does not inform Luke's theology, nor that Isa 49:6 is not important for understanding related passages such as Acts 1:8 and 26:23; it simply means that Luke is not attempting to refer to a specific passage.

89. Note that Matthew Bates has recently argued for a different (though syntactically possible) understanding of verse 45: "Then Jesus exposited the Scriptures so that the disciples could understand their meaning [νοῦς]." See Bates, "Closed-Minded Hermeneutics? A Proposed Alternative Translation," *JBL* 129, no. 3 (2010) 537–57; brackets in the quotation are original. While I remain unconvinced of Bates's proposal, the point I argue here is compatible with his argument.

90. Further, it is likely that the "citation" of 24:46–47 summarizes "all the things written" (πάντα τὰ γεγραμμένα) of 24:44.

91. Pao, *Acts*, 85, citing examples on p. 85, note 86. Keener follows Pao, here, without much elaboration (*Acts*, 703).

92. Pao, *Acts*, 86. Pao adds that the link between Luke 24:47 and Acts 13:46–47 could also be used as support (p. 86n91; cf. p. 86n92).

the subsequent mission to proclaim repentance to the nations. Thus it does not follow that Luke would have one particular passage "in mind" in Luke 24:46–47.[93] Indeed, the Isaianic New Exodus is not nearly as pervasive in Luke 24 as Pao suggests.

Luke's Usage of non-Isaianic Texts

The usage of non-Isaianic texts in key places in Luke and Acts significantly weakens the argument that the Isaianic New Exodus is a hermeneutical key. For example, in the highly significant Pentecost narrative (Acts 2:1–36), Isaiah is not cited, quoted, or clearly alluded to,[94] even though the role of the Spirit in Israel's restoration is discussed in Isaiah (as Pao earlier demonstrates).[95] When it comes to examining the Pentecost event, Pao moves quickly from the possible Isa 2:1 allusion of "in the last days" (Acts 2:17) to an examination of Acts 3:19–21, which he finds "more significant" for the discussion.[96] He argues that "times of refreshing" (Acts 3:19) is a reference to the outpouring of the Spirit that is related to Isa 32:15, an important passage for the Lukan writings.[97] Pao adds, "Moreover, the connection of the Spirit with the program of restoration can already be found in the quotation of Joel 2:28–32, a passage that depicts the hope of restoration, in Acts 2:17–21."[98] The problem is not in the suggestion that "times of refreshing" might refer to the role of the Spirit in the program of restoration. The problem is reading Acts 2 through the lens of Acts 3:19–20 and a possible allusion to Isa 32. As Pao seemingly acknowledges, Luke bases the program of restoration in Acts 2 not on Isaianic texts, but on the quotation of Joel 2:28–32 (Acts 2:17–21). The explanation of the Pentecost event by Peter depends on the Joel quotation (and other non-Isaianic Scriptures), not an allusion to Isa 32:15, even if the Isaianic allusion is present in Acts 3:19–20. This is simply to point out that Pao often does not adequately account for

93. Joseph A. Fitzmyer notes links between verses 46–47 and Acts, but calls the vague citation a "Lucan christologoumenon," one "reading the OT in the light of the Christian kerygma." See Fitzmyer, *The Gospel According to Luke*, AB 28–28A (Garden City, NY: Doubleday, 1981–1985) 2:1583–84; Darrell L. Bock notes a number of OT allusions possibly present. See Bock, *Luke: Volume 2, 9:51—24:53*, BECNT (Grand Rapids: Baker Academic, 1994) 1938–41.

94. Though it is possible that the phrase "in the last days" of Acts 2:17 alludes to Isa 2:1, as Pao notes (*Acts*, 131).

95. Ibid., 115–16.

96. Ibid., 132.

97. Ibid., 132–34.

98. Ibid., 133.

the use of non-Isaianic Scriptures in his attempt to connect words, concepts, and themes in Luke and Acts to Isaiah.

Another example of this can be seen in Pao's discussion of how the restoration theme of "rebuilding the Davidic kingdom" plays out in Luke and Acts. He begins with a passage that cites a part of the epilogue of Isa 40–55 (Isa 55:3 in Acts 13:34). However, since the Isaiah quotation is sandwiched between two related Davidic citations from the Psalms, Isaiah's unique influence remains to be seen. Pao next discusses two passages that link Jesus to David's throne (Acts 2:30 and Luke 1:32). He can then say, "These references to David's throne recall the statement in Isaiah 9 in which the imagery of the 'throne of David' is used to describe the reign for the eschatological figure during the restoration of Israel . . ."[99] Do these reference really "recall" Isa 9:6? Acts 2:30 rather seems to recall Ps 132:11 and 2 Sam 7:12. Davidic citations in Acts 2 are from Psalms (Ps 15:8–11 in Acts 2:25–28; Ps 109:1 [LXX] in Acts 2:34–35). In fact, much of the Davidic material in Luke and Acts derives from Psalms.[100] So here again one senses some strain in making connections to Isaiah.

Pao next examines the quotation of Amos 9:11–12 in Acts 15:16–18, arguing that it provides more evidence for the link between the Davidic kingdom and the restoration of Israel.[101] Pao thus successfully argues one point while undermining another: He shows from *multiple* scriptural sources used in Luke and Acts that the author in fact links the Davidic kingdom and the restoration of Israel, which undermines a claim of the *special* influence of Isaiah's own depiction of this connection on Luke and Acts. It may be more accurate to suggest that the restoration theme in Luke and Acts is not so distinctly "Isaianic." Pao notes: "The presence of the theme of restoration in other writings both within the Hebrew Bible and those that are developed in the Second Temple period should not undermine the significance of the theme in the Isaianic program."[102] Perhaps, but it may well undermine the claim that Luke derived his restoration theology primarily or especially from Isaiah.

---

99. Ibid., 136.

100. For a thorough examination of David in Luke-Acts, see Yuzuru Miura, *David in Luke-Acts: His Portrayal in the Light of Early Judaism*, WUNT 2/232 (Tübingen: Mohr/Siebeck, 2007).

101. Pao, *Acts*, 136–38.

102. Ibid., 111n1.

The Word of God in Acts as an Agent of Conquest

Questionable attempts to connect themes in Acts with Isaiah are similarly made throughout the book.[103] A representative example comes in a chapter where Pao argues that the "word of God/the Lord" in Acts is used in way similar to that of the Isaianic New Exodus—as an agent of conquest—and in fact the "word" becomes the main character of Acts.[104] Recall that when Pao speaks of the "word" appearing in a city, he refers to passages in the narrative where the Greek term λόγος is used in the text to show the presence of the "word" in a certain location (see note 49 above).

First, it is not clearly the case that the "word" in Acts is influenced uniquely by Isaiah. In addition to allowing for authorial creativity, one must recognize the possible influence of scriptural sources besides Isaiah.[105] Pao highlights three passages in Isa 40–55 (Isa 40:6–8; 45:23; 55:10–11) that show a dual Isaianic theme: The power of God's word and the fragility of the people.[106] Pao is aware of the possibility of non-Isaianic influence and includes a short excursus to address "λόγος-theology" in other texts.[107] He notes that notions of God's word as a powerful agent can be found in various places in the OT, as well as in Philo, the NT, and the Wisdom of Solomon. But rather than undermine the claim of particular Isaianic influence, Pao argues that his case is supported by this evidence since the relevant Lukan contexts where the λόγος terminology occurs exhibit Isaianic influence in other ways. This again fails to account for non-Isaianic use of Scripture in some of the same contexts.

Second, Pao's characterization of the "word" in Acts tends to overemphasize features that are used to connect it to Isaiah (e.g., features which emphasize the activity of the word, its independence, its prominence in the narrative, etc.). Pao argues that the "itinerary" of the "word" in Acts is just what is expected from Isaiah 2:2–4 where "the word of the Lord [will go forth] from Jerusalem"[108]—a passage, it should be noted, that is not cited or

103. For example, in addition to issues noted elsewhere in this essay, the anti-idol polemic Pao sees in Acts is neither as strong as Isaiah's nor distinctly Isaianic; so also is the theme of prophetic rejection in Luke 4:16–18 not distinctly Isaianic.

104. Ibid., 159.

105. Pao's discussion of the "word" in Isaiah, on which this part of his argument depends, is just a few paragraphs in length (ibid., 48–50).

106. Four other passages are suggested as examples where "the power of God (and his word) is contrasted with the impotence of idols" (Isa 40:18–20; 41:5–7; 44:9–20; 46:5–7). But God's word does not appear in any of the four passages listed as examples. Thus three examples of God's word in Isa 40–55 remain for Pao (ibid., 49).

107. Ibid., 177–80.

108. Ibid., 156–59.

quoted in Luke and Acts. Pao makes an extensive argument that attempts to show that the word of God (and related uses of λόγος) begins in Jerusalem and only appears once in any given city as it journeys out to the ends of the earth.[109] In depicting the word this way, Pao claims that Luke emphasizes the "conquest" of the word "in the midst of opposing forces" in a way fitting the Isaianic New Exodus.[110] But Pao has overstated the case.

In certain instances, the theme of hostility against the "word" is exaggerated. For example, in an attempt to emphasize hostility against the "word" in Acts 4:4, Pao seems too eager to find militaristic overtones based on scriptural contexts of "numbering men."[111] Also, the theme of hostility is inconsistently present where the "word" occurs (e.g., Acts 10:36 and 11:1). In Acts 13:5–6, there is no indication of hostility against the "word" until *after* Paul and Barnabas had "proclaimed the word of God" (κατήγγελλον τὸν λόγον τοῦ θεοῦ) and traveled through much of the island unto Paphos (13:6). In Acts 4:29–31, the "victory of the word" Pao speaks of is really the victory of God and the people (perhaps even victory for the Spirit that produces the bold speech). This is in fact a recurring problem: Pao seems to speak of the word as an active agent far more than the text of Acts does.[112]

Pao also places too much weight on the claim that the "word" never returns to the same geographical location twice, thereby emphasizing its conquest. If this is true, it is only true *textually* (i.e., where λόγος is used in the text), and in some instances it is not so clear this is the case. For example, after Samaria "received the word" Phillip preached, Peter and John are sent to the same city (8:14). But later, Acts 8:25 reports that Peter and John[113] had been speaking the "word of the Lord" (τὸν λόγον τοῦ κυρίου) *in the same city* and proceeded to evangelize other Samaritan villages (πολλάς

---

109. Citing Acts 4:4, Pao begins by noting that the "word" begins in Jerusalem as Isa 2:2–4 would anticipate (ibid., 150). It is difficult to establish Isaianic influence on this point since it seems natural that the gospel would emanate from Jerusalem. Note, too, that it would seem that Acts 2:41 should actually be the first reference given here, but this point makes no great difference to Pao's argument or my criticism of it.

110. Ibid., 156.

111. Ibid., 151.

112. E.g., in Acts 13:46 Pao speaks of the word of God *turning* to the Gentiles, but actually the text portrays Paul saying, "*we* are turning to the Gentiles" (στρεφόμεθα εἰς τὰ ἔθνη) (ibid., 153).

113. The Greek does not specify whether Phillip could be included as the subject of ὑπέστρεφον. He could "return" to Jerusalem (with Peter and John) since he had come from there earlier (8:1–4), though it seems more likely the verb takes only Peter and John as the plural subject since (1) Philip is absent in 8:14–24, and (2) Philip becomes the subject in verse 26.

τε κώμας τῶν Σαμαριτῶν εὐηγγελίζοντο).[114] The significance of Acts 10:36, where Pao says that the "word of God came to Cornelius," is also unclear.[115] Unlike the previous examples where Luke is narrating something about the "word," this instance of λόγος is actually on the lips of Peter, speaking not about Cornelius receiving the word, but "the word sent to the sons of Israel" (τὸν λόγον ἀπέστειλεν τοῖς υἱοῖς Ἰσραὴλ). In Acts 14:25, Pao notes the word is "deposited" in Perga, observing that, while Paul and Barnabas had already been in Perga (13:13), the "word" did not appear there.[116] The narrative, however, is not clear whether or not Paul and Barnabas were evangelizing in Perga in Acts 13:13.[117] In Acts 15:35, Paul and Barnabas are teaching and preaching the word of the Lord (διδάσκοντες καὶ εὐαγγελιζόμενοι . . . τὸν λόγον τοῦ κυρίου) in Antioch. Here it would seem the "word" appears where it has already had an effect: Acts reports persecuted believers fleeing to Antioch and evangelizing Jews (11:19) and the presence of a church established enough to have teachers and send out missionaries (13:1). Pao explains, however, that it is not until 15:35 that the word has "captured" Antioch.[118] However, there is no report of the effect of the preaching and teaching to provide Pao the necessary evidence for his assertion.

Pao supports his argument further by noting that the "word" is not mentioned when Paul returns to certain cities on a second journey (16:1–5). It is no surprise that the "word" does not appear again, however, since Paul had returned to many of these cities once already (14:21–25) and now, as in his previous return, his stated purpose is to build up the church, not evangelize (15:36, 41; 16:4, 5; cf. 14:21–25; 18:23). The absence of the "word" is actually much more striking in a few other passages, and these weaken Pao's argument further.

For example, the "word" does not appear textually in Acts 17:1–9, though clearly Paul successfully evangelized in Thessalonica by preaching (17:4; cf. 17:13 where Thessalonian Jews find out "the word of God" is being proclaimed in Berea "also," καὶ ἐν τῇ Βεροίᾳ κατηγγέλη ὑπὸ τοῦ Παύλου ὁ λόγος τοῦ θεοῦ). Nor does the "word" appear in Athens, though clearly some Athenians "believed" (17:34). Pao explains that the absence of the word in

114. Granted, one might argue that the word never left the Samaritan city and so technically did not return there. Even so, the case is not as clear as Pao makes it.

115. Pao, *Acts*, 152.

116. Ibid.

117. Further, Acts 14:21–25 seems to portray return visits to previously evangelized cities for the primary purpose of building up the church and appointing elders as Paul and Barnabas return to Antioch (esp. 14:22–23). It is possible Perga is an exception, but again, the case is not as clear as Pao presents it.

118. Ibid., 153n25.

Paul's first visit to Ephesus (18:19–21) confirms that Luke reserves explicit mention of the "word" for contexts that can show its conquest, as he does for Ephesus in 19:1ff.[119] Pao, however, fails to observe the following: (1) Paul's evangelistic activity (and that of Priscilla and Aquila who Paul leaves in Ephesus; cf. 18:18, 26) was not obviously without success during his first visit to Ephesus because there are believers there at his return (19:1), including certain brothers who commended Apollos for ministry in Corinth (18:27–28; cf. 19:1); (2) It is doubtful in light of the previous observation that the twelve disciples Paul meets in Ephesus (19:1–7) are the only disciples in Ephesus; and (3) Acts 19:10 does not indicate the "conquest" of the word (e.g., reports of conversions, "belief," etc.) but only the extent to which the word was *heard* in that region (ἀκοῦσαι τὸν λόγον τοῦ κυρίου).[120] In Acts 19:20, a summary statement about the word's growth is made. Pao claims: "Just as 6:7 summarizes the first stage of the conquest of the word in Jerusalem and 12:24 summarizes the conquest of the word in Judea and Samaria, 19:20 summarizes the third stage of the conquest of the word throughout the Gentile world"—this in keeping with the three stages of the Isaianic New Exodus found in Acts 1:8.[121] However, he fails to account for similar statements (i.e., 2:41, 13:49, and 28:30–31) that lessen the correspondence he suggests. Thus it is not the case that Luke gives one summary statement in each of the three "stages" of the Isaianic New Exodus. Coming to the last chapter of Acts, Pao argues that even though the word does not textually appear in Rome, "the same act of the word reappears in Rome although its activities are summarized in one concise statement."[122] Using such an argument, however, can we not see the presence and activity of the word in, say, Thessalonica and Paul's first visit to Ephesus, or in cities where Paul and others return (as suggested above)?

Finally, it is not obvious that Acts reflects the "hypostatization" of the word to the extent Pao claims. Certainly Acts depicts the word uniquely as "growing" and "multiplying" (6:7; 12:24; 19:20), receiving praise (13:48), and "building up and giving an inheritance" (20:32), as Pao notes. However, do these passages clearly show the word is an independent being, God's agent of conquest, and the main character of Acts, as Pao claims? It is unlikely, especially considering that the uses of λόγος which Pao sets out to examine are *most often* passive in nature and refer primarily to a message that is spoken by a character. In the end, it is difficult to see that

---

119. Ibid., 154.

120. Though see Acts 19:18.

121. Ibid., 154–55; see also p. 155n27.

122. Ibid., 156.

Luke's depiction of λόγος in Acts is nearly as calculated as Pao suggests or influenced particularly by Isaiah.

Conclusion

Pao fails to prove in a convincing manner that the Isaianic New Exodus is the "hermeneutical key" to Luke and Acts or that the Isaianic New Exodus pervades the text of Acts as extensively as he claims: (1) Luke's citation of Isa 40:3–5 in Luke 3:4–6, the foundation of Pao's argument, does not present itself as a hermeneutical key through which to read the whole of Luke and Acts, and it cannot bear the weight Pao places on it; (2) Most of the New Exodus and restoration themes found in Isaiah that Pao argues are developed in Acts are not uniquely Isaianic, nor are those themes developed in Acts to the extent Pao claims; (3) Many of the claims of allusions and echoes of Isaiah are strained and fail to provide adequate support for the pervasive influence of Isa 40–55 on Luke and Acts necessary for the larger argument, and the circularity inherent to this line of reasoning only weakens it further; (4) The use of non-Isaianic texts in Luke and Acts is not adequately accounted for, including scriptural texts and traditional sources (e.g., Mark, Q, and L material) that demonstrate influence much broader than Isa 40–55.

It is precisely because Luke's use of the Scriptures is so rich and varied that there are so many scholarly claims to explain it. F. Scott Spencer synthesizes the claims succinctly when he describes the use of the Scriptures in Luke and Acts as follows:

> The narrative opens with a pair of natal accounts heavily stylized after miraculous OT birth stories involving barren women . . . Beyond Luke 1–2, not simply isolated texts from "Moses," but also the broader template of a "prophet-like-Moses" (Acts 3:22; 7:37; cf. Deut 18:15–18) shapes the portraits of Jesus, Stephen, Philip, Peter and Paul . . . Moreover, as the glorified Moses discusses Jesus' impending *exodus* . . . with him on the Mount of Transfiguration, he sets the stage for Jesus' winding "wilderness journey," as it were, in Luke 9:51—19:27, providing instruction that both echoes and exegetes Moses' farewell sermon in Deuteronomy and prepares the way for a "new exodus" or restoration of God's exiled people, Jew and Gentile, envisioned in Isaiah and extended to "the ends of the earth" (Isa 49:6; Luke 2:32; Acts 13:47; 26:17–18). Along with this rich Moses/Exodus prototype, we should add the Elijah/Elisha model from Jesus' programmatic first sermon (Luke 4:25–27).[123]

123. F. Scott Spencer, "The Narrative of Luke-Acts: Getting to Know the Savior

Regardless of whether *all* of these scriptural allusions, types, motifs, patterns, etc., are really to be found in Luke and Acts in the way they are claimed, Spencer's summary should caution the interpreter not to abandon a careful reading of the narratives on their own terms to go in search for a singular hermeneutical key elsewhere. Accordingly, Foster's critique and consequent appeal deserves repeating:

> The danger of a study like this is that it appears to smuggle in an Old Testament theme which actually is not at the foreground of Luke's gospel and then suggest that this is the hermeneutical key for understanding the text. This whole enterprise of the study of echoes, allusions and intertextuality needs to be soundly reassessed. Here is another example of a theologically motivated juggernaut overtaking the restraints of close textual analysis."[124]

In sum, the use of Isaiah in Luke and Acts indicates its importance in understanding the narratives, and the theology of the Isaianic New Exodus appears to inform them. Even so, the Isaianic New Exodus neither pervades nor controls Luke and Acts in any kind of singular way. Indeed, Luke's use of Scripture is far too diverse for such a claim.

God," in *Issues in Luke-Acts: Selected Essays*, eds. Sean A. Adams and Michael Pahl, Gorgias Handbooks 26 (Piscataway, NJ: Gorgias, 2012) 127–28; italics original.

124. Paul Foster, Review of *The Reading and Transformation of Isaiah in Luke-Acts*, by Peter Mallen, *ExpTim* 119, no. 9 (2008) 451 (cf. notes 59 and 65 above).

7

"The Word Became Flesh and Tabernacled among Us"

A Primer for the Exodus in John's Gospel

Thomas N. Willoughby

Introduction

Perhaps no other book of the NT, if not the entire Bible, has come under greater scrutiny, or attack, than the Fourth Gospel (hereafter referred to as John). The explanations for such attention are varied, ranging from its numerous attestations of the divinity of Jesus to the rich, theological sophistication with which the author pens his arguments. The book drips with didactic verbal imagery unparalleled within the whole of the NT, save, perhaps, Revelation. It has captured the attention of scholar and schoolboy, preacher and parishioner. It refuses to be coupled with the Synoptics, yet reveals a message believed here to be consistent with the whole of Scripture.[1] It is a gold mine whose vast resources have been more than picked over, yet somehow, never entirely plundered. It is a mystery.

The purpose of this essay is in no way an attempt to fully remove the cloud that covers this incredible book; rather, it is a reflection upon a

---

1. For a fuller discussion regarding this, see D. Moody Smith, "Historical Issues and the Problem of John and the Synoptics," in *From Jesus to John: Essays on Jesus and New Testament Christology in Honour of Marinus de Jonge*, ed. M. C. de Boer, JSNTSup 84 (Sheffield: Sheffield Academic, 1993) 252–67; and Craig S. Keener, *The Gospel of John: A Commentary* (Peabody, MA: Hendrickson, 2003) 1:3–52.

portion of biblical text which the author seems most likely to have had in mind when composing John. The aim is simply to apprehend something more of the book's glorious content. The essential question is this: Is there evidence that elements of the exodus event shaped the composition of John? There is simply not space to give this topic its full and proper attention. This essay merely scrapes the surface by examining select passages in hopes of laying groundwork for future research and discussions.[2]

The Exodus and John 1:14

We begin our journey with a brief examination of some intriguing elements in John 1:14. Here the text states, "the word (ὁ λόγος) became flesh and tabernacled (ἐσκήνωσεν) among us." First, it will be noted that the term typically rendered "dwelt" (aorist of σκηνόω) has here been translated on the basis of its etymological meaning: "to tent" or "to tabernacle." The verbal form of this root is rare in the NT literature, appearing only here and four times in Revelation.[3] In each of its occurrences in Revelation, it is used specifically in conjunction with the idea of the divine abode.[4] Such an understanding of its usage then requires us to consider what possibilities are being described by its selection in John 1:14. One passage that might prove beneficial to this discussion is found at Mt. Sinai in Exod 19–35. While the specific term does not appear here in its verbal form in Greek, we do find the convergence of the root term "tent" or "tabernacle" (σκηνή) in conjunction with the notion of the abode of YHWH exhibited in the vast majority of occurrences within the Torah from the time of the inception of the Tabernacle.[5]

2. Much of the information contained within this work is the culmination of research first presented in lectures at Criswell College, Midwestern Baptist Theological Seminary, and Princeton Theological Seminary.

3. Rev 7:15; 12:12; 13:6; 21:3. Two different cognate verbs appear in Matt 13:32; Mark 4:32; Luke 13:19; Acts 2:26; and 2 Cor 12:9. However, the idea conveyed in each of these instances is that of "nesting" in the first four and "resting," which seems to imply a more temporal nuance, in the last.

4. Rev 7:15; 12:12; 13:6; 15:5; and 21:3 are the only instances of this verb within the NT other than John 1:14. In each case, context clearly reveals that the term references the Tabernacle, or the abode of YHWH. Cf. Kendell H. Easley, *Revelation*, HNTC 12 (Nashville: Broadman & Holman, 1998) 228, 273, 394–95.

5. Exod 25:9; 26:1, 6–7, 9, 12–15, 17–18, 22–23, 26–27, 30, 35; 27:9, 21; 28:43; 29:4, 10–11, 30, 32, 42, 44; 30:16, 18, 20–21, 26, 36; 31:7; 33:7–11; 35:11, 21; 36:8, 37; 38:21, 8; 40:32; 38:27, 30–31; 39:33, 40; 40:2, 5–6, 8–9, 12, 17–19, 21–22, 24, 26, 29, 33–36, 38; Lev 1:1, 3, 5; 3:2, 8, 13; 4:4–5, 7, 14, 16, 18; 6:16, 26, 30; 8:3–4, 11, 31, 33, 35; 9:5, 23; 10:7, 9; 12:6; 14:11, 23; 15:14, 29, 31; 16:7, 16–17, 20, 23, 33; 17:4–6, 9; 19:21; 23:34, 42–43; 24:3; Num 1:1, 50–51, 53; 2:2, 17; 3:7–8, 10, 23, 25–26, 29, 35–36, 38; 4:3–4, 15–16, 23, 25–26, 28, 30–31, 33, 35, 37, 39, 41, 43, 47; 5:17; 6:10, 13, 18; 7:1, 3, 5,

After the conclusion of the golden calf tragedy (Exod 32), Moses has an interesting dialogue with YHWH in Exod 33. In Exod 33:2, YHWH says that He will send an angel before the people in order to drive out the inhabitants of the land. His reasoning for this decision is given in verse 5 where He states very plainly that, should He go with the people for a single moment, He would destroy them because they are obstinate. Moses then interjects the argument that it was not his idea to deliver the people in the first place, but rather YHWH's. After a brief exchange, YHWH relents and in verse 14 says that His presence shall go with them and give them rest. In fact, in verse 17, YHWH says that He will also do "this thing" (את־הדבר הזה) which Moses had asked of Him. "The word/thing" (הדבר) seems to be the Tabernacle, which YHWH had instructed that the people make for Him. The purpose of this Tabernacle according to Exod 25:8 was that YHWH might dwell among the people. This Tabernacle would be the very abode of YHWH in the midst of His people.

The second intriguing element of John 1:14 in this context is found with the expression that the author "beheld his glory." The "glory" (כבוד) of YHWH first appears in Exod 13:21, although the term itself is not incorporated here, only its manifestation as a cloud that leads the Israelites by day and a pillar of fire that is seen by them in the darkness of the night. In Exod 16:7, in response to the outcry of the people for food, YHWH tells the people of His provision for them and that they will see His glory (כבוד, 16:10). In Exod 24:16–17, the glory (כבוד) is found upon the mountain for a period of six days before the Lord calls to Moses from it on the seventh day. In like fashion, the glory appears upon the mountain as both a cloud and fire. Earlier in the passage (24:1), Moses is instructed to bring with him Aaron, Nadab, Abihu, and the seventy elders of Israel, while Moses alone is commanded to come up further. The leadership that joins Moses on the mountain enjoys a meal together while having the privilege of seeing the God of Israel and the pavement of sapphire beneath His feet (24:9–11). In verse 12, Moses is instructed to part company with these men and to ascend the mountain even further before the Lord. This ascension seems to imply various points of proximity with respect to Divine communion.[6]

89; 8:9, 15, 19, 22, 24, 26; 9:15, 17–20; 10:3, 11, 17, 21; 11:16, 24, 26; 12:4–5, 10; 14:10; 16:9, 18–19, 42–43, 50; 17:4, 7–8, 13; 18:2–4, 6, 21–23, 31; 19:4, 13; 20:6; 24:6; 25:6; 27:2; 31:30, 47, 54; Deut. 16:31:14–15.

6. A similar image to this is found in the Tabernacle itself wherein the priests enjoyed the prebends apart from the congregation, yet the High Priest alone was afforded access into the Most Holy Place. This is not to imply that Moses is representative of the High Priest, but merely that such a division of proximity with respect to the Divine is displayed elsewhere within the Pentateuch. For, as Jacob Milgrom notes, Aaron is uniquely given access to the adytum even while the tent is filled with the divine cloud, something that

After spending a significant amount of time with the Lord upon the mountain and subsequently addressing the people because of their sin of making the golden calf, Moses enters into a period of dialog that is of special interest to our study. As noted above, in Exod 32:31—33:16 Moses intercedes on behalf of the people with YHWH. At the conclusion of this, YHWH does agree to go with the people into the land by doing "this word/ thing" (את־הדבר הזה), making the Tabernacle within which His presence might abide. Apparently, sensing his standing before YHWH in light of the Lord's proclamation in Exod 33:17, Moses entreats the Lord to show His glory to him. Certainly this is a notable request in that it sheds significant light upon the ability of Moses at this point to observe clearly the glory of the Lord. Remember that the Israelites were allowed to see it to some degree in Exod 13 and 16, the priests and elders were able to see it at yet another degree in Exod 24, and Moses was already enabled to see it at an unprecedented level in the dialog just recounted. However, this was still not enough for him. He wanted to see the fullness of the glory of the Lord.

This brings to light two specific points for consideration here. First, YHWH explains to Moses that no man can see Him and live (33:20). Second, it is equally interesting to note the extent to which YHWH goes in order to enable Moses to see as much as is humanly possible. He hides him in the cleft of a rock, covers him with His hand, and then causes His glory to pass by, only allowing Moses to look upon it from the rear. In light of this, it is an overwhelmingly powerful statement that the author of John makes when he says, "we beheld His glory . . . full of grace and truth." We will look at the second part of this statement below, but for now, suffice it to say that the ability to behold the glory and not simply a part, a side or, a shadow, but rather the fullness of the divine glory, is without precedent in biblical literature since the Garden narrative of Genesis apart from other encounters with Jesus.

A third intriguing element of John 1:14 is the expression, "full of grace and truth." This expression corresponds well with the Hebrew phrase חסד ואמת. These two terms are found numerous times throughout the HB with specific reference to covenant faithfulness.[7] In fact, continuing in the pas-

---

Moses is unable to do (Exod 40:35). See Milgrom, *Leviticus 1–16*, AB 3 (New York: Doubleday, 1991) 138. For a different perspective on this, see Douglas K. Stuart, *Exodus*, NAC 2 (Nashville: Broadman & Holman, 2006) 558–59. Stuart suggests that it is assumed that Moses *et al* went back down the mountain after the meal and then ascended again. His rationale for this additional undocumented descent is that he believes (A) the two events are substantially different, and (B) only Moses and Joshua are allowed to ascend at this point. William H. C. Propp *Exodus 19–40*, AB 2a (New York: Doubleday, 2006) 164–65, suggests that it could be interpreted either way. Cf. Carol L. Meyers, *Exodus*, NCBC (New York, Cambridge: Cambridge University Press, 2005) 298.

7. See Gen 24:27, 49; 32:11; 47:29; Exod 34:6; Josh 2:14; 2 Sam 2:6; 15:20; Isa 16:5;

sage in Exod 34:6, as the Lord passes by Moses while he remains covered within the rock, YHWH states of Himself that He is, among other things, חסד ואמת. This portion of the self-disclosure of YHWH to Moses is observed in John 1:14. It is clear that the author believes himself, and others, to have been the recipients of an unprecedented encounter with the Divine wherein they were able to see fully what Moses himself could only hear proclaimed and see in part.[8] Furthermore, he continues in John 1:16 by stating that out of this fullness of חסד ואמת, this group had all received an abounding portion as indicated by the expression, "grace upon grace." If this connection is correct, the term "grace" in this instance may serve as something of an abbreviated form of the fuller expression. Thus, the author would be indicating that the benefit received from Christ is a multiplied amount of חסד ואמת.

The explanation for this benefit is revealed by means of a contrast between Jesus and Moses found in John 1:17, which says the Law "was given through Moses, but grace and truth [חסד ואמת as we suggest] through Jesus Christ came into existence." In other words, Moses was able to convey the "Ten Words" (as they are called in the HB[9]) that were given to him; but, in contrast, חסד ואמת came into existence and was imparted by Jesus Christ "out of His fullness." This distinction is not only dramatic in light of the first century Jewish appreciation for the role of Moses as giver of Torah, but it is entirely possible that it establishes something of a framework upon which the rest of the book hangs.

If this exodus reading of John is accurate, then one would expect to see additional elements of the exodus account. One of the fundamental messages of the exodus is that YHWH came down to both meet and dwell with His people.[10] The preparation for this event is found in Exod 19.

The Revelatory "Three" in Exodus and John 1

In Exod 19, various boundaries are established to ensure that no one would break through and touch the mountain and be destroyed. But our attention is drawn just prior to these instructions to verses 10–11, where Moses

---

Mic 7:20; Zech 7:9; Pss 25:10; 26:3; 40:11–12; 57:4, 11; 61:8; 69:14; 85:11; 86:15; 89:15; 108:5; 115:1; 117:2; 138:2; Prov 3:3; 14:22; 16:6; 20:28.

8. It is also interesting to note that these two factors help to introduce the First Epistle of John, namely "That which we have seen and heard" in 1 John 1:3. It would seem that this fact was so significant that the author not only utilizes it within this gospel, but elsewhere as well.

9. Exod 34:28; Deut 4:13; 10:4.

10. Propp, *Exodus 19–40*, 164–65; Meyers, *Exodus*, 142.

instructs the people to wash themselves for two consecutive days and to be prepared, for on the third day, the Lord will come down upon Mt. Sinai. He reiterates that they are to be ready for the third day, because on that day, YHWH will come down "in the sight of the people" (19:9–11). The emphasis of the passage seems to be upon the idea that YHWH himself is descending upon Mt. Sinai to speak with Moses in the sight of all the people, thus validating Moses' testimony before them (19:9).

This observation illuminates two significant points. First, within the Pentateuch, nearly every time that the number three is used in conjunction with a period of time, it indicates a preparation for a revelation.[11] Second, the preparation for a revelation *via* washing is something that seems to carry along into the Tabernacle and later Temple periods, as the priests would wash themselves before entering into the presence of YHWH (Exod 30:18–21). But this was no anomaly, as evidence of a similar understanding (with respect to the reception of divine revelation) was present even among the community at Qumran. "Ritual purification anticipated the spirit bringing divine revelation already in Scripture," says Hanna Harrington of the practices at Qumran.[12] In 4Q213a we find evidence that the community at Qumran certainly understood that ritual purification was necessary prior to receiving divine revelation. To be sure, this is not an isolated instance, for much of the work and life of the community centered upon laws of purification. But it is this idea of washing, and specifically for three days prior to a revelation, that is most intriguing here. Harrington says,

> The quintessential type of revelation at Sinai was preceded by a three-day ritual purification process and this is partially mirrored in the *Temple Scroll's* requirement of a three-day quarantine and purification before entry in the Temple City. According to Josephus, the Essenes, the sect which best resembles the Qumran authors, did require ritual purification as a prerequisite

11. The following are all of the occurrences wherein the number three is used in conjunction with a period of time within the Pentateuch: Gen 31:22; 34:25; 38:24; 40:12–13, 18–19; 42:17; Exod 2:2; 3:18; 10:22–23; 15:22; 23:14, 17; 34:23; Lev 19:23; 25:18–22; Num 10:33; 22:28–32; 24:10; 33:8; Deut 14:28; 16:16. The one possible exception is Leviticus 7:17–18 where the text speaks of the sacrifice remaining until the third day. The idea here is that the sacrifice is to be eaten or burnt entirely on the third day. Whether this suggests an additional revelatory element is best left to further research.

12. Hannah K. Harrington, "Ritual Purity," in *The Dead Sea Scrolls and Contemporary Culture: Proceedings of the International Conference Held at the Israel Museum, Jerusalem (July 6–8, 2008)*, eds. Adolfo D. Roitman, Lawrence H. Schiffman, and Shani Tzorff (Boston: Brill, 2011) 345.

for the reception of prophecy; they utilized the books of the prophets and also "various forms of purification" (*BJ* 2.159).[13]

Having noted that the number three when connected to periods of time within the Pentateuch anticipates a revelation, and that washings were used in Exod 19 in preparation for the revelation of YHWH descending in the midst of His people, we are prepared to examine the text in John to see if there are any similar types of connections. Within the first chapter we find a rather unique structuring of the narrative surrounding the common expression in Greek, Τῇ ἐπαύριον ("the next day," John 1:29, 354, 43). Since John 1:1–18 comprises what is typically understood to be the Prologue, then we are left with 1:19–51 (according to the traditionally accepted break with 2:1 and following) to explain by way of narrative structure. Since 1:29 begins the section of the Τῇ ἐπαύριον, this leaves only 1:19–28 to explain.

Here we suggest that 1:19–28 should not be included in the daily numbering of events that start at 1:29 because 1:19–28 serves as the authentication for the witness that follows. In other words, 1:19–28 is consumed with revealing the identity and authority of John the Baptizer. The inquiry comes from an investigative entourage of priests and Levites who have been sent specifically by the Pharisees for this purpose (see 1:19, 24). The narrative indicates that the baptizing or washing of people is the work of only personalities associated or recognized by the cult. Thus John 1:19–28 establishes the authority not only of the washings of John, but also his prophetic office as fulfillment of the prophecy in Isa 40:3. One might question why such a validation would be needed. This is where the explanation of John 1:29, 35, 43 comes in.

Each of these verses has one major thing in common: the witness to the identity of Jesus. In John 1:29, John the Baptizer says, "Behold the lamb of God who takes up the sins of the world." In 1:36, he says, "Behold the Lamb of God." Two facets are worth noting. First, in both instances, the one bearing witness is John the Baptizer. It is his unique position as one washing the people that allows for him to play a dual role of priest and prophet. He is from a priestly family (his father Zacharias offered the incense in the Temple when the angel proclaimed his birth, Luke 1:8–23.). This, however, was apparently an unnecessary point, because although it is noted in other accounts, the Gospel of John says nothing of it. One reasonable explanation might be that this is a moot point due to the fact that the priests and Levites have already validated his cultic authority *via* John 1:19–28; and, in the same passage, he identifies himself before the priests and Levites as one fulfilling the prophetic call of Isa 40:3.

13. Ibid., 345.

Also, John's selection of identifiers for Jesus is unique. He calls Jesus "the Lamb of God," and he is the only NT writer to do so.[14] Clearly this foreshadows aspects that the gospel writer is seeking to illuminate. But more immediate than this is the fact that Torah prescribes that every sacrifice or offering be presented to the priest. Authority regarding cultic elements fell within the jurisdiction of the priesthood, as is evidenced in part with the persecution that comes to Jesus in John 2:18 for protesting the marketplace within the Temple without validated credentials.[15] The authority of the priesthood during this period is well documented. For example, Craig Keener says,

> Josephus (*Life* 1; cf. *Ant.* 4.218), Philo (*Spec. Laws* 1.131–55, esp. 1.131; 4.190–92), and the Dead Sea Scrolls (the "wicked priest" in 1QpHab 8.8–12; 9.4–7; 12.5; greedy priests in 4QpNah 1.11) indicate the prominence that priests retained in all parts of Judaism before the destruction of the temple.[16]

Clearly the pronouncement of a sacrificial lamb for the sins of the world falls within this sphere. Again, this would add emphasis to the need for the validation portion of John 1:19–28.

Of special note within these first two passages is the concept of "remaining" (μένεις). In 1:32–34, John the Baptizer shares that he had previously been ignorant of the identity of this lamb, even though we glean elsewhere (Luke 1:36) that he was the biological cousin of Jesus. Nevertheless, the one who sent him said to him that the person upon whom he saw the Spirit descending and remaining upon him, the same was to be the One Who would baptize in the Holy Spirit. The emphasis here is the remaining aspect of the Spirit.

In light of the exodus motif, it is the Spirit of YHWH Who is upon the Tabernacle as it moves from place to place. Whenever the presence of YHWH (manifested with His glory) moved, the people moved. Whenever He stopped, the people would stop. So we have in John 1:29–34 the Spirit descending and remaining upon Jesus. In 1:35–42 we have the second testimony of John the Baptizer with a truncated version of the prior day's proclamation, "Behold the Lamb of God." At the hearing of this, two of John's

---

14. Certainly Paul had this concept in mind in 1 Cor. 5:7 when he speaks of the Passover that was sacrificed, but he does not specifically use the term lamb as a title for Jesus in the same way that John does. Although a case might be made for elision, the term "lamb" does not appear. Also, in 1 Pet 1:19, Peter uses the term "lamb" as a simile and not as a specific title for Jesus.

15. Michael A. Daise, *Feasts in John: Jewish Festivals and Jesus' "Hour" in the Fourth Gospel*, WUNT 229 (Tübingen: Mohr/Siebeck, 2007) 26.

16. Keener, *John*, 1:431 (see pp. 1:429–33 for a fuller discussion of the significant influence of the priests during the period before the destruction of the temple).

disciples leave John to follow Jesus. Jesus asks them what they seek, and they respond that they want to know where He is "remaining" (μένεις). He invites them to come and see, so they follow Him; and, since it is late in the day, they remain with Him there. In fact, the syntactical structure of the sentence seems to add weight to this idea of remaining. John 1:39b says, "when they came and saw where He was remaining (μένεις), also with him they remained (μένεις) that day . . . " Admittedly, this in and of itself would prove virtually nothing, but placed within the context of the exodus theme, it seems to parallel the way in which the Israelites followed the Tabernacle when it moved and remained where it remained.

While it is relatively easy to identify the similarities between days one and two, it is the third day that is of special interest here. In John 1:45, Philipp finds Nathanael and explains that they have found the one foretold by Moses in the Torah (see Deut 18:15), Jesus the son of Joseph from Nazareth. Nathanael gives a skeptical response by asking if any good thing can come out of Nazareth, and he is subsequently issued the same invitation that Jesus issued in 1:39— "Come and see." Upon arrival, Jesus says to Nathanael, "Behold truly an Israelite in whom is no δόλος." The term δόλος is used of Jacob in Gen 27:35 for the way he had used deceit to take the birthright and blessing of Esau. It is further used in Gen 34:13 of the deceit used by his sons when avenging their sister, Dinah.[17] Jesus' use of the term here seems to reflect an understanding of Nathanael's integrity in light of such a questionable lineage. In doing so, Jesus, having His own testimony authenticated by John (whose own testimony was authenticated by the priests and Levites), authenticates Nathanael's testimony that follows. In response to Jesus' statement regarding His seeing Nathanael under his tent before Phillip even called to him, he exclaims, "Rabbi, you are the Son of God. You are the King of Israel." This testimony, having been painstakingly validated all the way back through both priestly and prophetic offices, is the focal point of the revelation expected by the narrative structure. But, as we will see, such profound statements will be further validated by divine attestation *via* the use of signs.

Finally, there is something of note in Jesus speaking of Nathanael seeing the heavens opened and the angels ascending and descending upon the Son of Man. Many have noted the parallel between this response of Jesus and Gen 28 where Jacob encounters YHWH at Bethel.[18] However, it is inter-

17. See D. A. Carson, *The Gospel According to John*, PNTC (Leicester: IVP, 1991) 160–61; Gerald L. Borchert, *John 1–11*, NAC 25A (Nashville: Broadman & Holman, 1996) 147–50.

18. See Carson, *John*, 163; Tom Wright, *John for Everyone, Part 1: Chapters 1–10* (London: SPCK, 2004) 17–18; Barclay Moon Newman and Eugene Albert Nida, *A*

esting to note the difference in the location of the Lord in Gen 28 (heaven) and Jesus speaking to Nathanael (earth). The idea is clearly that the Lord had descended and He has revealed Himself on the third day.

Finally, the third day of John 1:43–51 also stands out in contrast to the previous days in that it does not contain a washing. In light of the days of washing in preparation for a divine revelation, and the accompanying proclamation, not only by Nathanael, but by Jesus Himself, the stage is set for a series of divine validations of this remarkable testimony *via* various signs.

The Exodus and John's First "Sign"

The first of these signs occurs in John 2:1–11. Again, the efforts of NT scholars to provide an explanation to the opening terminology of 2:1, "Now in the third day" (Καὶ τῇ ἡμέρᾳ τῇ τρίτῃ) have resulted in no conclusive determination. Some have suggested a seven-day new creation motif leading up to the wedding at Cana.[19] Some have suggested that the Greek Καὶ at the beginning of 2:1 indicates the beginning of yet an additional day. However, if one translates it as an adjunctive Καὶ, "also in the third day" (as if to say the profound ending of the proclamational passage of Nathanael actually serves as a nice segway into the attesting sign before all the people in John 2), then the numbering at the beginning of John 2 actually makes sense by being connected to the previous days of washing. It is not a different day from Nathanael's proclamation, but one-in-the-same.[20] The link between the two passages has been acknowledged as readily apparent, as Beasley-Murray attests:

> It is evident that the second chapter is linked with the account of the call of the disciples in chap. I through the reference in 2:1 to the *third* day; the promise in 1:51 is given its first fulfillment in the miracle of the water into wine.[21]

Handbook on the Gospel of John, UBS Handbook (New York: United Bible Societies, 1993) 53; Borchert, *John 1–11*, 147–50; George R. Beasley-Murray, *John*, WBC 36 (Dallas: Word, 2002) 28.

19. E.g., Raymond E. Brown, *The Gospel According to John: I–XII*, AB 29 (New York: Doubleday, 1966) 4; Keener, *John*, 1:105–6 (see pp. 1:496–98 for an extensive list of perspectives on this issue).

20. Note that while some later codices have a space or other marking to identify a paragraph break between 1:51 and 2:1, Codex Sinaiticus clearly does not. While such a detail does not guarantee this view, it would seemingly leave open the possibility for such a reading. For more on this reading, see Daise, *Feasts in John*, 9–11.

21. Beasley-Murray, *John*, 31. Note, however, that he does not suggest the explanation for the third day offered here, merely that there is a clear connection between the passages.

While certainly there is much to say about this first of signs in John 2:1–11, we will only view here a couple of elements. First, it is a wedding ceremony that is identified by John as being the location of the first sign, or public manifestation of Jesus, designed to attest to the word of testimony that had been previously proclaimed.[22] The events at Sinai have oft been seen to be akin to a marriage ceremony, and are even seemingly validated as such in later writings where YHWH indicates that he will divorce His bride.[23]

Second, it is a large ceremony, as noted by the presence of the six stone vessels used for purification. Stone was a costly material to be used for large dishes and vessels.[24] Nevertheless, it was the material of choice for those who had the means to acquire it because it was the unique material that had the ability to not conduct impurities such as would defile the user. When over ninety percent of the region was noted to have lived at subsistence level,[25] the likelihood that a given family in such a rural community could afford a single vessel of this size made of stone was at best improbable. But to have six of them the size indicated by John not only speaks of wealth, but also gives a strong indication as to the size of the expected party. Weddings were noted to be public events anyway, but certainly one of such a wealthy household would have drawn attendants from the entire community. This may also lend some insight as to the magnitude of potential embarrassment upon the groom for running out of wine. It is here that Jesus performs his first attesting sign of turning water into wine, which has often been noted to have strong similarity to the first public sign presented before Pharaoh of turning the water into blood as a validation of the word of YHWH.[26] It is in this light that we see the Lord descend in the presence of the people.

22. This miracle is especially curious in that it is referred to as the first of Jesus' signs. The omission of such a detail within the Synoptics begs for explanation. However, if John is focusing upon the public manifestation of Jesus, his is a unique perspective indeed and would warrant such unprecedented recorded events.

23. Herbert M. Wolf, *An Introduction to the Old Testament Pentateuch* (Chicago: Moody, 1991) 180. Here Wolf offers as an example Jer 3:8 (but see also Isa 50:1).

24 Jodi Magness, *Stone and Dung, Oil and Spit: Jewish Daily Life in the Time of Jesus* (Grand Rapids: Eerdmans, 2011) 74.

25. Anthony J. Saldarini, *Pharisees, Scribes and Sadducees in Palestinian Society*, BRS (Grand Rapids: Eerdmans, 2001), cited in Magness, *Stone and Dung*, 14–15.

26. Peter Ainslie, *Among the Gospels and the Acts Being Notes and Comments Covering the Life of Christ in the Flesh, and the First Thirty Years' History of His Church* (Baltimore: Temple Seminary Press, 1908) 234, mentions the connection between Moses miracle and the water-to-wine. He does not expound upon it. See also A. Blum, "John," in *The Bible Knowledge Commentary: An Exposition of the Scriptures*, eds. J. F. Walvoord and R. B. Zuck (Wheaton, IL: Victor, 1985); Charles P. Baylis, "The Woman Caught in Adultery: A Test of Jesus as the Greater Prophet," *BSac* 146, no. 582 (1989) 174; and H. D. M. Spence-Jones, ed., *St. John Vol. I*, Pulpit Commentary (London, New York: Funk

The Exodus and the Purity Narratives in John 3–4

In what way did the descent of the Lord affect the narrative structure of John's Gospel? Certainly there are numerous points of interest that are worthy of investigation, and there is simply not space to discuss everything. Here we focus on two specific narrative blocks that are illuminated by the exodus and the cultural climate at the time of the writing of the Gospel.

In the first century, regardless of exactly what year one dates the authorship of John, the nation was divided by comparison with the time of the exodus. The one-time slaves had entered the land of promise and a monarchy had been established. It was under Solomon that the monarchy reached its apex. Tragically, after the death of his father and under the foolish counsel of his advisors, Solomon's son, Rehoboam, attempted to strengthen his grip upon his people in an effort to establish his authority as king in his father's stead. His inexperience caused a split within the nation that would seemingly never be overcome. In 722 BCE, Samaria, the capital of the newly formed northern kingdom (Israel), fell to the Assyrians. Its inhabitants were scattered and many of those that remained intermarried with other nations. For all intents and purposes, Israel (i.e., the northern kingdom) ceased to exist.

While it is difficult to speak of an "Israel" in the first century CE with any kind of true clarity because of the intermingled nature of the inhabitants of the land, it seems clear from the text that John has a special interest in the Samaritans (not as Gentiles, but rather as the remnant of Israel[27]), the current inhabitants of a land that served as the capital of the northern kingdom before its fall. A. Büchler states that it is difficult to know exactly what the status of the relationship between Jews and Samaritans was before 70 CE. In fact, their relationship was subject to an ebb and flow depending upon the state of current events. Be that as it may, by 65–66 CE,[28] the schools of Hillel and Shammai taught that Samaritan women were as those who menstruate from the cradle.[29] The idea behind this is that, in accordance with Levitical law, anything or anyone that the woman touched would be defiled. For example, when her husband would have relations with her, he would become defiled as well.

Defilement meant, among other things, the inability to perform worship duties within the prescribed Temple precincts. These kinds of purity issues were in large part the main points of division within Judaism in the

---

& Wagnalls, 1909) 102.

27. The dialogue of the Samaritan woman with Jesus evidences this in John 4.

28. A. Büchler, "The Levitical Impurity of the Gentile in Palestine before the Year 70," *JQR* 17, no. 1 (1926) 3.

29. Niddah 4:1.

first century CE. While the various sects held to differing perspectives regarding purity and defilement, according to Josephus, the dominant voice on these issues, at least within Jerusalem, was that of the Pharisees.[30] Indeed, the Pharisees were the ones who sent the priests and Levites in John 1:19 to inquire about John's authority for immersing people. Subsequently, no typical Jewish adherent of Temple law would ever be found speaking with such a one for fear of contamination and defilement. But Jesus was certainly *not* typical. This brings us to the two narrative blocks in question.

John 3:1–21

The first block is John 3:1–21.[31] Here, Nicodemus, a Pharisee and a "ruler of the Jews," comes to Jesus by night. He acknowledges that Jesus is a teacher sent by God, but he is clearly unaware that he is anything more than that. Jesus makes a rather peculiar remark to begin the dialogue: "Truly, truly, I say to you, unless one is born from above he cannot see the kingdom of God" (John 3:5). At first glance the expression "born from above" might strike the non-rabbi as odd, but the context that follows indicates that Nicodemus understood what Jesus was saying. In fact, the content of the discussion becomes much clearer the second time Jesus responds. He says in verse 5, "Truly, truly, I say to you, unless on is born of water and the spirit he cannot enter into the kingdom of God." This reference appears to reflect the prophecy of Ezek 36:16–38.

In Ezek 36:16–38, the prophet offers hope in the midst of despair. He speaks of a new work that YHWH will do among His people on behalf of His great name. The long awaited promise of the patriarchs seemed to have fizzled out with the conquest of Israel in 722 BCE and the exile of the majority of the inhabitants of Judah and the subsequent destruction of the Temple in 586. Nevertheless, YHWH offers a promise of restoration in Ezek 36. He makes it very clear that this restoration is not being done because of the people, but rather because of His great name.[32]

The problem is the defilement of the people with idols, which He likens to that of a woman during her menstruation. Their defilement has

---

30. Büchler, "Levitical Impurity," 4–7.

31. While there is some discussion among scholars regarding the section division here, for this essay, we will examine John 3:1–21 as an entire narrative unit. For samples of differing perspectives regarding the division of this passage, see D. A. Carson, *John*, 185; Wright, *John 1–10*, 27–34; Newman and Nida, *Handbook*, 86; Beasley-Murray, *John*, 45–46.

32. This point is repeated several times here (Ezek 36:20, 21, 22, 23, 32). See Lamar E. Cooper, *Ezekiel*, NAC 17 (Nashville: Broadman & Holman, 1994) 314–15.

separated them from YHWH. The remedy comes in Ezek 36:24–28 where creation and purification elements are utilized to describe how YHWH will essentially re-create His people. In verese 26, YHWH states that He will give them a new heart and put a new spirit within them. Also, verse 27 states that YHWH would put His Spirit within them and *cause* them to walk in His statutes—something that until now, the people had shown themselves incapable of doing. But perhaps the most intriguing point comes in verse 25, in which YHWH says that He will sprinkle "clean water" on them in order to cleanse them from their defilement and idolatry. The point of the passage is very clear: due to the sin and defilement of the people, they have been removed from the land of promise; nevertheless, YHWH would remove both of these impurities by means of sprinkling them with clean water[33] and a re-creation or rebirth.

In light of the perspective of the Pharisees on matters of purity and defilement,[34] the passage from Ezek 36 has much greater weight with respect to the discussion with Jesus in John 3. Given the recognized position of Nicodemus among the Pharisees,[35] it is doubtful that one could imagine someone better to embody the ideas of purity. Even his approaching Jesus by night may indicate an unwillingness to allow his contemporaries to recognize him having dialogue with such a questionable character. However, Jesus' opening remarks seem to cut through cultic attempts to accomplish and maintain a status of purity. He reflects the words of Ezekiel by stating that this birth is that which comes from above, not by means of human effort.

Although much more could be said on this, the important point is that a primary concern in John 3 is the inability of even the model Jewish rabbi to achieve a status of purity before YHWH apart from the internal transformation accomplished only *by* YHWH. This is perhaps revealed best by the question of Nicodemus (John 3:9) and the subsequent response of

33. The concept of sprinkling with "clean water" is expressed most notably in Num 19 where the rite of the red heifer is instituted. While scholars debate the extent to which the ashes of the heifer were required for removal of general impurities, they were certainly required for the removal of corpse defilement. Nevertheless, even if the ashes themselves were not used in the washings, the "clean water" was to be comprised of "living" or flowing water. Depending on the type of defilement, the contaminated person would bathe on the third and fifth days (and sometimes the seventh). For more on purification and ritual cleansing, see Hannah K. Harrington, "Ritual Purity," in *The Dead Sea Scrolls and Contemporary Culture*, 329–47; Hannan Birenboim, "*Tevul Yom* and the Red Heifer: Pharasaic and Sadducean Halakah," *DSD* 16, no. 2 (2009) 254–73; Jacob Milgrom, "The Paradox of the Red Cow," *VT* 31 (1981) 62–72; Keener, *John*, 1:550–52.

34. Cf. Josephus, *Ant.* 18.1.3–4. It is here explained that the Pharisees greatly influenced even the Sadducees because of the respect given them by the larger Jewish community.

35. See Borchert, *John 1–11*, 169.

Jesus: "Are you the teacher of Israel and do not understand these things?" (3:10). The use of the definite article with reference to "teacher of Israel" perhaps speaks to the idea that Nicodemus is at the very least, one of the more prominent rabbis of the day, if not *the* most prominent.[36] Surely if he does not grasp the concepts being outlined by Jesus' questions, how could the Jewish people ever understand them? However, the narrative block ends with Nicodemus failing to embrace the message of Jesus at this juncture.

John 4:1–42

The second block is John 4:1–42.[37] As stated above, at least by the time of the writing of John, Jews considered Samaritan women to be perpetually defiled. The woman whom Jesus encounters here is not simply another Samaritan, which is demonstrated by the time of day that she comes to draw water as well as the ensuing discussion. We see in verse 6 that it is noon when both Jesus and the woman arrive at the well. This would be much too hot a time of day to come and draw water. As the narrative continues, it becomes apparent (by the woman's response to Jesus regarding her previous husbands and current paramour) why she is not well received among the Samaritans. Although the theology with respect to the Temple location was a matter of contention with Jews, their views regarding purity were much the same as the mainstream thought of Judaism, which may explain her apparent ostracism.[38]

Jesus engages the woman with a provocative request for a drink of water. In the Jewish mind at that time, nothing transmits impurity more quickly than fluids. The woman's response that the Jews have no dealings (συγχρῶνται) with Samaritans may convey this.[39] Although the evidence is potentially open to the charge of an etymological fallacy, this particular context seems to benefit from the nuance. He seems to be asking the woman for a drink in order that He might in turn offer the woman the water that she truly needs.

Jesus' reference in verse 10 seems to refer back to the discussion with Nicodemus about the gift of God (3:16). The description that Jesus uses with

36. See Daniel B. Wallace, *Greek Grammar Beyond the Basics: An Exegetical Syntax of the New Testament*, (Grand Rapids: Zondervan, 1996) 223; Keener, *John*, 1:558–59.

37. For our purposes, it seems best to treat this segment as a whole. See Carson, *John*, 214; Beasley-Murray, *John*, 58–59.

38. See Wright, *John 1–10*, 41.

39. Its root indicates sharing utensils or vessels. This would certainly be unacceptable for a purity conscious Jew to do with a Samaritan woman in light of the teachings of the day. See Borchert, *John 1–11*, 202.

respect to the water is especially noteworthy. The woman understands the concept of "living water" as being that which does not end (but is flowing) and asks that she might have some of this endless water supply. These kinds of wells were incredibly valuable in nomadic cultures,[40] but that is not what Jesus is speaking about. He says in John 4:14 that the water He gives is a well that springs up from within the person and leads to eternal life. When read with John 3, this is the water referred to in Ezek 36 that can only come from above. Its purpose is not to quench a temporary thirst, but to purify perpetually against all that would defile the person.

The narrative block ends with this woman who has been an outcast from society (both at home in Samaria and abroad throughout Judaism) embracing the "gift" by believing in Jesus as the Christ. She is thus compelled to share her finding with others, and they too come to believe in Him. In verse 42, the people of Samaria give the bold testimony that this is "the Savior of the world" because they have heard for themselves.

John 3:22–36 as a Purity Connector

One might suggest that we are reading a bit much into the text by asserting that these two blocks are connected by a purification backdrop; but, the intervening passage is crucial. In John 3:22–36, a dispute arises between the disciples of John the Baptizer and "a Jew" regarding purification. The identity of the "Jew" is left anonymous.

If the author of John (who throughout the work omits his own name) happened to be "the Jew" in question, then the scene would make more sense. As a former disciple of John, he would theoretically be baptizing people with Jesus' other disciples in the same area as John. It makes sense that he would engage John's disciples when they questioned why the disciples of Jesus were baptizing. The reason for the questioning would be that John's authority to perform such immersions with Temple authority had already been validated by the priests and Levites in John 1. But the question stands as to what right Jesus had to be performing this cultic activity. John was a priest, but Jesus was not from a priestly lineage.[41] To make matters worse, multitudes were coming to Jesus rather than John for immersion. Something of professional jealousy erupted and John had to step in to settle nerves.

---

40. See Kenneth A. Mathews, *Genesis 11:27—50:26*, NAC 1B (Nashville: Broadman & Holman, 2005) 410.

41. Both Matt 1:3 and Luke 3:33 indicate that Jesus was of the lineage of Judah, not Levi.

His remarkable attitude is again a testimony to the authenticity of the events being witnessed. He remarks very candidly that while he, himself, is the friend of the bridegroom, Jesus *is* the bridegroom. The point is that the friend of the bridegroom is not the focus of the wedding, but the bridegroom himself. In this instance, he once again identifies that bridegroom as none other than Jesus. He then makes a very profound statement indicative of a major thematic truth throughout John's Gospel, "He must increase and I must decrease." In other words, the baptism that looks forward to the revelation must give way to the baptism that is itself the revelation. John 4:2 makes this clear that Jesus is not baptizing, but only His disciples. The fact that John employs the nominative case when speaking of the disciples here indicates that it was the disciples and not Jesus who were doing the baptisms. This ritual of water immersion is not the baptism that Jesus came to bring.

The Exodus Connection

So how does the exodus link these two blocks together? As we have seen, both of these accounts share the issue of purity as a fundamental aspect. Within the culture at that time there was no reason to discuss matters of purity regarding the Samaritans as they would not have been permitted within the Temple due to their status as those who are perpetually impure.[42] There is no effort to speak in terms of Gentiles being purified within this gospel, only the Samaritans. Within the motif of the exodus, there was not a Judah and an Israel—there was only Israel, the covenant people of YHWH.

The fundamentally divisive point for these two groups centered upon worship, and specifically for the Pharisees (whose influence we have already recognized) was the matter of purification. This text demonstrates that the purification that was impossible to accomplish through cultic activity among the people actually came through "the gift" that God provided.

Conclusion

While indeed a great deal more material could have been covered here, we have merely sought to lay the groundwork for further research into this biblical text and its meaning in light of the exodus theme. Although it is highly unlikely that this essay has resolved all of the questions surrounding some of the difficult passages it has addressed, it is our hope that the utilization of the exodus backdrop to the text has illuminated these passages in a fresh way.

42. A. Büchler, "Levitical Impurity," 3, 5, 10.

We have considered the connotation inherent in John 1:14 if an exodus theme were present in the mind of the author. We have considered another possibility for the accounting of days recorded in John 1:29—2:1. We have considered the process of cultic validation for the purpose of witness. Finally, we have examined a possible connection between two narrative accounts on the basis of the cultural backdrop of purity rites and customs. Such a connection may open wide the possibilities for further research within this gospel in light of the exodus theme.

It would be interesting to see in what ways, if any, the exodus theme illuminates accounts such as the feeding of the five thousand and its position within the gospel relative to the scene of Jesus walking on the water. The notion of purity and its various manifestations throughout the gospel would be intriguing as well in light of the purity laws that governed the exodus camp. One might also wonder if there is any correlation to be found between the upper room narrative and the events of the Tabernacle. Such undertakings are likely to yield much fruit in the vast field of Johannine studies.

8

Ephesians and the Hermeneutics of the New Exodus

DAVID STARLING

Ephesians and the Old Testament

IT IS IMPOSSIBLE TO read Ephesians without noticing that there is a relationship of some sort between this letter and the scriptures of the OT. The most obvious way in which that relationship is expressed is in the handful of direct OT citations that occur through the course of the letter (Eph 2:17; 4:8; 5:31; 6:2–3). A reader familiar with the OT will also notice a string of unmistakable allusions to OT texts (e.g., 1:20, 22; 4:25, 26, 30; 6:14–17) and may also detect a host of fainter echoes and concepts that appear to have their source in the OT scriptures (e.g., "inheritance" in 1:18; or "fragrant offering" in 5:2).

While the existence of some sort of relationship between Ephesians and the OT is unmistakable, the extent and nature of that relationship is not so easy to determine. Scholarly discussions of the topic in recent decades have come to widely divergent conclusions. Three treatments of the topic by Markus Barth, Andrew Lincoln, and Thorsten Moritz provide a representative sample of the diversity of scholarly views.

Markus Barth's influential commentary includes a brief but important discussion of the literary relationship between Ephesians and the OT.[1]

---

1. Markus Barth, *Ephesians 1–3*, AB 34 (Garden City, NY: Doubleday, 1974) 27–31.

Against the current of more than a century of German NT scholarship,[2] Barth concludes that the principal background against which the ideas of the letter are to be understood is not the thought-world of Gnosticism but the thought-world of the OT scriptures, and that the manner in which those scriptures are read and interpreted in Ephesians is entirely consistent with the way in which the OT is used in the undisputed Pauline letters. In Ephesians, Barth argues, the OT scriptures tend to be used with a purpose that is hymnic and hortatory, rather than polemical, celebrating the inclusion of Gentiles within the one people of God, and urging them to live in the light of that.[3]

Andrew Lincoln's subsequent study comes to strikingly different conclusions. Lincoln focuses only on actual quotations from the OT (particularly Eph 4:8–10; 2:17; 5:31–32; and 6:2–3) while paying close attention to Eph 3:5, which plays a key role in his argument. On the basis of this verse and his analysis of the OT quotations, Lincoln concludes that within Ephesians there is no trace of a promise/fulfillment use of the OT that is a characteristic feature of the undisputed Pauline letters. Within Ephesians, "OT traditions are one source among a number of authoritative traditions which can be employed to further the writer's purposes."[4] In Christological and ecclesiological contexts (e.g., 1:20, 22; 2:17; 4:8–10; 5:31–32), "OT texts are clearly interpreted authorities, being read in the light of what the writer knows to be true independent of the text and their meaning being derived from that independent source."[5] When OT texts are employed ethically, and their original meaning is largely unaltered (e.g., 4:25–26; 5:18; 6:2–3), "they are still not an ultimate authority but rather convenient vehicles and supports for ethical exhortations the writer is able to ground in other ways."[6]

The most extensive recent treatment of the topic is that of Thorsten Moritz. The distinctive element of Moritz's approach is his argument that Ephesians is Colossians rewritten for a church with a more significant Jewish Christian component; hence, Moritz suggests, the greater prominence of the OT in Ephesians compared with Colossians. He suggests that some of the OT references are used with a deliberate polemic against Jewish interpretive traditions (e.g., Ps 68:18 in Eph 4:8–10). In other instances,

2. Ibid., 12–18; 404–5.

3. Ibid., 30.

4. Andrew T. Lincoln, "The Use of the Old Testament in Ephesians," *JSNT* 14 (1982) 49.

5. Ibid.

6. Ibid.

he argues, the OT is quoted because "the author is trying to show that Christian ethical teaching is compatible, and in no way inferior to, that of the Jewish Torah."[7]

The wide divergence between the conclusions arrived at in these three studies of the hermeneutics of Ephesians suggests that there is still work to be done on resolving the questions that are raised by the use of the OT within the letter. In this chapter I suggest an alternative approach to the question, focusing on the new exodus hermeneutical framework established in the first three chapters of the letter and reinforced in the exhortations of the final chapter, then showing how it helps to resolve the particular interpretive challenges posed by two puzzling instances of the use of the OT in the second half of the letter (the use of Ps 68:18 in Eph 4:8–10 and the use of Exod 20:12 in Eph 6:2–3).

Ephesians 1–3: Salvation History for Gentile Believers

The argument of Ephesians is built on the foundation of solemn salvation-historical recitals, cast in the form of doxology (Eph 1:3–14) and reminder (2:1–10, 11–22) and strikingly redolent of the salvation-history recitals of the OT scriptures. Lincoln's summation of the function of these salvation-histories is apt: "The writer is concerned to motivate his readers, and he knows that a deeper sense of their corporate Christian identity and a greater desire to please God in wise and holy living will flow out of the sort of remembering of God's activities on their behalf that is accompanied by thanksgiving."[8]

Exodus-Shaped Blessings (Eph 1:3–14)

The doxology (Eph 1:3–14) immediately follows the greeting contained in the opening verses and takes the form of a *berakah*—a liturgical form derived from the OT and from the prayers of Jewish synagogue worship, which ascribes blessing to God on the basis of his saving deeds.[9] The *berakah* is not an intrinsically or necessarily narrative form; the grounds on which God is blessed may simply be a catalogue of divine attributes or actions. More often than not, however, the content of a *berakah* is declarative

---

7. T. Moritz, "The Use of Israel's Scriptures in Ephesians," *TynBul* 46 (1995) 395.

8. Andrew T. Lincoln, *Ephesians*, WBC 42 (Dallas: Word, 1990) lxxxvi.

9. Cf. Ibid., 10–11, for a useful summary discussion of the *berakah* form.

rather than descriptive praise;[10] it is concerned with the proclamation of God's saving acts.

Here in Eph 1, the *berakah* is not merely a list or catalogue. The blessings for which God is praised are strung together in a loosely narrative sequence, commencing with the readers' election before the foundation of the world (1:4) and tracing its outworking through their adoption as sons of God (1:5), their redemption (1:7), their receipt of the revelation of God's will (1:9), and (in prospect) their eventual entrance into the inheritance which is theirs as the people of God (1:11–14).

The language used to describe these blessings and the sequence in which they are arranged are reminiscent of the exodus narrations of the OT. For example, the grounding of the salvation story in the readers' prior election in Christ echoes the way the exodus narrations within the early chapters of Deuteronomy are grounded in God's election of Israel, which is in turn based on his prior love for the patriarchs (e.g., Deut 4:37–38; 7:7–8). Similarly, the adoption language of Eph 1:5 echoes the strong connection within the OT between the exodus and the special position of Israel as the "son" of YHWH[11] (e.g., Exod 4:22–23; Hos 11:1); the language of "redemption" echoes the favorite word employed in Deuteronomy to describe the liberation of the Hebrew slaves from Egypt (e.g., Deut 7:8; 9:26; 13:5; 15:15; 21:8; 24:18; cf. Exod 6:6; 15:13); the assertion that "he has made known (γνωρίσας) to us the mystery of his will" echoes the sequence of the OT exodus narrations, in which the exodus event was immediately followed by the great act of revelation at Sinai, in which God made known (LXX: ἐγνώρισα) his law to Israel at Sinai (e.g., Ezek 20:11; Neh 9:14); finally, here in Ephesians as in the OT exodus narrations, the climax of the story is the "inheritance" into which the redeemed people are brought as the destination of their journey (Exod 15:17; Deut 32:9).[12]

In both form and content, then, the opening benediction (Eph 1:3–14) is replete with echoes of the OT exodus traditions. Not only is the exodus evoked through concepts such as election, adoption, redemption, revelation, and inheritance—all of which are part of the basic vocabulary used in

10. Cf. Claus Westermann, *The Praise of God in the Psalms*, trans. K. R. Crim (Richmond, VA: John Knox, 1965) 81–142.

11. Cf. James M. Scott's study of υἱοθεσία in the undisputed Pauline letters, in which he demonstrates convincingly that the most plausible background to the metaphor in Pauline usage is not the Hellenistic legal procedure but the OT exodus tradition. Scott, *Adoption as Sons of God*, WUNT (Tübingen: Mohr/Siebeck, 1992) 267.

12. Significantly, the language of inheritance (κληρονομία, κληρόω) can be used within the Eph 1 *berakah* (1:11, 14) and the OT exodus narratives (e.g., Exod 15:17; Deut 32:9) to describe both the promised land as the inheritance of Israel as well as the people of Israel as the inheritance of the LORD.

the OT for the narrating of the exodus story—it is also evoked through the way those concepts are placed in sequence and embedded in the form of a *berakah*, giving praise to God on the basis of his saving deeds.

The *berakah* of Eph 1:3–14 is foundational for the letter's soteriology and hermeneutics. Paul wants his readers to know that they have a salvation history of their own—analogous to and emerging from within the salvation history of Israel's scriptures—with the implication that they are to understand their salvation in Christ in the light of the Scriptures, and to understand the Scriptures in the light of their salvation in Christ. Specifically, it is the schema and vocabulary of the exodus story that he has appropriated typologically to eulogize the saving work of God accomplished in Christ. This typological appropriation of the exodus story is not a Pauline novelty, but is grounded in the typology of the OT itself. Within the books of the prophets in particular, the exodus story becomes a paradigm for the future salvation that is promised (e.g., Hos. 9:1–3; 11:10–11; Mic 7:15–17; Ezek 20:33–38; Isa 43:16–21; 51:9–11).[13]

If the shape and content of the *berakah* implies that, at one level, the readers' salvation in Christ is a typological echo of the exodus salvation of Israel, it also offers a number of hints that the readers should view their salvation as the fulfillment of the second exodus and new covenant promises of the prophets. Like the promised new covenant of the second exodus—but unlike the scriptural narrations of the original exodus[14]—the deliverance that they have experienced is described as being, at its heart, not merely a defeat of hostile powers but a "forgiveness of . . . trespasses."[15] Additional hints are added in Eph 1:13 with references to "the gospel of your salvation"[16] and "the promised Holy Spirit,"[17] both of which imply that the prophetic promises of the post-exilic restoration of Israel have somehow been proclaimed to and fulfilled among the Gentiles.

13. See esp. Michael Fishbane, "The 'Exodus' Motif: The Paradigm of Historical Renewal," in *Text and Texture: Close Readings of Selected Biblical Texts*, ed. Fishbane (New York: Schocken, 1979) 125–40.

14. While the bleak history of Ezek 20 includes reference in verses 7–9 to the Israelites' complicity in the idolatry of Egypt, there is no suggestion even there that the four hundred years in Egypt was a punishment imposed on Israel for the sins of the patriarchs.

15. Cf. Jer 31:34; 33:8; Ezek 16:63; Ps 130:4, 8.

16. Cf. Isa 52:7 (LXX).

17. Cf. Isa 32:15; 44:3; Ezek 36:26–27; 37:14; 39:29; Joel 2:28–29.

New Exodus Salvation (Eph 2:1-22)

The pattern of depicting the salvation experienced by the readers as a partici-pation in the fulfillment of the second exodus promises of the exilic prophets is even more marked in the second and third salvation-history recitals, Eph 2:1–10 and 2:11–22. While there are close connections between chapter 2 and the account of the triumph of Christ in 1:20–23[18] as well as affinities between 1:20—2:22 and OT Divine Warrior narratives such as the "Song of the Sea" in Exod 15 (suggesting a continuing exodus typology in the salvation-history narratives of chapter 2),[19] the strongest inter-textual echoes to be found in this chapter are not direct echoes of the exodus story itself; rather, they are second-hand echoes *via* the end-of-exile promises of the prophets.[20]

The narrative in Eph 2:1–10 is in essence a story of salvation through resurrection, a reminder to the readers of the letter that they were once dead through trespasses and sins, but have now been made alive together with Christ, becoming participants in the triumph of his resurrection. While the language of "Jews" and "Gentiles" is absent, the references 2:1–3 to "you" and "we" show that the discussion of 1:11–14 has not been forgotten,[21] and, they play an important role in preparing the way for the more explicit dis-cussion of the overcoming of the estrangement of the Gentiles from Israel and from God in 2:11–22.[22]

The salvation narrative in Eph 2:1–10 begins in 2:1–3 with a description of the plight from which the readers have been delivered.[23] The focus in

18. There are several close and important parallels between 2:1 and its immedi-ately preceding and following context: ἐγείρας αὐτὸν ἐκ νεκρῶν . . . Καὶ ὑμᾶς ὄντας νεκρούς . . . καὶ ὄντας ἡμᾶς νεκρούς (1:20; 2:1; 2:5). Καὶ ὑμᾶς (2:1) thus functions as a kind of hinge, holding together a double connection vital to the flow of the text: αὐτόν [Χριστόν] . . . καὶ ὑμᾶς; καὶ ὑμᾶς . . . καὶ ἡμᾶς.

19. Cf. Timothy G. Gombis, "Ephesians 2 as a Narrative of Divine Warfare," *JSNT* 26 (2004) 403–18.

20. Prophetic end-of-exile and post-exilic restoration texts are also alluded to else-where in the letter, in 4:25 (Zech 8:16), 4:30 (Isa 63:10), 5:2 (Ezek 20:41), 5:14 (Isa 26:19; 60:1–2) and the cluster of Isaianic references in 6:14–17 (discussed below). Cf. P. Qualls and J. D. W. Watts, "Isaiah in Ephesians," *RevExp* 93 (1996) 249–59; and Frank Thielman, "Ephesians," in *Commentary on the New Testament Use of the Old Testament*, eds. G. K. Beale and D. A. Carson (Nottingham: IVP, 2007) 813–33.

21. This reading of the "you" and "we" in verses 1–3 is followed by Barth (Barth, *Ephesians*, 216), though not by Lincoln (Lincoln, *Ephesians*, 97). If the we/you distinc-tion in verse 3 is a Jew/Gentile distinction, then it is presumably Gentiles who are the οἱ λοιποί at the end of the verse.

22. Cf. N. T. Wright, *Justification: God's Plan and Paul's Vision* (London: SPCK, 2009) 145.

23. Peter Tachau, *"Einst" und "Jetzt" im Neuen Testament* (Göttingen: Vandenhoeck

2:1–2 is on "you" (i.e., Gentiles) and their plight is depicted as one of death "through trespasses and sins" (2:1)—the trespasses and sins which were once the readers' characteristic lifestyle. The world (2:2) whose ways they followed is not merely "*the* world" but "*this* world"—more literally, "the age of this world" (τὸν αἰῶνα τοῦ κόσμου τούτου), defined in opposition to the age of the world to come and ruled by hostile powers opposed to God and his people (cf. 6:12).[24] "The sons of disobedience" is an obvious Hebraism, which occurs again in 5:6 as a description of unconverted Gentiles (describing the same people referred to as τὰ ἔθνη in 4:17), and it is reasonable to suppose that the expression has the same Gentile connotations here in 2:2.

Having painted the blackest possible picture of the pre-conversion life of the Gentiles, Paul goes on in Eph 2:3 to say the same things emphatically about himself and his fellow-Jews, both in their conduct and in their nature. The "among whom" language of 2:3 (ἐν οἷς καὶ ἡμεῖς πάντες ἀνεστράφημέν) carries an implied spatial metaphor, reminiscent of the situation of Israel in exile.

If that is the case, then there is good reason to hear in the verse an allusion to the description of the house of Israel in Ezek 36, living "among the nations" (LXX ἐν τοῖς ἔθνεσιν), under God's wrath and profaning his name by both their conduct and its punishment.[25] A further parallel with Ezek 36 can be found in the the language and imagery of death throughout that chapter (i.e., an unclean people, hearts of stone, a desolate land), spilling over into the vision of the valley of dry bones in the chapter that follows, and echoing the warnings of Deuteronomy about death as the punishment for disobedience to the law of God (cf. Deut 30:15–20; 32:22, 39).[26] While the restoration promised in Ezek 36–37 is not directly identified within those

---

& Ruprecht, 1972) 134–43 (cited in Lincoln, *Ephesians*, 86), suggests that 2:1–10 should be classified formally as the first part of a ποτέ . . . νῦν contrast that is completed only in 2:11–13. A more useful application of the ποτέ . . . νῦν schema, however, would be to treat each half of the chapter as a "once . . . now" contrast in its own right. Despite the absence of an explicit νῦν statement, the contrast between being "dead" and being "made alive" is clearly completed within 2:1–10.

24. Assuming that αἰών is to be read with temporal force, as it is in 1:21 and 2:7.

25. The language of Israel 'among the nations' is a byword throughout Scripture for the shame of exile, but it is language that is especially prevalent in Ezekiel, nowhere more so than in 36:19–23, where the phrase (LXX ἐν τοῖς ἔθνεσιν / εἰς τὰ ἔθνη) occurs six times in the space of five verses. Similarly, the language of "wrath" (LXX ὀργή and θυμός) is particularly prevalent within Ezekiel, typically in the context of descriptions of the exile as a judgment from God on the Israel's idolatry and bloodshed.

26. Cf. the similar observations in Ralph P. Martin, *Reconciliation: A Study of Paul's Theology* (Grand Rapids: Academie, 1999); Robert H. Suh, "The Use of Ezekiel 37 in Ephesians 2," *JETS* 50 (2007) 715–33.

chapters as a typological echo of the exodus, an explicit connection of this sort is made in the closely parallel passage of Ezek 20:33–44.[27]

The narrative in the second half of the chapter (Eph 2:11–22) opens with a command to "remember" (διὸ μνημονεύετε) that is reminiscent of the similar commands to Israel that punctuate the book of Deuteronomy (e.g., Deut 5:15; 15:15; 16:12; 24:18, 22).[28] If the movement in Eph 2:1–10 is one from death to life, the movement in 2:11–22 is one from separation to inclusion, narrating the salvation of the letter's Gentile readers as a recapitulation of Israel's return from exile, once more in language and imagery borrowed from the exilic prophets. The centerpiece of the section is 2:17, which provides the link between the language of "far off" and "near" foreshadowed in 2:13 (summarizing 2:11–13) and the language of "peace" foreshadowed in 2:14 (introducing 2:14–16).[29]

The principal theme of the section is soteriological. While it certainly speaks of the unity of Jews and Gentiles in the church, it does so within the frame of the overarching story of the salvation of the letter's Gentile Christian readers. The predicament which the opening verses describe is not so much the alienation of Jews from Gentiles as it is the alienation of Gentiles from God (and consequently from his people). The reconciliation of Jew and Gentile is obviously on Paul's mind as he writes, but the internal logic of his argument requires that to be understood as the corollary of the reconciliation of Gentiles to God.[30]

Thus, when Paul appeals to the OT scriptures in Eph 2:17, it is not an appeal to texts explicitly addressing the eschatological inclusion of Gentiles but rather to soteriological texts (Isa 52:7; 57:19) about the proclamation of peace and salvation to Israel in exile. That is, the "far off" in the original

27. See further in Rebecca G. S. Idestrom, "Echoes of the Book of Exodus in Ezekiel," *JSOT* 33 (2009) 489–510.

28. Cf. Peter T. O'Brien, *The Letter to the Ephesians*, PNTC (Grand Rapids: Eerdmans, 1999) 185.

29. Gombis's account of the chapter's structure—Lordship (1:20–23), conflict-victory (2:1–16), victory shout (2:17), celebration (2:18), and house-building (2:20–22)—takes inadequate account of the structural markers in the syntax and vocabulary of Eph 2 that indicate a break between verses 10 and 11 and bind verses 11–22 together as a unit. See Gombis, "Ephesians 2 as a Narrative of Divine Warfare," 408.

30. The reverse emphasis can be found in R. Schnackenburg, *Ephesians: A Commentary*, trans. H. Heron (Edinburgh: T. & T. Clark, 1991) 102, who summarizes the theme of the whole section from 2:11—3:21 as "an ecclesiology developed from Christology," which is "the whole substance of the author's theology." He is left to speculate on the circumstances unknown to us which had created problems to do with the relationship between Gentile- and Jewish-Christians within the Ephesian church, necessitating the reminders in 2:11–22 (see p. 119).

context of Isa 57, for example, is unmistakably a reference to exiled Israelites, not to Gentiles.

In context (i.e., Isa 57), Isa 57:19 conceives of "peace" in new exodus categories (reminiscent of the ideas and imagery of Ezek 36–37) alluded to in the first half of Eph 2. The paragraph commences with an echo of the opening verses of Isa 40: "Build up, build up, prepare the road! Remove the obstacles out of the way of my people" (Isa 57:14). What follows is a promise that God, whose name is holy,[31] will "revive"[32] the spirit of the contrite and the lowly, creating praise on their lips as he brings them home to once more "inherit the land" and "possess [his] holy mountain" (Isa 57:13).[33]

At every point of significance within Eph 2:11–22, the new exodus story is narrated in Christological terms. So the excluded Gentiles described in 2:11–12 are described as being separate "from Christ"; it is "in Christ" (2:13) that they have been brought near; the dwelling-place for God's presence into which they are now being built (2:19–22) is a building that has "Christ Jesus himself" as the chief cornerstone; and, most significantly of all, the excursus in 2:14–18 is focused on the fact that "he himself is our peace."

The final paragraph of this section (Eph 2:19–22) picks up the thread of the ποτέ . . . νῦν contrast introduced in 2:11–13 and reiterates it, with slight variation in language (οὐκέτι ἐστὲ . . . ἀλλὰ ἐστέ) and with stress not on the "once . . ." but on the "now . . ." half of the contrast. The climactic statement in 2:21–22 tells how the situation of the Gentile readers has been so thoroughly transformed from their former alienation that they are now being built into a holy temple, which is to be a "dwelling place" (κατοικητήριον) for God. The sanctuary imagery of these verses is another echo of the exodus and new exodus narratives of the Old Testament, in which the story of Israel's salvation culminates in them being brought (back) into the sanctuary of the promised land (e.g., Exod 15:17; Ezek 37:26–27; Zech 2:10–12).[34]

Both in the structure and movement of its narrative form, as well as the Scriptural allusions and quotations which it makes, the account of the readers' salvation in Eph 2:11–22 is thus strongly suggestive of the idea that the readers should understand their salvation in Christ as a participation in the fulfillment of OT second exodus promises originally given to exiled Israel.

---

31. Cf. Ezek 36:21–23.

32. Cf. Ezek 37:1–14.

33. Cf. Ezek 37:14; Exod 15:17.

34. The oracle in Zech 2:6–12 is clearly framed in new exodus categories: verse 7 speaks of an escape (LXX ἐκπορεύομαι) from Babylon, Israel is described in verse 8 as the "apple of the Lord's eye," echoing the language of the exodus-hymn in Deut 32, and verse 9 paints a picture of the liberated slaves plundering their former overlords.

The text explicitly acknowledges that these promises were not originally given to them in Eph 2:12, where Paul describes his readers as having once been "aliens from the commonwealth of Israel, and strangers to the covenants of promise." The story of how this alienation was overcome is brought into sharper focus in 2:14–18 as Paul elaborates on the "peace" which has been preached to the readers in Christ. Here the abolition of the "dividing wall of hostility" between Jew and Gentile (including the abolition of the Gentiles' estrangement from the covenants of promise) has taken place in the death of Jesus, which has "abolished the law of commandments in ordinances" (2:15).[35] For Paul, the death of Christ is thus not only a soteriological event (reconciling Jew and Gentile to God) and an ecclesiological event (reconciling Jew and Gentile to one another within the "new humanity" of the church) but also a hermeneutical event, transforming the relationship of his readers to the scriptural promise, law, and covenants.[36]

Ephesians 6: The New Exodus and the Armor of the Divine Warrior

The final chapter reinforces the new exodus hermeneutic established in the salvation-history narratives of Eph 1–2. In Eph 6:10–17, Paul exhorts his readers to "be strong in the Lord and in the strength of his power." While the accent of the salvation histories in chapters 1–2 is on the deliverance already accomplished by Christ on behalf of his people, the exhortation in the final chapter addresses the readers as still an embattled people, engaged in a continuing conflict against the same powers over which Christ triumphed in his resurrection (1:20–23).

The description of the armor which they are urged to put on for this conflict (as most commentators observe) is laced with intertextual references to the language and imagery of Isaiah. The "belt of truth [fastened] around your waist" (Eph 6:14) echoes the language of Isa 11:5 ("righteousness shall be the belt around his waist, and faithfulness [LXX ἀλήθεια] the belt around his loins"); the "breastplate of righteousness" (Eph 6:14) and the "helmet of salvation" (6:17) echo the language of Isa 59:17 ("He put on righteousness like a breastplate and a helmet of salvation on his head"); and the exhortation of Eph 6:15, "as shoes for your feet put on whatever will make you ready to proclaim the gospel of peace," echoes the language and

---

35. Author's translation.

36. For a discussion of the hermeneutic *via* which Paul encourages his readers to see themselves as Gentiles implicated in the promises originally given to exiled Israel, see Starling, *Not My People*, 167–94.

imagery of Isa 52:7 ("How beautiful upon the mountains are the feet of the messenger who announces peace, who brings good news").

The armor spoken of in Eph 6:14–17 (and in most of the Isaianic texts standing behind that passage) is thus the armor of God (Isa 59:17) and of the Messiah (Isa 11:5) before it is the armor of his people. In doing battle against the powers that oppose them, the readers should see themselves as participating in the conflict and triumph of God himself, the Divine Warrior of Isa 59 who intervenes to save and whose arm brings him victory—an image that is itself an echo of the language and imagery of Exod 15.[37]

Testing the Hypothesis: Two Case Studies in Ephesians 4–6

Having traced the outlines of the new exodus hermeneutic which (I have argued) is established in Eph 1–2 and reinforced in 6:10–17, my intention in the remainder of the chapter is to demonstrate the way in which this hermeneutical framework assists in the interpretation of two much-debated instances of Paul's use of the OT in 4:8–10 and 6:2–3.

Psalm 68:18 in Ephesians 4:8–10

The way in which Ps 68:18 is quoted and appropriated in Eph 4:7–10 is something of an interpretative *crux*, and discussion has centered on two issues in particular.

1. Why does Eph 4:8 read "gave when Ps 68:18 (at least in the textual traditions behind the LXX and MT) reads "received"?

2. When Paul draws the conclusion that the "ascent" spoken of in the psalm implies that the one who ascended "also descended into the lower parts of the earth," what is the "descent" to which he is referring?

"Received" and "gave"

In relation to the first question, a number of theories have been proposed:

1a. Paul simply misquotes the psalm to make the text fit his point.[38]

This common theory is difficult to reconcile with the equally common idea

---

37. See esp. Timothy G. Gombis, *The Drama of Ephesians: Participating in the Triumph of God* (Downers Grove, IL: IVP, 2010)155–80.

38. E.g., Joseph A. Fitzmyer, "The Use of Explicit Old Testament Quotations in Qumran Literature and the New Testament," *NTS* 7 (1961) 297–333, esp. 325; Frank

that Paul's use of the Old Testament follows the *gezera shava* principle, given that the key word "gave" is the very word that Paul has to insert into the verse to make it serve his purpose. If this theory is followed, then, it requires another explanation for why Ps 68 is quoted at all and why he felt at liberty to make the change to its wording.

1b. Paul is working from a variant form of the OT textual tradition that reads "gave" rather than "received."[39]

1c. Paul understands that in a number of OT contexts, "receive" implies an intention to "give," particularly in the context of booty seized in battle and divided among the troops.[40]

1d. In the original context of the psalm, the "captives" are not Gentile enemies but Israelites; and, the "taking captive" and "receiving" in the psalm is a reference to Num 8 and 18 in which the Levites are taken by the LORD as his own possession, and then given back to Israel as servants and ministers.[41] It is hard to reconcile this theory with the fact that the "gifts" and "spoil" and "tribute" elsewhere in the psalm (Ps 68:12, 29, 30, 31) are clearly material and not human, and few if any unambiguous clues in the psalm to the idea that the Levites are any more in view than the whole gathered congregation of Israel.

"He also descended"

Three main theories have been proposed in answer to the second question, regarding the nature of the "descent" of which Eph 4:9 speaks:

2a. The "descent" is a descent of Christ into Hades or into the grave. This interpretation was common among the Church fathers, and one can still find a number of advocates for it among recent commentators.[42] According to this theory, τὰ κατώτερα μέρη τῆς γῆς is read as "the lower parts

---

Thielman, *Ephesians*, BECNT (Grand Rapids: Baker, 2010) 267–68.

39. Cf. R. A. Taylor, "The Use of Psalm 68:18 in Ephesians 4:18 in the Light of Ancient Versions," *BSac* 148 (1991) 319–36. There is evidence in the Peshitta and Targum of such a manuscript tradition having existed. Thus, e.g., the Targum on verse 18 reads: "You have ascended to heaven, that is, Moses the prophet; you have taken captivity captive, you have learnt the words of the Torah; you have given it as gifts to men."

40. This is perhaps the reasoning behind Chrysostom's frequently-quoted but somewhat cryptic comment, cited in O'Brien, *Ephesians*, 291: "The one [word] is the same as the other."

41. This is the argument of G. V. Smith, "Paul's Use of Psalm 68:18 in Ephesians 4:8," *JETS* 18 (1975) 181–89.

42. E.g., Clinton E. Arnold, *Power and Magic: The Concept of Power in Ephesians*, 2nd ed. (Grand Rapids: Baker, 1997); Thielman, *Ephesians*, 271.

of the earth" (cf. NRSV). This theory stumbles at a number of points, including the awkwardness of the comparative τὰ κατώτερα as a reference to the "lowest" regions of a three-story universe,[43] the fact that a two-step descent to Hades *via* earth is poorly balanced by the one-step ascent mentioned (4:8, 10), and the fact that the cosmology of the letter elsewhere speaks of "all things" as being made up of "heaven and earth" (not "heaven, earth and things under the earth") and describes the current abode of the rebellious principalities and powers as "the heavenly places."[44]

2b. The descent of Christ was his in his incarnation (and death). According to this theory, τὰ κατώτερα μέρη τῆς γῆς should best be read as "the lower, earthly regions" (cf. NIV), treating τῆς γῆς as a genitive of apposition.[45]

2c. The descent was the descent at Pentecost of the exalted Christ in the Spirit.[46] This reading relies on the rejection of the poorly attested textual variant that inserts πρῶτον after κατέβη, and requires that the descent take place after the ascent and not before. In support of this theory it is often pointed out that rabbinic tradition, as reflected in the Targum and elsewhere, associated the "ascent" of Ps 68:18 with Moses' ascent of Sinai and identified the thing that is "received" or "given"—depending on which text is followed—as the Torah. This rabbinic interpretation of the psalm correlated with the liturgical use of Ps 68 in the synagogue as a Pentecost psalm, and (it is argued) lies behind the reference to the ascended Christ "receiving" and "pouring out" the Spirit in Acts 2:33.[47]

One significant weakness of this interpretation is the way in which it struggles to explain the logic of Paul's rhetorical question in Eph 4:9. An ascent of God may well imply a *previous* descent, but why does an ascent imply a *subsequent* descent? If the subsequent descent is necessitated by anything, it is necessitated by the *giving* (if one assumes that God needs to come down to earth in order to give) and not the *descending*.

---

43. References in the LXX to subterranean depths (e.g., LXX Pss 62:10; 138:15) use the superlative κατώτατα rather than the comparative κατώτερα.

44. Cf. O'Brien, *Ephesians*, 294–95; Markus Barth, *Ephesians 4–6*, AB 34A (Garden City, NY: Doubleday, 1974) 433–34.

45 E.g., Barth, *Ephesians 4–6*, 432–34.

46 E.g., G. B. Caird, "The Descent of the Spirit in Ephesians 4:7–11," in *Studia Evangelica*, ed. F. L. Cross (Berline: Academie, 1964) 535–45; W. H. Harris, *The Descent of Christ: Ephesians 4:7–11 and Traditional Hebrew Imagery* (Leiden: Brill, 1996) 192–97; Lincoln, *Ephesians*, 244–48.

47. Cf. John R. W. Stott, *God's New Society: The Message of Ephesians* (Downers Grove, IL: IVP, 1979) 157–58, and Lincoln, *Ephesians*, 241–42.

An alternative approach

An alternative approach is to examine the possibility that Paul reads Ps 68 in the light of the sort of hermeneutic suggested above, in which the story of Christ is understood as a typological echo of the original exodus and a fulfillment of the OT hopes and promises of a new exodus.[48] Such an approach begins by reading Ps 68:18 in the original context of the psalm, and noting the rich background of exodus and new exodus imagery surrounding it.

Psalm 68 begins with a call to God to come and rescue his people (68:1–3). It goes on to address praises to God for his past acts of deliverance and provision, with clear allusion to the story of the exodus, the wilderness wanderings, and the conquest of the land (68:4–10). Before the triumphant progress of the LORD, the kings of the nations are scattered (68:11–14); and, having triumphed over his enemies, the LORD marches from Sinai to Zion to ascend the holy mountain that he has chosen for his dwelling (68:15–18). There (68:18) he receives gifts from (or among) people, and takes up his dwelling place.

The remainder of the psalm evokes the continuing significance of the story for the worshipping community of Israel. The God whose triumph is narrated in the exodus story and who now dwells among his people is "the God of salvation" (68:19–20) who has promised the overthrow of his enemies (68:21–23); the processing tribes of Israel re-enact his triumphs and declare his praises (68:24–27), appealing to him to do once more what he did in the exodus (68:28), so that the kings of the nations will be scattered and defeated (68:30) and come to his temple in Jerusalem bearing gifts and singing praises (68:29, 31–35).

The message of the psalm is clear: the hope of Israel is grounded in the exodus story, and the ultimate destination of the exodus is Zion—a glorious Zion in which the LORD rules over the nations who joyfully come to bring their gifts and submit themselves to him.

The key verse for our purposes, Ps 68:18, is translated somewhat unhelpfully in the NRSV: "You ascended the high mount, leading captives in your train and receiving gifts from people, even from those who rebel against the LORD God's abiding there." At least two points the NRSV translation is open to question.

In the first place, the translation "*from* people" (HB בָּאָדָם; LXX variously ἐν ἀνθρώπῳ or ἐν ἀνθρώποις) is overly interpretive. While the verb "received" might suggest "from" as one possible meaning for בְּ, it is certainly a most unusual way of translating the preposition, and it is hard to

---

48. Cf. the similar proposal argued for in Timothy G. Gombis, "Cosmic Lordship and Divine Gift-Giving: Psalm 68 in Ephesians 4:8," *NovT* 47 (2005) 367–80.

explain why the author of the psalm would have chosen this way of expressing himself in preference to the less ambiguous מֵן־. If בָּאָדָם is translated less interpretively as "among people," the option is left open that the "people" surrounding the LORD in the context of the gift-giving are not the givers of the gifts but the surrounding retinue of the LORD's people who are indirectly enriched by the tribute given to the LORD.

In the second place, the way the NRSV translation concludes the verse—"even from those who rebel *against the LORD God's abiding there*"— is equally strained, and gives a somewhat implausible account of the way the infinitive construct לִשְׁכֹּן (to dwell; LXX τοῦ κατασκηνῶσαι) fits into the syntax of the verse. A more likely translation is one that reads לִשְׁכֹּן not as the thing opposed by the rebellious but as the purpose for which the LORD took the riches that were given to him as tribute—the LORD receives the treasures of the nations (as booty and as tribute) in order that he might have a glorious dwelling in the midst of his people Israel.

The verse thus translated would emerge as something like the rendition of Ps 68:18b in the RV: "Thou hast received gifts among men, Yea [among] the rebellious also, that the LORD God might dwell [with them]."[49] Thus, against the backdrop of the psalm, we might read 68:18 as a picture (enacted, perhaps, in cultic procession) of the LORD ascending in triumph from his exodus victory to his dwelling on Mt. Zion, a dwelling in the midst of his people that is gloriously enriched with the treasures of the nations.

The enriching of God's people and his dwelling with the treasures of the nations is one of the recurring motifs of OT exodus and new exodus traditions. Thus, in Exod 12, the people of Israel depart from Egypt in such triumph that they are showered with gifts by the Egyptians, a circumstance foretold in Gen 15 and recalled in Ps 105:37, 44. Also, when the prophets of the new exodus speak about its gloriousness, one of the recurring images is that the LORD's triumph over the nations will be expressed in the enrichment of his people and his house with all the treasures of the nations (e.g., Isa 18; 45; 60–61; Hag 2).

Here in Ps 68, that appears to be the motif in view in the final verses of the psalm, which describe the triumph of Israel's God over the nations as resulting in gifts being brought "because of your temple at Jerusalem" (Ps 68:29), even from Egypt and Ethiopia (68:31; cf. Isa 18; 45), and conclude with an invitation to the kingdoms of the earth to sing praises to the Lord, who is "awesome in his sanctuary," giving power and strength to his people (Ps 68:35).

---

49. According to this translation, the "rebellious" are presumably rebellious nations (cf. the use of הַסּוֹרְרִים in Ps 66:7); the gifts are received in the presence of both the "men" [of Israel] and the "rebellious" [defeated enemies].

If that is at least a plausible reading of Ps 68:18 in its original context, it is not difficult to see how Paul (whether or not he is aware of the textual tradition reflected in the Peshitta and the Targum) feels justified in paraphrasing "received gifts among people" as "gave gifts to people," given that the "people" among whom the gifts are received are not the ones giving the gifts but the ones who are indirectly enriched by them.

The exodus and new exodus imagery of the psalm also sheds some light on the interpretation of "he also descended" in Eph 4:9.[50] On the one hand, there is an obvious exodus background for the interpretation that sees the descent as being a descent at Pentecost, viewed as a typological fulfillment of Moses' descent from Mt. Sinai. This reading fits comfortably with at least one (apparently quite common and relatively early) strand of Rabbinic interpretation of the psalm and with the liturgical use of the psalm in association with the festival of Pentecost, but it struggles to give any sort of coherent account of the psalm's original sense, in which the LORD comes *from* Sinai *to* the holy place (Ps 68:17), which suggests that the "high mount" in 68:18 is not Sinai but Zion. It also struggles (as I have argued above) to account for the logic of Eph 4:9–10 in which the descent is seen as a necessary implication of the subsequent or previous ascent.

If we follow the more plausible reading of Paul's logic in Eph 4:9–10 and take the descent as being a reference to Christ's descent in the incarnation, this fits quite comfortably with the psalm's exodus imagery. According to this reading, the previous "descent" implied by the LORD's victorious ascent of Mt. Zion is his descent as the warrior-redeemer in the events of the exodus (cf. the "coming down" of the LORD in Exod 3:8; Isa 64:1–3), suggested (if not explicitly described) in Ps 68:7–8.

What emerges, then, when Eph 4:7–10 is read in the light of a hermeneutic in which the story of Christ is understood a typological echo of the exodus story and a fulfillment of new exodus prophecies and hopes is a coherent account of how Paul appropriated and understood Ps 68:18.

In the psalm, God's past triumph over the nations in the exodus led to his establishment of a glorious dwelling place in the midst of his people, enriched with the treasures of the nations (extracted as booty or willingly given as tribute). In the context of (cultic?) remembrance of that tradition, a prayer is uttered for a similar future deliverance, so that the nations may be scattered and defeated and, once more, the dwelling of God may be enriched with their treasures.

For Paul, this prayer has been answered in the new exodus salvation accomplished in Christ. In the incarnation, Christ has descended in power

---

50. Author's translation.

for the deliverance of his people; in his resurrection and ascension he has triumphed over the nations (and over the principalities and powers that stand behind their hostility). Now, in the body of Christ, the fruits of that victory are being poured out, as grace is showered upon the people of God (Eph 4:7) and as the body of Christ is being enriched and built up (4:11–13). Further, if the body of Christ, the church into which the gentile believers of Ephesus are being built, is now the "temple" in which God dwells by his Spirit (2:21), and the "fullness" by which his eventual filling of the universe is anticipated (1:23), then it is not drawing too long a bow to suggest that Paul views the church as the sphere in which we see the eschatological vision of Ps 68:28–35 beginning to be fulfilled, as the treasures of the nations and the spoils of Christ's victory enrich the place of his dwelling, and some even from among the nations gather to sing his praises.

Exodus 20:12 in Ephesians 6:2–3

Paul's use of Exod 20:12 in Eph 6:2–3 raises hermeneutical questions no less difficult than the questions raised by his use of Ps 68 in Eph 4:8–10. The command to children in Eph 6:1 that they obey their parents is followed immediately (and without any connective or introductory formula) by a citation in 6:2–3 of the fifth commandment of the Decalogue and the promise that accompanies it.

Two main hermeneutical questions arise. The first question (arising out of the commandment) is about whether and in what sense Paul viewed the OT law as addressed to and authoritative for his Gentile Christian readers. The second question (arising out of the promise) is about how Paul understood that a promise of long life and blessing in the promised land might be fulfilled for those same readers.

The first question becomes particularly acute when Eph 6:2 is placed alongside Eph 2:15, in which Paul has already asserted that the unification of Jew and Gentile in Christ has taken place by means of the fact that Christ in his death has "abolished the law with its commandments and ordinances."

Numerous attempts have been made to qualify the starkness of that assertion (e.g., the suggestions that it is the ceremonial and not the moral law that is abolished,[51] that the law in its divisiveness and not in its commanding force is what is abolished,[52] or that the thing done away with by

---

51. E.g., Walter C. Kaiser, "Response to Douglas Moo," in *Five Views on Law and Gospel*, ed. Wayne G. Strickland (Grand Rapids: Zondervan, 1996) 397.

52. E.g., Barth, *Ephesians 1–3*, 287–91.

Christ's death is not law but "legalism").[53] It is still fair to say, however, that the most natural reading of Eph 2:15 is that the only qualification intended by Paul is the one that he himself implies—that it is the law "of commandments in ordinances" (τῶν ἐντολῶν ἐν δόγμασιν) that is abolished. In other words, the Law of Moses is no longer a directly commanding authority over the believer in Jesus (and hence its dividing walls between Jew and Gentile are broken down).

If that is the most natural reading of Eph 2:15, then the tension between 2:15 and 6:2–3 remains as long as 6:2–3 is read as a commandment and promise directly addressed to the Gentile Christian readers of the letter. The fact that most commentators assume this reading of 6:2–3 is one of the reasons why they feel compelled to hedge the bold statement of 2:15 with additional qualifications, so that the Law of Moses can still remain authoritative enough to command children in 6:2 to honour to their parents. As I shall argue below, however, this is not the only or even the most natural reading of the function of 6:2–3 in the flow of the letter.

The second hermeneutical problem 6:2–3 raises is the question of how a promise of long life and blessing in the promised land addressed to Israel at Sinai was understood by Paul to apply to Gentile Christians in Ephesus. The assumption adopted by most commentators is that Paul intends his readers to hear themselves directly addressed in the words of the promise in 6:3. For this reason (it is argued) he abbreviates the quotation from Exod 20 so that the final phrase ἐπὶ τῆς γῆς τῆς ἀγαθῆς ἧς κύριος ὁ θεός σου δίδωσίν σοι becomes simply ἐπὶ τῆς γῆς, which the readers of Ephesians would have understood as meaning "on the earth." Almost without exception,[54] this assumption underlies English translations of the verse, too, in their rendition of ἐπὶ τῆς γῆς.

This interpretation creates more problems than it solves, however, and leaves commentators clutching at straws to explain what Paul means when he promises his readers long life and earthly blessing in return for obedience to their parents. O'Brien retreats to the argument that the promise is a "general principle" which "holds true for obedient Christian children."[55] Lincoln suggests that the writer (whom he does not believe to be Paul) has simply failed to "[integrate] its Jewish this-wordly perspective consistently with his interpretation of inheritance in the first half of the letter." Mitton proposes that the promise should best be interpreted communally to

53. E.g., Heinrich Schlier, *Der Brief an die Epheser: Ein Kommentar* (Düsseldorf: Patmos, 1957) 125–26.

54. One notable recent exception is the ESV, which renders ἐπὶ τῆς γῆς as "in the land."

55. O'Brien, *Ephesians*, 444. Similarly, Thielman, *Ephesians*, 400–401.

mean that "a society in which the aged are respected and cared for by their children is a healthy and stable one."[56] Needless to say, such motivations and promises (whether as cast-iron guarantees or as vague generalizations) are entirely absent from the remainder of the letter; and, the way in which the OT promises about life in the land of Canaan are translated into this-worldly blessings for obedient Christians sits uncomfortably with the way in which OT categories and types are appropriated in the first half of the letter (as Lincoln acknowledges).

An alternative approach

Within the flow of the letter, the command to children in Eph 6:1 is located not only within the immediate context of the household table (5:22—6:9), but also within the wider context of the ethic for which Paul lays the foundation for in 4:17—5:21. Within 6:1-9 in particular, this latter connection is particularly prominent. Thus, Snodgrass points out the connections between 6:1 and 5:3, 4, 9; between 6:4a and 4:26-27, 31; between 6:4b and 4:20-21; between 6:8 and 4:28-29; and between 6:8-9 and 5:5-6.[57]

If that is the case, then, it makes sense that we read the commands in Eph 6:1-9 as belonging in an ethical framework that is explicitly and emphatically eschatological. The ethic of 4:17—15:21 is about a way of life motivated and shaped by the fact that the readers have experienced a decisive transfer from the "darkness" of life under the powers of the present age into the "light" of life in Christ (e.g., 4:21-23; 5:7, 14). What is "right" (6:1, δίκαιον) is to be understood in these terms as "the fruit of the light" (5:9), and the "darkness" and "light" themselves are to be understood as defined eschatologically by the coming judgement and salvation of God—the works of darkness are those things upon which the wrath of God comes (5:6), and the things that are "proper" among the saints are the things that correspond with "an inheritance in the kingdom of Christ and of God" (5:5, cf. 4:30). This is the background that is being evoked in the explicitly eschatological motivations attached to the commands that are given to masters in 6:8-9.

When the command to children is read against that backdrop, it seems almost inconceivable that Paul would have reverted in Eph 6:3 to an ethic motivated by promises of this-worldly long life and blessing and forgotten the "inheritance" typology established in 1:13-14 and evoked as recently

---

56. Mitton, *Ephesians*, 213, paraphrased in Lincoln, *Ephesians*, 405. Mitton himself acknowledges that his suggested reading is a modern re-interpretation and is unlikely to have been the sense intended by the original writer.

57. Klyne Snodgrass, *Ephesians*, NIVAC (Grand Rapids: Zondervan, 1996) 320.

in the letter as 4:30 and 5:5. If that typological framework is still securely in place here in Eph 6, then there is no need for the promise about "life in the land" to be turned into a promise about "life on the earth"; "the land" is still "the land," but the readers are expected to know that the promise being quoted is a word addressed to Israel at Mt. Sinai and that the corresponding promise for them—as the new exodus community—is a promise about life in the eschatological kingdom in which they have obtained an inheritance through Christ.

If that is the approach that Paul would have expected his readers to take in appropriating the promise in Eph 6:3, it is reasonable to assume that he expects a similar hermeneutical sophistication in the approach that they should take to the command in 6:2: like the promise, it is a word addressed to Israel at Sinai, a speech-event within the story of the original exodus, and not a word directly addressed to his Gentile Christian readers.

Once again, it would seem the new exodus hermeneutic which Paul establishes in the soteriological narratives of Eph 1–2 provides the most convincing framework for understanding the way in which he appropriates the Exod 20:12 command and promise in these verses. The problems raised by the interpretation of Eph 6:1–3 that is assumed by most commentators (the tension between the direct application of the Law of Moses to Gentile Christians and the word about its abrogation in 2:15, and the difficulties in explaining the promise of long life and prosperity on the earth as a motivation for obedience) dissolve when the promise and command are read as words addressed to Israel, and applicable to Gentile Christians only second-hand, *via* the typological transformations between the exodus and new exodus communities.

Summary

Across the six chapters of Ephesians, therefore, there is evidence that Paul encourages his readers to understand the story of Christ as a typological echo of the original exodus and a fulfillment of the OT hopes and promises of a new exodus. This new exodus hermeneutical framework is established in the *berakah* of 1:3–14 and the salvation-history narratives of 2:1–10 and 2:11–22 and reinforced in the exhortations of 6:10–17 as the letter draws to a close. In between, it helps to explain some of the more puzzling instances of Paul's use of the OT within Ephesians, including his use of Ps 68:18 in Eph 4:8–10 and his use of Exod 20:12 in Eph 6:2–3.

One important function of this new exodus typology is to contribute to Paul's identity-forming purposes within the letter,[58] reinforcing his readers' confidence in the power of God and his saving love for them (cf. Eph 1:15–23; 3:14–19) so that they understand themselves as his redeemed people and play their part in the continuing demonstration of the victory of God in Christ over every hostile power (cf. 1:23; 3:10; 3:21; 4:1; 5:1–2; 6:10–20).

---

58. Cf. Lincoln, *Ephesians,* lxxviii, lxxxvi; Arnold, *Ephesians,* 45; Ben Witherington III, *The Letters to Philemon, the Colossians, and the Ephesians: A Socio-Rhetorical Commentary on the Captivity Epistles* (Grand Rapids: Eerdmans, 2007) 223.

περὶ τῆς ἐξόδου . . . ἐμνημόνευσεν,
"He Spoke about the Exodus"

Echoes of Exodus in Hebrews

RADU GHEORGHITA

Introduction

THE IMPORTANCE OF THE book of Exodus for the Author to the Hebrews (henceforth, the Author) and its contribution to the argument of the epistle can easily be underestimated. With only three explicit citations,[1] the second

---

1. There is no consensus on the tally of Scriptural quotations in Hebrews, nor on the quotations from Exodus. Possible candidates are Exod 25:40 in Heb 8:5, Exod 24:8 in Heb 9:20, and Exod 19:12–13 in Heb 12:20. The UBS4 lists all three passages as quotations, but the NA27 only the first two. Monographs follow a similar pattern: Schröger and Ellingworth consider all three, whereas Guthrie and Steyn do only the first two—see Friedrich Schröger, *Der Verfasser des Hebräerbriefes als Schriftausleger* (Regensburg: Pustet, 1968); Paul Ellingworth, "The Old Testament in Hebrews: Exegesis, Method and Hermeneutics," PhD diss., University of Aberdeen, 1978; George H. Guthrie, "Hebrews," in *Commentary on the New Testament Use of the Old Testament*, eds. G. K. Beale and D. A. Carson (Grand Rapids: Baker Academic, 2007) 919–95; Gert J. Steyn, *A Quest for the Assumed LXX Vorlage of the Explicit Quotations in Hebrews* (Göttingen: Vandenhoeck & Ruprecht, 2011). Commentators are also divided: Ellingworth and Cokerill count all three, but Attridge, Koester, O'Brien, and possibly Lane, just two—Harold W. Attridge, *Hebrews*, Hermeneia (Philadelphia: Fortress, 1989); Gareth Lee Cockerill, *The Epistle to the Hebrews*, NICNT (Grand Rapids: Eerdmans, 2012); Paul Ellingworth, *The Epistle to the Hebrews: A Commentary on the Greek Text*, NIGTC (Grand Rapids: Eerdmans, 1993); Craig R. Koester, *To the Hebrews*, AB 36 (Garden City, NY: Doubleday, 2001); William L. Lane, *Hebrews 1–8*, WBC 47A (Dallas: Word, 1991); Lane, *Hebrews 9–13*,

book of the Pentateuch is barely visible at the level of Scriptural quotations, a far less substantial representation than other books (i.e., the Psalter). Even among the epistle's allusions, the readers of Hebrews could hardly find, *prima facie*, an impressive footprint of the book of Exodus. Yet, as this chapter seeks to prove, a careful reading of Hebrews evinces that no book of the Jewish Scriptures surpasses Exodus's presence in its fabric. To relegate Exodus to a secondary tier of the Author's theological interests would be shortsighted and lead to an incorrect assessment of the Scriptures' influence on the Author and his epistle.

Investigations of the NT use of the OT[2] often focus on the subdivisions within the discipline, such as the analysis of direct and indirect OT quotations, the detection of explicit or implicit allusions, verbal and lexical parallels, and theological concepts.[3] Yet, the standard methodology is not entirely helpful as far as the use of Exodus in Hebrews is concerned. Unlike other scriptural material, an analysis of Hebrews's use of quotations from Exodus distinct from the use of allusions presupposes an approach that has no warrant in the Author's practice of Scripture usage. The Author's exploration of Exodus material does not depend on the type of Scripture import, whether quotation or allusion.[4] This study proposes an alternate approach in order

---

WBC 47B (Dallas: Word, 1991); Peter T. O'Brien, *The Letter to the Hebrews*, PNTC (Grand Rapids: Eerdmans, 2010).

2. The terminology used here follows the traditional conventions, even though the alternative "the Jewish Scriptures" would have been a more appropriate option.

3. The literature on this subject is voluminous, not only in the general use of the OT in the NT, but specifically on the use of OT in Hebrews. The latest volume by Steyn (*Quest*) is an outstanding *tour de force*, setting the standard for future studies. Just as useful is Guthrie, "Hebrews." While there has been a continuous stream of general dissertations, *inter alia*, Kenneth J. Thomas, "The Use of the Septuagint in the Epistle to the Hebrews," PhD diss., University of Manchester, 1959; Schröger, *Verfasser*; J. C. McCullough, "Hebrews and the Old Testament," PhD diss., Queen's University, 1971; Ellingworth, *Old Testament*; Dale F. Leschert, *Hermeneutical Foundations of Hebrews* (Lewiston, NY: Mellen, 1994); Herbert W. Bateman, *Early Jewish Hermeneutics and Hebrews 1:5–13*, AUS 7/193 (New York: Lang, 1997); Radu Gheorghita, *The Role of the Septuagint in Hebrews*, WUNT 2/160 (Tübingen: Mohr/Siebeck, 2003); Susan E. Docherty, *The Use of the Old Testament in Hebrews*, WUNT 2/260 (Tübingen: Mohr/Siebeck, 2009). A monograph devoted exclusively to Exodus was published only recently, King L. She, *The Use of Exodus in Hebrews*, StBL 142 (New York: Lang, 2011).

4. The best way to substantiate this assertion is to compare the Author's use of Exodus material both in a quotation and an allusion. Hebrews 8:5 quotes from Exod 25:40. Even though it is the lengthiest quotation from Exodus, the text is marked by terseness as it comprises merely eleven words, ὅρα . . . ποιήσεις πάντα κατὰ τὸν τύπον τὸν δειχθέντα σοι ἐν τῷ ὄρει, "See . . . that you make everything according to the pattern that was shown you on the mountain" (ESV). Short as it is, however, the quotation provides the scriptural foundation for many of the Author's crucial points in the central section of the epistle. It launches the complex contrast between the earthly and heavenly

to do justice to the evidence: tracing the use of Exodus in Hebrews not by the type of textual import but by following a thematic culling of the material under three headings. First, it focuses on the way in which Hebrews remembers the momentous event at the heart of the book of Exodus—the exodus proper, the exodus *qua* event. In the second part, the attention shifts from the event to its aftermath, namely, the Mosaic covenant, with its inseparable components: the Law, the priesthood, the tabernacle, and the accompanying paraphernalia. Lastly, to do justice to the Exodus material in Hebrews, the study concludes with a brief consideration of the Author's depiction of Moses, the quintessential leader of God's people, appointed and repeatedly confirmed as such in Exodus.

As a perfunctory matter, the reader must assess the legitimacy of focusing on the influence of Exodus on Hebrews, apart from the role played by the Pentateuch as a whole, to avoid implementing an artificial construct in tracing scriptural influences in the epistle. Even though, for pragmatic reasons, the present chapter focuses on Exodus, the reader must remember that the events in Exodus are foretold and prepared in the book of Genesis and are frequently taken up and developed in the subsequent books of Leviticus, Numbers, and Deuteronomy.[5] Tracing the echoes of Exodus in

---

tabernacles and provides scriptural support for at least three key stages of the argument, 9:11–12, 23–24; 10:19–20. Alternatively, the Author alludes to Exodus's description of the tabernacle in Heb 9:2–3, and a similar pattern is discernible. The brief allusion to the demarcation between the Holy and the Holy of Holies becomes the scriptural basis for several ideas in the ensuing argument, primarily in Heb 9:6–7 and 10:19–20. While generally it is warranted to treat separately the quotations and allusions, as far as Exodus is concerned, there seems to be no substantial benefit other than the text critical implications.

5. The actual division of the Pentateuch into five books could easily obscure the reality of a unified *opus*. Regardless of the complex history of the Pentateuch's coming together as a book, it is evident that the Author, not unlike his apostolic contemporaries, considered the Pentateuch as a unified whole. For them, the Pentateuch stood as the definitive literary, historical, and theological account of the Sinaitic covenant, the complex, multileveled, defining reality of God's election of the Jewish people as the covenant people; see, *inter alios*, John H. Sailhamer, *The Pentateuch as Narrative: A Biblical-Theological Commentary* (Grand Rapids: Zondervan, 1992). Any critical analysis of this literary masterpiece, while dealing with its convoluted story line, doublets, various literary strata, recapitulations with variations, alleged chronological incongruences, and plethora of enigmatic names, places, times, and many other idiosyncrasies, must not obfuscate the self evident truth that the Author did not approach the Pentateuch with modern scholarly presuppositions. He read it as the authoritative account of the factual, historical event of the Sinaitic covenant. Any modern attempt to understand Hebrews's use of Exodus must proceed along similar lines. Source, form, redaction, and narrative criticisms have a legitimate place for a thorough understanding of the Pentateuch; yet, to project them on the way the Author read and used Exodus would do injustice to his encounter with the Pentateuch.

Hebrews would need to accommodate to the Author's holistic treatment of the Pentateuch as a whole, not as a story segmented in five books. With these considerations in place, the presence and the impact of Exodus material in Hebrews can now be rightfully assessed.

Exodus—The Event

Hebrews reminisces about the Israelites' exodus from Egypt in two textual clusters. The first one, Heb 11:23–29, roughly a third of the space allotted for the historical panorama of God's people, provides the most elaborate NT reminiscence of the event. A second cache of texts placed strategically throughout the epistle augments the perspective. Each group will be treated separately.[6]

The Exodus according to Hebrews 11

The most convenient way to analyze this material is to reconstruct the Author's timeline of events in Exodus, acknowledging all the while that their true prolegomenon is the Abrahamic covenant in Genesis.[7] The trail of the exodus events commences in Heb 11:23, with a reference to Joseph, the grandson of Abraham, who prophetically foretold the exodus, Heb 11:22. The anaphoric "by faith," used throughout the chapter, partitions the exodus narrative in five distinct episodes.

Nowhere is this aspect more obvious than in the story of the exodus event. The exodus stands as a singular, paramount historical event, whose story as a literary-theological depiction of the event has a multifarious presence throughout the Pentateuch. It would be difficult, and certainly unfair to the Author, to differentiate among the five Pentateuch books and treat them as distinct scriptural sources for Hebrews. E.g., Heb 12:21 includes a quotation from Deut 9:19, even though the event itself happened within the timespan of Exodus. Similarly, Heb 3–4 considers the events at Meribah and Massah as a single unit, most likely rolling into one the events in Exod 17 and Num 20.

6. See also Nathan MacDonald, "By Faith Moses," in *The Epistle to the Hebrews and Christian Theology*, eds. Richard Bauckham et al. (Grand Rapids: Eerdmans, 2009) 374–82.

7. As the backdrop for the exodus, Heb 6:14 quotes Gen 22:17, God's seminal promise to Abraham. Already in Exod 2:6, God reveals his intention to liberate and to adopt these descendants as his own people (Exod 3:18; 6:7). The adoption ensued in the midst of a savage and ethnocidal slavery (Exod 1–2) and consisted of an unequivocal promise of deliverance from slavery (Exod 3:17).

The first episode—Moses' parents (Heb 11:23; cf. Exod 2:2)

The story starts with Moses' parents and their act of civil disobedience as they protectively hid the infant for three months. The Author detects behind the action their implicit faith in the promised redemptive plan of God. Their perception of the boy's qualities (ἀστεῖον τὸ παιδίον, Heb 11:23; cf. Exod 2:2) and their fearlessness in braving the kingly decree (τὸ διάταγμα τοῦ βασιλέως, Heb 11:23; cf. Exod 1:15, 22) adequately justified their courageous deed.

This particular reading of Exodus displays two key characteristics of the Author's Scriptural approach. First, the retelling of the story follows Exodus in the Greek textual tradition, the LXX. Two of the details provided in Hebrews—the qualities of the boy and the duration of the hiding—are traceable to both the HB and LXX. Making both parents responsible for the hiding, however, is based solely on the LXX.[8] Second, the Author marks their faith as the basis for their action. The anaphoric πίστει ("by faith") is the common denominator of his perspective not only on the events of Exodus, but also on the entire history of God's people. Its legitimacy is addressed at the end of the section.

The second episode—Moses' early life (Heb 11:24–26; cf. Exod 2:2–4)

Next, the Author moves to the episode covering Moses' early life. It is the longest episode in the Moses cycle; and, it corresponds to the storyline starting with Exod 2:11, from which the phrase μέγας γενόμενος Μωυςῆς ("Moses becoming mature") serves to launch Hebrews's account, Μωϋσῆς μέγας γενόμενος (Heb 11:24). The text highlights Moses' choice of siding with God's people rather than clinging to the position, the power, the prestige, and the privileges offered by Egypt.

Two elements in the episode deserve closer attention. First, the Author equates the treasures and privileges of Egypt with "the fleeting pleasures of sin" (πρόσκαιρον ἔχειν ἁμαρτίας ἀπόλαυσιν, Heb 11:25). While in his theology, sin is usually associated with overt disobedience to God's commands,[9] it also encompasses every choice that undermines God's plans.[10] Had Moses decided to remain in Egypt, the choice would have inevitably altered the

---

8. The HB specifically singles out Moses' mother as the agent responsible for the hiding. See John William Wevers, *Notes on the Greek Text of Exodus*, SBLSCS 30 (Atlanta: Scholars, 1990) *ad loc.*

9. See, *inter alia*, Heb 10:28 or Heb 12:1–2.

10. O'Brien, *Hebrews*, 431.

course of his life, his allegiance to God and, ultimately, his availability for God's plan and mission.[11]

Second, the phrase "the disgrace of Christ" (ὁ ὀνειδισμός τοῦ Χριστοῦ, Heb 11:26)—stated as the reason for his choices—deserves hermeneutical unpacking. The term "disgrace" (ὀνειδισμός), while present in neither Exodus nor the Pentateuch, is the lexical unit of choice denoting the Israelites' oppression in Egypt. Due to its semantic potency, the Author employs it to describe not only the plight of Christ,[12] but also that of his readers.[13] While the lexical choice itself (ὀνειδισμός) is not surprising, its qualifier (τοῦ Χριστοῦ) is. There are several syntactical possibilities for this difficult genitive construction. The least likely option would be to read it as a subjective genitive (i.e., the sufferings experienced by Christ during his earthly life). The Author knew about them (Heb 5:5), but Moses did not. More likely, given the Author's Christological outlook, the phrase should be construed as a genitive of relation (i.e., the sufferings that ensue because of and in association with the messianic agenda).[14] The phrase becomes just another marker of the Author's Christological reading of the Jewish Scriptures.

The third episode—the departure from Egypt
(Heb 11:27; cf. Exod 2:11–13 or Exod 12:37–39)

The episode continues the exclusive focus on Moses with a reminiscence of his departure from Egypt. In Heb 11:27, the phrase "he left Egypt" (κατέλιπεν Αἴγυπτον) carries a slight ambiguity of referent. The Author could refer to the first, solo departure of Moses from Egypt to Midian (Exod 2:11–13) or, more likely, to his final departure as leader of the liberated people (Exod 12:37–39). The Author's comments on Moses' fearlessness before an outraged Pharaoh and his ability to see, virtually, the Unseen One, favor the latter option.[15] In this episode, faith is evidenced by Moses' perseverance

11. The Author makes no comment on the fact that Moses' first departure was precipitated by the killing of the Egyptian, cf. Exod 2:11–12.

12. Most likely a subjective genitive, "bearing the reproach he endured," τὸν ὀνειδισμὸν αὐτοῦ φέροντες.

13. A reminder of the beginning stages of their faith, "being publicly exposed to reproach and affliction," τοῦτο μὲν ὀνειδισμοῖς τε καὶ θλίψεσιν θεατριζόμενοι.

14. The most probable referent in all occurrences. See the discussions in O'Brien, *Hebrews*, 432, and Cockerill, *Hebrews*, 573.

15. The chronology of events in *Exodus* mark the preparation for the Passover meal as the harbinger of the flight from Egypt. If the chronology in Heb 11 mirrors strictly the one in *Exodus*, then Heb 11:27 refers to Moses' first departure. It should be remembered, however, that chronology in Hebrews is not always strict, (cf. Heb 11:32).

in pursuing the ultimate goal of liberation in spite of an obstinate Pharaoh, fueled by the encounter with the Unseen God and motivated by the promise of a reward.[16] The tenacity he displayed as "he endured" (ἐκαρτέρησεν) stands as the true marker of faith not only for him, but also for the epistle's addressees. The Author repeatedly exhorts them to perseverance, "you need to persevere" (ὑπομονῆς γὰρ ἔχετε χρείαν, Heb 10:36), the synonymic correspondent to Moses' endurance (cf. Heb 12:3, 7).

The second detail in the passage, "as seeing the unseen" (τὸν γὰρ ἀόρατον ὡς ὁρῶν) carries several exegetical challenges, ranging from the construal of the conjunction "as" (ὡς) to the exact historical event referenced by the Author. He could have been referring to the burning bush encounter in Exod 3.[17] Also possible, Heb 11 is echoing Exod 24:10–11, a text in which the Hebrew and the Greek textual traditions diverge. While the MT states repeatedly that Moses and the elders "saw the God of Israel," the LXX translators, perhaps reluctant to translate literally the phrase, adopt the circumlocution, "seeing the place of God."[18] Moses' request to see the face of God (Exod 33:12–14) could also have provided the backdrop for Hebrews's account.[19] Since none of the options fits easily into Hebrews's chronology, it is plausible that the Author rolled all these passages into one referential experience.

The fourth episode—the Passover (Heb 11:28; cf. Exod 12–13)

This episode marks a shift of focus from Moses to the whole congregation of Israel. While Heb 11:20 implicitly commences with Moses, "by faith he kept/instituted the Passover" (πίστει πεποίηκεν τὸ πάσχα), the Passover observance includes necessarily the whole people. From this point on, the

---

Therefore, a reference to the final departure is more likely.

16. Exodus records no less than eleven appearances before Pharaoh, in each Moses making the same demand.

17. The narrative displays a peculiar interest in ophthalmic experiences, both with reference to the people, Exod 4:2, 3, 4, and to God, Exod 4:9.

18. The Hebrew text of Exod 24:10, ויראו את אלהי ישראל ("they saw the God of Israel,") is translated as καὶ εἶδον τὸν τόπον οὗ εἱστήκει ἐκεῖ ὁ θεὸς τοῦ Ισραηλ. The same translational choice is repeated in the following verse, Exod 24:11, "they beheld God" (ויחזו את־האלהים), which reads καὶ ὤφθησαν ἐν τῷ τόπῳ τοῦ θεοῦ (Exod 24:11); see Weaver, Exodus, ad loc.

19. In light of the Author's definition of faith (Heb 11:1), a completely different option is possible: "seeing the unseen" could be a reference to the deliverance experienced, "hoped for but not yet seen." Moses' faith brought about the fulfillment of the promise for deliverance, since faith can bring the things hoped from the realm of not-yet-seen into reality.

congregation of Israel takes the center stage in Hebrews's storyline. Hebrews 11:28 summarizes the lengthiest part of Exodus, the entirety of Heb 12 containing the instructions for Passover observance. The lexical connections between LXX Exodus and Hebrews are multiple. In Heb 11:28, the destroying angel (ὁ ὀλοθρεύων) echoes the participle of the same verb in the LXX account, "he will not let the destroyer" (καὶ οὐκ ἀφήσει τὸν ὀλεθρεύοντα, Exod 12:23). Similarly, the sprinkled blood (ἡ πρόσχυσις τοῦ αἵματος) picks up the Exodus emphasis on the protective blood to be sprinkled (πρόσχειν) on the door posts (24:6; 29:16, 21) and elevates it to theological prominence in the epistle's central section.[20] Just as the sprinkled blood in Exodus fulfilled a salvific role for the first born of Israel by preventing the destroyer from touching them (12:13), and, consequently, leaving the rest unprotected (12:29), the sprinkled blood of the new covenant, as its typological correspondent, performs a dual role in Hebrews. For those availing themselves of it, the blood cleanses (Heb 9:14), perfects (10:14), and enables (13:20); for those rejecting it, the blood condemns (10:29).

The fifth episode—the crossing of the Red Sea (Heb 11:30; cf. Exod 14:1–31)

The final episode deals exclusively with the Israelite commonwealth as they departed from Egypt. The significant shift in focus underscores a deep theological truth: faith operates not only on an individual level, but also a communal one. From this point on, the roll of faith replaces "by faith, he" with "by faith, they," highlighting that the individual and communal faith are both at their best when they complement each other. Similar to the role of the sprinkled blood, the parting waters of the Red Sea performed a dual role: a salvific one for the believing people (Heb 11:29a) and a damning one (Heb 11:29 b) for Pharaoh's army who sought the reversal of the deliverance plan. The reference to the Red Sea (ἡ ἐρυθὰ θάλασσα), the name of the body of water crossed by the people, confirms the Author's dependence on the LXX. The LXX Pentateuch translates סוף-ים as ἡ ἐρυθὰ θάλασσα, "the Red Sea."[21] For the sake of brevity (cf. Heb 11:32), the Author ends here the storyline of exodus, event and book, and, in fact, of the Pentateuch as a whole.

---

20. The noun is not used in Exodus, but the verbal cognate is (cf. Exod 24:6; 29:16, 21).

21. See Exod 10:19; 13:18; 15:4, etc.

The Exodus outside Hebrews 11

Texts related to the exodus of the second cache are dispersed throughout the epistle and they complement the sketch drawn from Heb 11. Two such passages deserve a closer look. The first comes in the epistle's exposition of Ps 95 [94 LXX] in connection with the theme of "rest." The Author exhorts the readers, the new house of God (Heb 3:5), to maintain firmly their confidence and hope. His plea strengthens when he appeals to Ps 95 [94 LXX], which he unequivocally equates with the voice of the Holy Spirit addressing the congregation when the Scriptures are read, (Heb 3:7a). A complex hermeneutical exercise is underway as the Author applies this portion of Scripture to his own generation, the readers of the epistle. The Davidic Ps 95 [94 LXX], written for the psalmist's generation, develops the Pentateuch theme of "rest," originally addressed to yet another generation—the original recipients of God's oath barring them from the promised Land (Num 14:23, 28, 30).

This original generation is, actually, the very generation of the exodus. Three interrogative clauses parse out their identity and failures. In answering the first clause, "who were those who heard and rebelled?" (Heb 3:16a), the Author identifies the exodus generation: "Those that came out of Egypt, under Moses" (πάντες οἱ ἐξελθόντες ἐξ Αἰγύπτου διὰ Μωϋσέως, Heb 3:16b). By their failure to live out an obedient faith, they are marked out as a counterexample for Hebrews's readers. Here is a most privileged generation: witnesses of the miraculous deliverance from slavery; beneficiaries of the uninterrupted miracles during the forty subsequent years; recipients of the word of God; members of the Sinaitic covenant; and yet, a generation that forfeited all these privileges because of unbelief and disobedience (Heb 3:19).

The second passage is also part of a quotation, this time from a prophetic passage, Jer 31 [38 LXX] in Heb 8, the longest quoted text in the epistle. Similarly to Ps 95 [94 LXX], the Jeremiah passage speaks of the exodus generation in negative terms. In the passage, the prophet reminisces of God's entering into covenant with the house of Israel and house of Judah, "I took by their hand and led them out of Egypt" (ἐπιλαβομένου μου τῆς χειρὸς αὐτῶν ἐξαγαγεῖν αὐτοὺς ἐκ γῆς Αἰγύπτου, Heb 8:9; cf. Jer 38:32 LXX). These people identified as the original generation of the covenant are the exodus generation. Yet, because of their unfaithfulness, "they did not remain in my covenant" (αὐτοὶ οὐκ ἐνέμειναν ἐν τῇ διαθήκῃ μου, Jer 38:32 LXX) and have forfeited their covenant status. As in Ps 95, the Author detects in the Jeremiah passage evidence for an irreparable breach in the covenantal relationship, "I also disregarded them" (καὶ ἐγὼ ἠμέλησα αὐτῶν, Heb 8:9; cf. Jer

38:32 LXX).[22] It was so definitive and categorical that only a new covenant could bring hope and restoration.

Both of these passages show that the Author, while informed by Exodus on matters related to the Sinaitic covenant, enhanced his theology by reflecting on the subsequent Scriptures' interpretations of the exodus. Both Ps 95 [94 LXX] and Jer 31 [38 LXX] are examples of Jewish scriptural interpretations of Exodus antedating the Author's intersection with the text and traditions of Exodus.

As mentioned earlier, an assessment of the Author's portrayal of the exodus must consider the larger hermeneutical issue raised by anaphoric "by faith." Readers of Heb 11 have often been intrigued by a slight *non sequitur* between the biblical record and the Author's interpretation. The people whose faith is praised throughout the chapter have neither consistently nor predominantly displayed faith. Not only does the biblical narrative lack explicit references to their faith, but, these heroes displayed, more often than not, quite the opposite of faith. On what basis, then, did the Author choose faith as the key ingredient to the lives of the OT saints?

Such a short space is inadequate for treating thoroughly a significant theological and hermeneutical issue.[23] As an absolutely necessary minimum, however, one must acknowledge behind Heb 11 an axiomatic theological system at work. For the Author, faith is the hermeneutical key that unpacks the story of God's people. But as such, it emerges out of a theological system that recognizes faith as the primary axiom, Heb 11:6.[24] The system is anchored in the Author's view of God and in his understanding of the inner dynamic of God's salvation plan, Heb 11:1. Every example selected from the history of God's people, from the civil disobedience of Moses' parents to the Red Sea crossing, moved God's plan of salvation a step further towards its fulfillment. The faith of all these people provided the substance out of which the things promised—"hoped for, yet not seen"—became reality (Heb 11:1). The Author inferred the presence of faith in their lives not necessarily from

22. The Author's dependence on the LXX text is evident again. The MT language of covenantal unfaithfulness to her Lord/husband, הפרו את־בריתי ואנכי בעלתי בם, "my covenant . . . they broke, though I was their husband," (ESV) has the LXX correspondent, αὐτοὶ οὐκ ἐνέμειναν ἐν τῇ διαθήκῃ μου καὶ ἐγὼ ἠμέλησα αὐτῶν, "they did not abide in my covenant, and I disregarded them," the latter being used in Hebrews without major modifications. See Steyn, *Quest*, 248–50.

23. See the thorough studies of Victor (Sung-Yul) Rhee, *Faith in Hebrews: Analysis within the Context of Christology, Eschatology, and Ethics*, StBL 19 (New York: Lang, 2001); and Dennis R. Lindsay, "*Pistis* and *'Emunah*: The Nature of Faith in the Epistle to the Hebrews," in *A Cloud of Witnesses: The Theology of Hebrews in Its Ancient Contexts*, eds. Richard Bauckham et al. (London: T. & T. Clark, 2008) 158–69.

24. Guthrie, "Hebrews," 968, holds to a similar position.

explicit or implicit biblical references, but rather from the working out of his own theological axioms, "faith is the substance of the things hoped for, the evidence of things not seen" (NKJV; ἔστιν δὲ πίστις ἐλπιζομένων ὑπόστασις, πραγμάτων ἔλεγχος οὐ βλεπομένων, Heb 11:1). Their faith gave substance to God's promises and ensured their progress from the moment of locution to its concrete fulfillment. Such is the nature and importance of faith, that the fulfillment of God's promises would have been impossible without it. It is, therefore, no surprise that faith is the *sine qua non* ingredient for a life pleasing to God. If and when, as the Author would assert, the fulfillment came, not least the redemptive word and work of the Son, it would be the undeniable and ultimate proof that the lives of the participants were essentially characterized by faith, despite temporary bouts of disbelief.

Exodus—The Aftermath

An event of the magnitude of the exodus would inevitably mark the subsequent history of the people involved in it. It established the premises for a new set of fundamentals needed to guide and secure the future of the nation. Exodus delves into such fundamentals. It narrates the liberation events and expounds on the distinctives of the Jewish religion. YHWH, the God of the Patriarchs, initiates, commands, institutes, and ratifies the covenant with the Jewish people in fulfillment of his earlier promises. Patterned after the suzerainty treaties of the time, the Sinaitic covenant stipulates the reciprocal responsibilities of the two covenanting parts: God adopts and marks out the Israelites as His people, just as He pledges Himself to be their God (Exod 19:5); on their part, the people of the covenant must fulfill their responsibilities, among which two requirements—the exclusive allegiance to their sovereign and obedience to the covenant laws—eclipse every other aspect. After the breathtaking deliverance from Egypt, the book focuses on the covenant: the Sinai theophany (19:1–25), the Decalogue (20:1–21), a first pack of laws and regulations (20:22—23:33), the actual making of the covenant (24:1–18), the instructions for the tabernacle and the priesthood (25:1—31:18), and the building of the tabernacle (35:1—40:35).[25] Thus the premises enabled the people of God to live up to the standard required by their redeemed status and fulfill their God-given mission.

---

25. The importance of the "external regulations" (δικαιώματα σαρκός, Heb 9:10) cannot be overestimated. More than a third of Exodus (25–40) is devoted to the cultic dimension of the covenant, including the tabernacle and the priesthood. After a detailed description of the instructions for the tabernacle (25–31), the book rehearses the same details almost verbatim (35–40) when it reports the completion of the work.

The Author explores five such fundamentals of the Sinaitic covenant with more readiness than any other aspect related to Exodus. In a logical rather than chronological order, these are: the covenant; the Law; the priesthood; the tabernacle; and the sacrifices. To grasp the true dimension of Exodus's footprint in Hebrews, it is worth noting that, while all these covenant matters are explored more fully in other books of the Pentateuch,[26] every single one of them made its seminal entry, historically as well as scripturally, in Exodus. This section considers them separately as part of Exodus's reverberations that informed and contributed to the message of Hebrews.

The Covenant

The analysis of the Sinaitic covenant, never named as such by the Author, is foundational for the epistle's contribution to the NT covenant theology, which is more profound and nuanced than any found in the other canonical writings. The epistle uses the word "covenant" (διαθήκη) more often than the rest of the NT. The labels chosen—either simply διαθήκη; or qualified, "the first covenant" (ἡ πρώτη διαθήκη); or, most often elliptically, "the first" (ἡ πρώτη)—are not novel in the NT.[27] What stands out in Hebrews is an exploration that invariably contrasts the old and the new. There is no interest in or reference to the Sinaitic covenant without an unfavorable comparison to the new covenant.

The epistle's preoccupation with the Sinaitic covenant does not have a linear progression. While it is introduced implicitly as early as Heb 2:1–4, its full development resurfaces only in Heb 8–10, the core section concerned with the multifarious relationship between the two covenants. Lexical statistics confirm this assessment: the section has no less than fifteen explicit usages of the word διαθήκη, while there are only three outside it.[28] Hebrews 8:6 wistfully picks up the examination of the covenant, "if the first had no problem . . ." (εἰ γὰρ ἡ πρώτη ἐκείνη ἦν ἄμεμπτος . . . , Heb 8:6). George Caird observed correctly that, each time the Author uses this formula, his intention is to draw attention to a scriptural self attestation about the insufficiency of that reality and its eschatological fulfillment.[29] The first cov-

---

26. The laws and regulations on sacrifice are addressed systematically in Leviticus.

27. There are Pauline precedents discernible, e.g., in reference to the apostles as the "ministers of the new covenant" (διακόνους καινῆς διαθήκης, 2 Cor. 3:6) or to the reading of Scriptures, "when they read the old covenant" (ἐπὶ ἀναγνώσει τῆς παλαιᾶς διαθήκης, 2 Cor. 3:14).

28. The statistic is even more persuasive when one considers the implicit references as well.

29. See George B. Caird, "The Exegetical Method of the Epistle to the Hebrews,"

enant can be rightly assessed only in light of the new covenant, which is its eschatological fulfillment and replacement. The Jeremiah quotation which follows stands as the *locus classicus* of the self-attested insufficiency of the old order.[30] In this depiction of the Sinaitic covenant, the Author's reflections are tributary to several ideas traceable to Exodus.

First, the lexical unit διαθήκη, as used in reference to the Sinaitic covenant, has obvious Exodus origins. Throughout Exodus (and indeed, the Pentateuch) διαθήκη stands as the translators' lexical choice for the Hebrew ברית. For reasons both of consistency and disambiguation, the LXX translators opted for this equivalence, even when the HB text employed the alternative articular noun העדת (as in, e.g., Exod 27:21; 31:7; 39:15).[31] Not simply a matter of convenience for the Author, this lexical unit's intrinsic double entendre—"a will" as well as "a testament"—assumes a key role in Heb 9:15–20.

By using the term διαθήκη in relation to the Sinaitic covenant, Exodus forges two important lexical links. Looking backward, it sets the covenant established in the wake of the exodus, "keep my covenant" (καὶ φυλάξητε τὴν διαθήκην μου, 19:5) in line with the earlier one made with the Patriarchs, "his covenant with Abraham, Isaac and Jacob" (τῆς διαθήκης αὐτοῦ τῆς πρὸς Αβρααμ καὶ Ισαακ καὶ Ιακωβ, 2:24). Looking forward, it enables the connection with the aforementioned Jeremiah passage and its prophetic announcement of a new covenant, καίνη διαθήκη.

Second, Exodus qualifies every aspect pertaining to this covenant, crucially important for Hebrews, by means of genitive constructions. The most frequent are: "the book of the covenant" (τὸ βιβλίον τῆς διαθήκης, Exod 24:7); "the blood of the covenant" (τὸ αἷμα τῆς διαθήκης, 24:8); "the ark of the covenant" (ἡ κιβωτὸς τῆς διαθήκης, 31:7); and "the tablets of the covenant" (αἱ πλάκες τῆς διαθήκης, 34:28). The Author uses the same pattern: the blood (Heb 10:29), the ark, and the tablets (Heb 9:4, 5) are all qualified in the same way. For Exodus, as well as Hebrews, the covenant, διαθήκη, is the unmovable lexical unit; everything revolves around it. It marks a reality that demands exclusive loyalty to God, explicitly forbidding competing allegiances to other gods—"do not make covenant with . . . their gods" (οὐ συγκαταθήσῃ . . . τοῖς θεοῖς αὐτῶν διαθήκην, Exod 23:32)—or to other people—"do not make covenant with the dwellers of the land" (μήποτε θῇς διαθήκην τοῖς ἐγκαθημένοις . . . ἐπὶ τῆς γῆς, 34:15).

CJT 5 (1959) 44–51, one of the most seminal investigations of Hebrews's use of the OT.

30. Caird, "Exegetical," 47.

31. The cognate verb "to dispose, to decree," διατιθέναι, follows the same pattern in Pentateuch; its Hebrew correspondent "to cut," כרת, is part of the idiom "to cut a covenant כרת ברית, with the meaning "to initiate / enter into a covenant."

Third, the recipients of the first covenant were the people of Israel, with the exodus generation constituting its archetypal, first generation. Jeremiah's quotation in Hebrews reconfirms the ethnical exclusivity as an inherent part of the first covenant. This covenant made in the days of the exodus was in fact an ethnically exclusive covenant made with "your ancestors" (τοῖς πατράσιν αὐτῶν, Jer 38:31 LXX; cf. Heb 8:9). Hebrews presupposes this ethnical dimension whenever the Author refers to the first covenant.[32] Yet he understands that the Jeremiah oracle foresaw a time when the ethnical exclusivity would come to an end. The new covenant, while engaging "the house of Israel and the house of Judah" (τὸν οἶκον Ἰσραὴλ καὶ . . . τὸν οἶκον Ἰούδα, Jer 38:30 LXX; cf. Heb 8:8) would also incorporate "your neighbor . . . your brother . . . all of them" (τὸν πολίτην αὐτοῦ καὶ . . . τὸν ἀδελφὸν αὐτοῦ . . . πάντες, Jer 38:34 LXX; cf. Heb 8:11). Belonging to the new covenant would not be the result of blood or kin particularities but of fideistic allegiance.

Fourth, the first covenant had legal requirements and stipulations, imperatives that the people had to obey. Every willful disobedience, the Author reminisces, was punishable without mercy (Heb 10:28). These covenant laws, however, were written on "tablets of stone," (πλάκες λίθιναι, Exod 32:15; cf. Heb 9:4). The Author, as well as Jeremiah before him, deplores this impediment that stifled the obedience under the first covenant. The provisions of the new covenant include also an inner change, the etching of these laws on the minds and hearts of people—"I will put my laws in their minds and I will inscribe them on their hearts" (διδοὺς νόμους μου εἰς τὴν διάνοιαν αὐτῶν καὶ ἐπὶ καρδίας αὐτῶν ἐπιγράψω αὐτούς, Heb 8:10).

Lastly, the qualifiers the Author uses to refer to the Sinaitic covenant must be revisited. The Author's preferred term, the "first covenant" (ἡ πρώτη διαθήκη), is juxtaposed to a range of phrases: "the new covenant" (ἡ καίνη διαθήκη, Heb 8:8; 9:15; and ἡ νέα διαθήκη, 12:24), or even "the better covenant" (ἡ κρείττονος διαθήκης, 7:22; 8:6). Had the original readers found these adjectives derogatory, they had correctly construed the Author's theology of the covenants. How else could one read "if the first one had been faultless" (εἰ γὰρ ἡ πρώτη ἐκείνη ἦν ἄμεμπτος, 8:7) or "he has made the first one obsolete; and what is obsolete and outdated will soon disappear" (πεπαλαίωκεν τὴν πρώτην τὸ δὲ παλαιούμενον καὶ γηράσκον ἐγγὺς ἀφανισμοῦ, 8:13)?[33] The Author's

---

32. See the repetition of the reference to "the ancestors" (οἱ πατέρες, Heb 1:1; 3:9; 8:9).

33. There seems to be a growing trend at least in Hebrews research advocating for a revision of this NT language and its historical correctness. See, e.g., the non-secessionist reading of Hebrews in Alan C. Mitchell, "'A Sacrifice of Praise': Does Hebrews Promote Supersessionism?," in *Reading the Epistle to the Hebrews: A Resource for Students*, eds. Eric F. Mason and Kevin B. McCruden, SBLRBS 66 (Atlanta: SBL, 2011) 251–68. This

theological perspective on the Sinaitic covenant includes his charge against its temporality, insufficiency, and inferiority to the covenant to be ushered in by the eschaton. Backed by the Jeremiah oracles, he is unapologetic about his severe assessment: out with the old, in with the new. While the Author's assessment of the insufficiencies and imperfections of the Sinaitic covenant does not come directly from Exodus, it does emerge from reading Exodus in light of the subsequent prophetic oracles in the Hebrew canon.

It is just as important to acknowledge that the Author read Exodus not only in light of subsequent scriptures but also in light of the life and work of Christ. The phrase that defined the institution of the first covenant, "this is the blood of the covenant which God has commanded you to keep" (τοῦτο τὸ αἷμα τῆς διαθήκης ἧς ἐνετείλατο πρὸς ὑμᾶς ὁ θεός, Heb 9:20), and one of the few direct quotations for Exodus "behold the blood . . ." (ἰδοὺ τὸ αἷμα, Exod 24:8)[34] are equally predominant in the new covenant. Echoing the apostolic kerygmatic tradition, "this is the blood" (τοῦτο τὸ αἷμα, Heb 9:20) marks in the Gospels (Matt 26:28; Mark 14:24) as well as in the Pauline corpus (1Cor 11:23) the inauguration of the new covenant in the blood of Jesus. For Hebrews, this new covenant has ushered in better promises (Heb 8:6), better hope (7:19), better sacrifice (9:23), and in sum, a better covenant altogether (7:22). This radical covenantal overhaul is attributable to the pneumatological substructure of the new covenant, a theme that cannot be addressed here.[35]

The Law

The Law of Moses, named as such in Heb 10:28 (ὁ νόμος Μωϋσέως), is arguably the most important component of the Sinaitic covenant and establishes a firm presence in Hebrews. The Author clusters his exposition on this topic

---

looks more like a classical case of eisegesis, in which the subsequent history, painful and tragic as it was, is allowed to influence the more natural, direct understating of the biblical passage. Also illuminating is the earlier exchange on this topic between Hays and Skarsaune: Richard B. Hays, "'Here We Have No Lasting City': New Covenantalism in Hebrews," in *The Epistle to the Hebrews and Christian Theology*, 151–73; and Oskar Skarsaune, "Does the Letter to the Hebrews Articulate a Supersessionist Theology?," in *The Epistle to the Hebrews and Christian Theology*, 174–82.

34. See Steyn, *Quest*, 272–74, for a thorough textual analysis of the quotation.

35. While the Author did not develop his pneumatology as extensively as his Christology, the Holy Spirit holds a very important part in the epistle's understanding of the implementation and the dynamics of the new covenant. Cf. Steve Motyer, "The Spirit in Hebrews: No Longer Forgotten?," in *The Spirit and Christ in the New Testament and Christian Theology: Essays in Honor of Max Turner*, eds. I. Howard Marshall, Volker Rabens, and Cornelis Bennema (Grand Rapids: Eerdmans, 2012) 213–27.

in the central part of the epistle, the same section where the word "covenant" dominates. Any investigation of the lexeme "law" needs to address the semantic variance between the Hebrew word תורה and its Greek counterpart, νόμος—an enterprise well outside the scope of the present study.[36] Suffice it to say that the Author uses the word "law" (νόμος) squarely within the semantic range of the LXX denotations, which is merely stating a truism about a writer who used exclusively the Greek Scriptures.

The LXX translator(s) of the Pentateuch used the noun "law" (νόμος) as the primary lexical equivalent for the noun תורה more than fifty of some sixty occurrences. It connotes the law as a whole, a body of regulations and requirements accompanying the Sinaitic covenant.[37] This legislative body—the Law—incorporated a variety of "commandments" (LXX ἐντολαί, HB מצוה) and "requirements" (LXX πρόσταγμα, HB הק) which the covenant people needed to know, to keep, to perform, to read, to write, and to obey. The Lord commands Moses to teach these to the people as precepts for life, "the ways in which they must walk" (τὰς ὁδούς ἐν αἷς πορεύσονται, Exod 18:20).

Both lexical units, "the Law" (ὁ νόμος, singular) and "a stipulation" (ἡ ἐντολή, i.e., a command therein, usually plural), resurface in Hebrews with identical connotations. The Author regularly distinguishes between these two lexemes. He uses "the Law" (ὁ νόμος) when he refers to the prescriptive body of regulations attached to the covenant, as in Heb 7:19, "the Law made nothing perfect" (οὐδὲν γὰρ ἐτελείωσεν ὁ νόμος). Most singular usages (e.g., Heb 8:4; 9:19; 10:8) carry the same connotation. Alternatively, the Author employs the lexical unit "command" (ἡ ἐντολή) when he refers to the stipulations and commands the Law contains and demands, as in Heb 9:19, "after every command of the Law has been read" (λαληθείσης γὰρ πάσης ἐντολῆς κατὰ τὸν νόμον).

Several noteworthy aspects about the Author's concept of the Law are directly related to Exodus material pertaining to the Sinaitic Law in Hebrews. Foremost, one has to acknowledge the fundamental bond between the Law and the covenant under which it operates. The epistle axiomatically assumes the existence of an indissoluble triad, whose components, the covenant, the Law, and the priesthood (see *infra.*) stand or fall together. When one operates, the Author ascertains, the other two

36. See Douglas J. Moo, "Law," in *Dictionary of Jesus and the Gospels*, eds. Joel B. Green, Scot McKnight, and I. Howard Marshall (Downers Grove, IL: IVP, 1992) 450–61; Frank Thielman, "Law," in *Dictionary of Paul and His Letters*, eds. Gerald F. Hawthorne, Ralph P. Martin, and Daniel G. Reid (Downers Grove, IL: IVP, 1993) 529–42.

37. Two other LXX lexical equivalents for "statute," חק and חקה, are responsible for the rest of the occurrences. When these lexemes are translated by νόμος, they also refer primarily to the Law in its entirety, viewed as a whole.

maintain their functionality as well. Alternatively, when one becomes obsolete and needs replacing, the other two need altering as well. While the Author provides no direct scriptural quotation or allusion in support of the triad, it is worth noting that Exodus introduces all three components in an identical tightly knit system.

Secondly, the Author assesses the function of the Law within the historical framework of God's plan of salvation. This Pauline-*esque* idea is markedly visible in the Author's comparison between the Law and the Melchizedekian oath (to be distinguished from the Abrahamic oath), the two towering moments in the historical unfolding of the covenant. The Author claims in no uncertain terms that the worth of the oath surpassed that of the Law. The comment is defended on the basis of an observation about the historical succession of the two, "but the word of the oath, which came after the Law" (ὁ λόγος δὲ τῆς ὁρκωμοσίας τῆς μετὰ τὸν νόμον, Exod 7:28).[38] The full implication of this aspect will be taken up again in an analysis of the priesthood of the Sinaitic covenant.

Third, the Law, as a system operating within the perimeter of the Sinaitic covenant, was perfectly capable of fulfilling the role for which it was given, but disappointingly unable to do more. The positive side of the statement is visible throughout the epistle. The Law had the cardinal role in regulating every aspect of worship and sacrifice within the Sinaitic covenant. Everything had to be done "according to the Law" (κατὰ νόμον): the regulations (Heb 9:19), the offering of gifts and sacrifices (8:4; 10:8), and the cleansings and various washings (9: 22). Given that the commands were not optional, the covenant people needed to read them, to hear them, to assume them as their own, and to obey them scrupulously. Any deliberate, willful disobedience of the requirements resulted in merciless dying (10:28).

On the negative side, however, the Law was incapable to offer the worshipers a status which the Author calls "perfection" (τελειότης, 10:1). This inability of the Law surfaces several times in the epistle. In perfect parallelism with the criticism of the covenant, the Author asks wistfully about the priesthood and the Law, "if perfection could have been possible through the Levitical priesthood—for under it the people received the Law" (εἰ μὲν οὖν τελείωσις διὰ τῆς Λευιτικῆς ἱερωσύνης ἦν, ὁ λαὸς γὰρ ἐπ'αὐτῆς νενομοθέτηται, 7:11). The paragraph concludes with a reiteration, "the Law made nothing perfect" (οὐδὲν γὰρ ἐτελείωσεν ὁ νόμος, 7:19), leaving no room for ambiguity about the intrinsic inabilities of the Law. The devastating indictment, however, comes at the beginning of Heb 10, where the Author acknowledges

---

38. The Author refers here not to the Abrahamic oath (Heb 6:13) but to the Melchizedekian one, the second of two oracles, which form the substance of Ps 110 [109 XXX], the most important scriptural passage for the argument of Hebrews.

not only the Law's inability to grant perfection, but also the reasons behind it.[39] The Law is ontologically limited and unable to represent the heavenly realities—"the Law is only a shadow of the heavenly realities" (σκιὰν γὰρ ἔχων ὁ νόμος τῶν μελλόντων ἀγαθῶν, 10:1); it is exclusively concerned with externals—"they are external regulations imposed until the new order came" (δικαιώματα σαρκὸς μέχρι καιροῦ διορθώσεως ἐπικείμενα, 9:10). It is unable to perform the inner work necessary for achieving sanctification and perfection. It only provides safe passage until the time of the new order, until the time of the eschaton.

Spatial constraints prevent a debate on what influenced the Author's background of thought—whether it was a Platonic/Neo-Platonic or Jewish eschatological background in control of his language, thought, and metaphors.[40] Suffice it to say that, regardless of the controlling dualism, spatial or temporal, the Author perceived the Law as operating chronologically prior to and axiologically inferior to the coming of eschatological realities.

No analysis of Hebrews's understanding of the Law would be complete without addressing the aforementioned Jeremiah passage and its explicit link to the Sinaitic covenant of Exodus. The legislative stipulations feature prominently in the oracle. As a distinct mark of the New covenant, God will internalize them: "[he] will put [his] laws in their minds and [he] will inscribe them on their hearts" (διδοὺς νόμος μοθ εἰς τὴν διάνοιαν αὐτῶν καὶ ἐπὶ καρδίας αὐτῶν ἐπιγράψω αὐτούς, 8:10). Here is an inward mechanism resulting in hearts and minds bent on fulfilling God's demands due to genuine inner compulsion rather than external coercion. God's address in the Son (1:2) inaugurated a reality which brought to an end and rendered obsolete all preparatory stages, including the Law of Moses.

39. There are notable differences between Hebrews and Pauline assessments of the limits of the Law. Unlike the Apostle Paul, who seems to put the blame on the reality of "sin" and its destructive effect on the human person (Rom 7:7–13), the Author blames the Law's inability to offer perfection on its intrinsic nature: it is only a shadow of the good things that are coming, not the realities themselves (Heb 10:1–4).

40. For a well-worn path of this debate, see C. K. Barrett, "The Eschatology of the Epistle to the Hebrews," in *The Background of the New Testament and Its Eschatology*, eds. W. D. Davies and D. Daube (Cambridge: Cambridge University Press, 1956) 363–94; Ronald Williamson, *Philo and the Epistle to the Hebrews* (Leiden: Brill, 1970); James W. Thompson, *The Beginning of Christian Philosophy: The Epistle to the Hebrews*, CBQMS 13 (Washington, DC: Catholic Biblical Associations of America, 1981); and, most recently, James W. Thompson, "What Has Middle Platonism to Do with Hebrews?," in *Reading the Epistle to the Hebrews: A Resource for Students*, 31–52.

The Priesthood

The priesthood and its intrinsic subset, the high-priesthood office, complete the virtual triad of the Sinaitic covenant. Together with the themes of covenant and law, it stands high among the theological peaks of Hebrews. It is noteworthy the Author's exclusive theological interest in the Levitical priesthood and its new covenant counterpart. No other NT book or writer goes to such lengths in exploring the sacerdotal background and nature of Christ's work and its relationship to the Levitical priesthood and the Aaronic high-priesthood grounded in the Sinaitic covenant.

Lexical statistics support the assertion. Among the epistolary corpus, Hebrews's seventeen usages of "high priest" (ἀρχιερεύς) have no counterpart in the Pauline or the General epistles. Likewise, while the Gospels and Acts do employ the term, they limit it to references about the office and its representatives in the NT times. A similar count is true for the word "priest" (ἱερεύς). The epistolary material records fourteen usages, all in Hebrews. The other fourteen instances in the Gospels and Acts invariably refer to the priestly office during that era. Another cognate term, "priesthood" (ἱερωσύνη), a NT hapax-legomenon, further confirms the epistle's unique interest in these matters.[41] NT theology owes a debt of gratitude to the Author's exploration of this subject matter. Without his innovative and creative theological interest, the canonical writings would have been devoid of a canonical perspective on the priesthood, its contribution to connecting the covenants, and its Christological implications.

As already asserted, the Author developed his theology of the priesthood on the Pentateuch assumption that the covenant, the Law, and the priesthood stand or fall together (Heb 7:12).While the levitical priesthood receives its main coverage in other books of the Pentateuch, its origins are rooted firmly in Exodus. For the Author, the priesthood in Exodus comes with its inherent limitations, observable especially when assessed with Christological hindsight. Nowhere is this fact more evident than in Heb 7 and its sustained contrast between the Levitical priesthood and its Aaronic high-priesthood, on the one hand, and the high-priesthood of Christ, on the other.

Several characteristics of the priesthood / high-priesthood with roots in Exodus emerge in Hebrews. First, it should be noted that, according to Exodus, the priestly and high-priestly offices have both overlapping and distinctive elements, a point Hebrews mirrors in various moments. The priest and the high priest are both called by God into ministry (Heb 5:1; 8:3). They perform their service on behalf of the people (5:2) by offering gifts

---

41. As a lexical unit, "priesthood" (ἱερωσύνη) does not occur in the LXX Pentateuch. It is used occasionally in the apocryphal books.

and sacrifices (5:1; 8:3). They both are subject to weakness and sin (7:28), and consequently, they perform a ministry for their own behalf and for the people (5:3; 9:7). Yet, there are important differences explored in Hebrews with Exodus warrant. Only the high priest had the right to perform the sacerdotal act linked with the Day of Atonement (9:6, 7). The Author follows this distinction to engage in a multi-leveled contrast between the Aaronic high-priesthood and the one of Christ (see *infra.*).[42]

The Author's critique of the Sinaitic priesthood / high-priesthood follows the pattern already established in discussing the law and the covenant, "if perfection could have been achieved under the levitical priesthood" (7:11). In his assessment, the OT priesthood was imperfect, ineffective, and insufficient; internal faults marred it in the same way in which its covenant suffered. Following this stern indictment, the Author moves the argument even further by means of another conditional statement, "if he were on earth" (εἰ μὲν οὖν ἦν ἐπὶ γῆς, 8:4). The implications point to another flaw of the levitical priesthood: While they performed competently the duties prescribed to them by the sacrificial legislation, they were completely outclassed when there was a need for a sacerdote to minister in the true, heavenly tabernacle.

To back his assessment, the Author draws attention to the following aspects. First, there is the inherent human weakness of all the appointees to the office, "men in their weakness" (ἀρχιερεῖς ἔχοντας ἀσθένειαν, 7:28). They are no different than the people on whose behalf they are appointed to minister: They are men marred by weaknesses (5:2; 7:28); they are sinners (5:3; 9:7); and they need sacrifices just as much as "the ignorant and the wayward" (5:2). Repeatedly, the Author reminds the reader that the priests had to perform the sacrifices for themselves as well as for the people (καθὼς περὶ τοῦ λαοῦ, οὕτως καὶ περὶ αὐτοῦ, 5:3; cf. 9:7) A further limitation to the office was the ephemerality of the priests' lives, since death prevented them to remain in office (7:23). A ministry conducted by such priests could continue only in as one generation passed it on to the next. While the Author does not explore further this train of thought, it is clear that this is a negative assessment. The third limitation revolves around the locus where they performed their ministry, an earthly tabernacle set up as a man-made structure. This earthly sanctuary[43] was only a shadow, a copy of the true

42. The Author developed his view on the priesthood not only by merging the Melchizedekian passages of Gen 14 and Ps 110 [109 LXX], but also by investigating the vast information available in the Pentateuch, both in and outside Exodus.

43. The explicit target of the Author is the tabernacle, not the Jerusalem temple. Whether he did it because he considered it more important to address the primary archetypal sanctuary, or to avoid being caught up in a volatile, easy to misconstrue

tabernacle in heaven (ὑποδείγμα καὶ σκιᾷ τῶν ἐπουρανίων, 8:5). The ministry these priests could perform was inefficient and inconsequential by the
demands and standards of the true sacred space, the heavenly tabernacle.

The Author finds the solution for the flaws of Sinaitic priesthood in
the Melchizedekian oracle (Ps 110:4), but since his considerations use texts
outside Exodus, the argument will not be traced further. A sufficient closing
lies in the Author's belief that the role of the priest was admirably fulfilled
by Jesus Christ, "such a high priest truly meets our needs" (τοιοῦτος γὰρ ἡμῖν
καὶ ἔπρεπεν ἀρχιερεύς, Heb 7:26). All the qualifications required for a high
priest in the eschatological setting of the heavenly tabernacle are indeed
fulfilled by Jesus Christ.

The Paraphernalia: the Tabernacle, the Sacrifices

The fundamentals of the Sinaitic covenant traceable in Exodus and their
exploration in Hebrews could end justifiably with the aforementioned triad.
Yet, in fairness to the Author's complex theology, a closing word about that
covenant's paraphernalia is in order. Belonging to this group are the tabernacle as the place of worship, and the sacrifices required to maintain the
status and well-being of the covenant members. While intrinsically essential
to the covenant, these aspects nevertheless belong to a second tier of prominence. Attention will be directed also to the Author's particular interest in
the Mt. Sinai theophany and its implications for the new covenant.

The tabernacle

The Author's interest in the tabernacle complex is not incidental. Exodus
gives considerable attention to these matters; it not only records the detailed
instructions for its construction, but it also repeats them with as many details when the work was performed. The tabernacle was the cultic sacred
space associated with the Sinaitic covenant,[44] the only legitimate place in
which worship, service, sacrifice, and communion with the God of the covenant could take place (Exod 25:8). The Author acknowledges its centrality
in his opening statement, "the first covenant had regulations for worship
and an earthly place of holiness, for a tent was prepared" (Εἶχε μὲν οὖν ἡ

---

dispute over the Jerusalem temple (cf. Acts 7) continues to perplex scholars; see Andrew T. Lincoln, *Hebrews: A Guide* (New York: T. & T. Clark, 2006) 39.

44. Marie E. Isaacs, *Sacred Space: An Approach to the Theology of the Epistle to the
Hebrews*, JSNTSup 73 (Sheffield: Sheffield Academic, 1992), continues to be the most
thorough investigation of the cultic and sacred space in Hebrews.

πρώτη δικαιώματα λατρείας τό τε ἅγιον κοσμικόν. σκηνὴ γὰρ κατεσκευάσθη, Heb 9:1–2).

Due to limited time and space, the Author is selective in the list of components: the Holy place, with the lampstand and table with its consecrated bread; the most Holy place, with the alter of incense, the ark of the covenant (containing the jar of manna, Aaron's staff that has budded, and the stone tablets of the covenant), the cherubim of the glory and the atonement cover; and the curtain separating them (9:2–5). Scholarship on Hebrews has extensively scrutinized these issues, the selection as well as the noted idiosyncrasies such as position of the altar of incense (θυμιατήριον) in the Most Holy place, the reference to a second curtain (τὸ δεύτερον καταπέτασμα), and the gold used for some components. This chapter cannot undertake a thorough investigation of these matters. It would underline, however, that any attempt to explain the Author's description should start by taking in consideration the sources at his disposal. First, the LXX, his Scriptures, display some of the most notorious divergencies between the Hebrew and Greek textual traditions in this very section of Exodus. A reader of the LXX account of the tabernacle could have ended up with a mental picture of the tabernacle similar to the Author's.[45] Second, the representation of these elements in the Author's time, both in the literature and at the Jerusalem Temple, otherwise an edifice of no interest to the Author, could likewise explain the Author's particular take on these components.

The Exodus tabernacle, God-commissioned as the original sanctuary of the Jewish cult, was nevertheless considered by the Author as an inferior, imperfect, man-made, earthly, replaceable, and temporal place of worship (9:11, 24). Hebrews's interest in the Exodus narrative of the tabernacle focuses on the task of setting it up. God commissioned Moses to build a replica of the heavenly tabernacle, "see to it that you make everything according to the pattern shown you on the mountain" (ὅρα γάρ φησιν, ποιήσεις

---

45. The lack of consensus on the tabernacle cycle in LXX Exodus is well known. The differences between the Hebrew and Greek textual traditions, including significant omissions, or at times even additions, and most baffling changes in order provide a notoriously complex textual situation. The major studies have explained the differences between the Hebrew and Greek textual traditions in a variety of ways, from the translator's incompetence and unprofessional work— David W. Gooding, *The Account of the Tabernacle: Translation and Textual Problems of the Greek Exodus* (Cambridge: Cambridge University Press, 1959)—to the existence of a different *Vorlage*—Anneli Aejmalaeus, "Septuagintal Translation Techniques—A Solution to the Problem of the Tabernacle Account," in *Septuagint, Scrolls and Cognate Writings*, eds. George J. Brooke and Barnabas Lindars, SBLSCS 33 (Atlanta: Scholars, 1992) 381–402—or a combination of the two—Wevers, *Exodus*. For the current state of the debate, see Martha Wade, *Consistency of Translation Techniques in the Tabernacle Accounts of Exodus in the Old Greek*, SBLSCS 49 (Atlanta: SBL, 2003).

πάντα κατὰ τὸν τύπον τὸν δειχθέντα σοι ἐν τῷ ὄρει, 8:5). The blueprint had to be scrupulously followed. Yet, this earthly tabernacle constituted only an ephemeral entity, a shadow (σκιά), a copy (ὑπόδειγμα) of the true structure.[46] Once Christ, the superior High priest (7:26) and the mediator of a better covenant (7:22), performed his better ministry (8:6) by offering a better sacrifice (9:23) with better blood (9:12) in the better and more perfect tabernacle (9:11), the earthly tabernacle and its ministry would inevitably become obsolete, outdated, and, ultimately, replaced.

The sacrificial system

The Sinaitic covenant incorporated an elaborate sacrificial system, pedantically regulated in every aspect pertaining to it: the types of sacrifices and offerings, the correct procedures, the proper place and time of the offerings, and the qualifications of the ministering personnel. These issues form the subject matter of the book of Leviticus. The roots of this system, however, are firmly grounded in Exodus. Several assertions in Hebrews are intrinsically related to Exodus's material on sacrifices. The sacrificial system is ultimately necessary because of sin (Heb 5:3). The variety of sacrifices, listed in Heb 10 by means of the quotation from Ps 40 [39 LXX], mirror the sacrificial instructions in Leviticus. The issue of their periodic repeatability, however (and more importantly, its significance), is traceable to Exodus (cf. Exod 29:38–46). The Author construed this repeatability as another self-attested insufficiency of the old system. He asks rhetorically, "otherwise would they not have stopped being offered?" (Heb 10:2). With the arrival of the eschaton, however, and with the benefits from the redemptive work performed in the true tabernacle (9:14), these sacrifices are no longer necessary (10:18). Christ's self sacrifice offered under the auspices of the New covenant, the singularly perfect as well as perfecting sacrifice, rendered them obsolete and replaced them (10:12–14).

Exodus—The Man, the Leader

The echoes of Exodus in Hebrews would be incomplete without a brief reflection on Moses, the key character in the story of exodus. His unrivaled role in the Pentateuch and the Sinaitic covenant is axiomatic in the entire NT canon,

---

46. As already mentioned, while the neo-Platonic background of thought cannot be completely ruled out (Thompson, *Beginning*), the tensions within the Jewish eschatological system explain the language and imagery of the passage in a more direct way; cf. Barrett, "Eschatology," 392–94; Williamson, *Philo*, 157.

and a well developed portrait of him in Hebrews is not entirely unexpected. One needs to look no further than the two opening syncrises. The first one compares Jesus favorably to angels (Heb 1:4—2:18), and the second one, to Moses (3:1–5). The consecution proves Moses' towering and unchallenged superiority in all Jewish thought. Even for the Author, Jesus' superiority to angels was easier to demonstrate than his superiority over Moses. Since the man Moses made his entry into the history and story of Israel in Exodus, the Author's portrait of Moses would necessarily include echoes of Exodus material, the only ones considered in the following comments.[47]

The dominant features of Moses' portrait emerge from his key role in the Sinaitic covenant, discussed above. Providentially protected by God in his infancy, provided with privileges during his formative years, and chosen as the recipient of an awe-inspiring God's self revelation at the bush, Moses was reared as the commander to lead the people out of Egypt in the unique event of the exodus. For all these facets, Exodus stands as the primary source.

Besides Heb 11, however, there are passages that add important elements to his portrait. Notable among them is Moses' role in the giving of the Law, the initiation of the covenant, and the building of the tabernacle. Without these dimensions—all drawn from Exodus—his portrait would be incomplete.[48]

Moses' unique place vis-à-vis the Sinaitic Law is manifest in the paradigmatic phrase "the Law of Moses" (νόμος Μωϋσέως, Heb 10:28). The genitive construction is exclusively reserved for the name of Moses as *nomen rectum*. Moses was the quintessential law-giver. This predication is repeated either explicitly, as in the aforementioned phrase, or implicitly, in phrases such as "Moses said nothing about . . ." (οὐδὲν Μωϋσῆς ἐλάλησεν, 7:14). Moses' role was not limited to the reception of the Law but also to disseminating it among the people, "when Moses spoke every law to all the people" (λαληθείσης γὰρ πάσης ἐντολῆς κατὰ τὸν νόμον ὑπὸ Μωϋσέως παντὶ τῷ λαῷ, 9:19). Moses' words and instructions for the people were indeed God's words and instructions for them; when Moses spoke, God spoke (7:14). Hence the severity of punishment for those who would disobey those words (2:2), or not believe them (4:2), or rejected them (10:28), or

47. It would be good to acknowledge that Hebrews's portrait of Moses rests on the Author's reading of the Pentateuch as a whole, and not just of Exodus. This is another case in which a book-by-book segmentation of the Pentateuch is not entirely useful.

48. Hebrews 3 is the first passage in the epistle that makes explicit reference to Moses, but the scriptural support is not from Exodus. Moses is called as the faithful "servant" (θεράπων) in God's house (3:5). While the Author builds the argument on Num 12:1–9, it is actually Exodus that introduces this particular designation for Moses. It stands in Exod 4:10 as Moses' preferred form of self address; later on it becomes the people's ascription to him (14:31).

turned away from them (12:25). While Moses' role as spokesman for God resurfaces repeatedly throughout the Pentateuch (cf. Num 12:7–8), Exodus portrays him fulfilling this role for Aaron (Exod 4:15), Pharaoh (4:22), and the people (33:11).

Secondly, Moses' unrivaled role in instituting the Sinaitic covenant emerges in the narration of the initiation rites. The Author uses an Exodus passage as the backdrop for his perspective on the event. The covenant inauguration included the reading of the stipulations (Exod 24:7), the people's response (24:7), and the sprinkling of the blood over the people and the pronouncement, "this is the blood of the covenant" (24:8). At this juncture, the Author ascertains, the covenant was set into motion. This is precisely Hebrews's narrative of the covenant initiation, under the leadership of Moses, who performed every step of the ritual: he read the comments, took the blood of the covenant, sprinkled with it the book and the people, spoke about this blood and God's covenant, and further sprinkled the tabernacle and the utensils (Heb 9:19–21).[49]

Thirdly, the Author, similar to the attention devoted to the covenant inauguration, considers Moses' crucial role in the setting up of the tabernacle. Hebrews 8:5 traces this dimension based on the narrative and the imbedded quotation from Exodus. Moses had the privileged position of offering the people the earthly correspondent of the heavenly Temple. While Moses was not the only human being privileged with beholding God's heavenly Temple,[50] the charge and the responsibility to build its replica on earth have been uniquely given to Moses.

Lastly, Moses' portrait receives the final touch in Heb 12 within the Author's climactic contrast between the two covenants and everything associated with them: the representative sacred space; the privilege of entering God' presence; and the efficiency of the sprinkled blood. In this grand finale, the Author focuses on those covenant particularities which terrified even a man of Moses' stature—"I tremble with fear" (ἔκφοβός εἰμι καὶ ἔντρομος, 12:21). While the main quotation comes from Deut 9:19, the other accompanying quotation as well as the narrative follow the events in Exodus. The context reports the preliminaries for the meeting between the God of the covenant and the people of the covenant (Exod 19). Hebrews faithfully records the terrifying atmosphere, the gloom, the darkness, the storm, the sound of the trumpet, and, foremost, the unbearable command to stay away from God (Heb 12:18–21). The contrast in Hebrews cannot be

49. Leviticus records the sprinkling of the tabernacle and its utensils, not Exodus; see Mayjee Philip, *Leviticus in Hebrews: A Transtextual Analysis of the Tabernacle Theme in the Letter to the Hebrews* (New York: Lang, 2011).

50. The prophet Isaiah experienced a similar vision (see Isa 6).

more dramatic: the covenant that terrified even its most eligible representative and emphatically forbade the people to come into God's presence has now, in Christ, been replaced with one that repeatedly summons people to enter his presence with boldness (4:16; 10:22).

In light of this multifaceted portrait, as the one who declared the word of God, who initiated the covenant, who insured its proper role and its sacred space, who offered the blood, who was a faithful servant of the first covenant, who received the plans for its earthly sanctuary, who built it, and who sanctified it, Moses represented for the Author the perfect antitype of Christ. There was no one greater than Moses in the economy of the first covenant. Because of this stature, the Author of Hebrews, not unlike the rest of the NT writers, found the typology of Christ as the New Moses the most appropriate theological angle for their exploration of the new covenant.[51]

Conclusion

Heb 11:22 recounts how Joseph "spoke about the exodus" (περὶ τῆς ἐξόδου . . . ἐμνημόνευσεν) in the prophetic foretelling of the Israelites' liberation from slavery. This most defining historical moment became the ferment for many theological reflections of their prophets, psalmists, and subsequent writers. The Author of Hebrews likewise reflects, in retrospect, on this multifaceted event, the exodus, and the ensuing covenant, the Law with its commands, the priesthood and the sacrificial system, the tabernacle and the worship regulations, and on the imposing figure of Moses. Moreover, his reflection on these matters comes from the vantage point of an even greater event: God's word and work through Jesus Christ, marking the dawn of the eschaton, (Heb 1:1–2). To express best the significance of this ultimate event, the Author, informed by his reading of Exodus, used the theological template provided by the exodus event. Christ also brings a much needed and longed for liberation, not from the slavery of Egypt, but from the enslaving fear of death (2:14) and the entrapment of sin (9:15; 12:1–2). With these liberated people, Christ also establishes a covenant, incomparably superior to the previous one, in which the Spirit of God enables faith in God, knowledge of God, and obedience to God unimagined under the first one. Moreover, just as once Moses did it, Christ, as pioneer and perfecter of their faith, leads the new covenant people into the very presence

51. A convincing argument is advanced by John Lierman, *The New Testament Moses: Christian Perceptions of Moses and Israel in the Setting of Jewish Religion*, WUNT 2/173 (Tübingen: Mohr/Siebeck, 2004).

of God, a journey with better goals and rate of success than any previous attempts under the old one.

Three components of Exodus's rich theological matrix caught the attention of the Author's theological acumen: the exodus as event; the covenant, as its aftermath; and the man Moses, the faithful servant of God. Indebted to such rich literary and theological heritage, he would unequivocally rank Exodus among his paramount scriptural influences, not a whisper, but a reverberating thunder.

10

The Exodus and Biblical Theology

Robin Routledge

Introduction

THERE SEEMS LITTLE DOUBT that the events associated with the exodus—including the plagues and the first Passover, the escape from Egypt, the miraculous deliverance at the Red Sea, the covenant at Sinai, the giving of the Law, and the desert wanderings—play an important and continuing role in the story of God's people. The account of the exodus is, of course, important in itself. It points to the special relationship between God and the people he has chosen and called: to his presence with them, to the demands that he makes through the Law, and to the way he has compassion on them and redeems them from slavery in Egypt and from further threats on their way to occupy the land he promised to them. However, the significance of the exodus extends more widely: according to John Bright, "Israel early and late remembered the exodus events as the supreme exhibition of the divine grace whereby her God had delivered her from bondage and established her in her land"[1]; and Michael Fishbane suggests, "the exodus tradition was used, from the first, as a paradigmatic teaching for present and future generations."[2]

1. John Bright, *Covenant and Promise: The Prophetic Understanding of the Future in Pre-Exilic Israel* (Philadelphia: Westminster, 1976) 29.

2. Michael Fishbane, "The 'Exodus' Motif/The Paradigm of Historical Renewal," in *Text and Texture: A Literary Reading of Selected Texts*, ed. Fishbane (Oxford: One World, 1998) 121–40, esp. 121.

In this chapter, I look at the exodus motif from the perspective of biblical theology,[3] and consider its role in some important theological themes found in both Old and New Testaments. Three of these seem particularly significant. First, the exodus figures prominently in the way both OT and NT writers understand what it means to be the people of God. Second, closely related to what the people of God *are*, is what they do; and the challenge to live out their divine calling as those who have been called into covenant relationship with God, which has its focus in the events of the exodus, again has continuing theological implications. And third, for writers of both testaments, Israel's redemption from slavery in Egypt sets a pattern for further acts of divine redemption—including the return from exile in Babylon and Christ's redemptive work. While they do not exhaust every reference to the exodus, these three things—the relationship between the exodus and community identity, the responsibility of living as the covenant people of God, and the significance of the exodus as a pattern for divine redemption—seem to cover the main contexts in which the exodus motif is found, and will form the main areas of discussion. One further theme, which will not be considered separately because it is so integral to everything else, but which will figure in the discussion, is the significance of the events of the exodus for the understanding of the nature and character of God.[4]

Community Identity

As already indicated, the events associated with the exodus were formative to the way the OT people of God understood both their relationship with God and, closely related to it, their identity as a nation. Israel traced its ancestry back to Abraham, and Abrahamic elements figure prominently in the OT; nevertheless, it is the exodus that is widely regarded as marking the birth of the nation.

3. The definition of biblical theology adopted here is "theology that derives from and accords with the bible." As such, it is a synthetic task, which considers the theological significance of individual texts and, while recognizing diverse elements, looks for what gives the bible its essential coherence. See further, Robin Routledge, *Old Testament Theology: A Thematic Approach* (Nottingham: Apollos, 2008) 37–39, 73–75; see also James Barr, *The Concept of Biblical Theology: An Old Testament Perspective* (London: SCM, 1999); R. W. L. Moberly, "How May we Speak of God? A Reconsideration of the Nature of Biblical Theology," *TynBul* 53, no. 2 (1992) 177–202; Charles H. H. Scobie, *The Ways of Our God: An Approach to Biblical Theology* (Grand Rapids: Eerdmans, 2003).

4. Sylvia C. Keesmaat notes the significance of the exodus in similar terms. See Keesmat, "Exodus and the Intertextual Transformation of Tradition in Romans 8.14–30," *JSNT* 54 (1994) 29–56, esp. 37–38.

It was through the events of the exodus, and particularly the covenant at Sinai, that God established Israel as his own people (e.g., Exod 19:5–6).[5] This was in partial fulfillment of the covenant made with Abraham, which included the promise that God would make Abraham the ancestor of a great nation (Gen 12:2).[6] The significance of the exodus for the ongoing understanding of the people and of their relationship with God is seen in the frequent reference to God as the one who "brought Israel out of Egypt."[7] This presents the exodus as an historical fact—and in the light of the frequency and theological import of such statements it is difficult to justify the view that the exodus, in some recognizable form, did not take place.[8] However, God's activity in delivering Israel from Egypt is more than just an historical event. Within the OT, God reveals himself through history. God is known, not primarily through theological propositions (which are rare in the OT), but through what he does: through his saving activity in the life of his people. And these prominent references to God as the one who brought

5. Walther Eichrodt says the Sinaitic Covenant is "the concept in which Israelite thought gave definite expression to the binding of the people to God and by means of which they established firmly from the start the particularity of their knowledge of him." See Eichrodt, *Theology of the Old Testament* (London: SCM, 1961–67) 1:36. See further, Scott Hahn, "Covenant in the Old and New Testaments," *CBR* 3 (2005) 263–92; Scott J. Hafemann, "The Covenant Relationship," in *Central Themes in Biblical Theology: Mapping Unity in Diversity*, eds. Hafemann and Paul R. House (Leicester: Apollos, 2007) 20–65; P. R. Williamson, *Sealed with an Oath: Covenant in God's Unfolding Purpose*, NSBT 23 (Leicester: Apollos, 2007).

6. On the continuity between the Abrahamic and Sinaitic covenants, see Routledge, *OT Theology*, 166–69. The patriarchal narratives anticipate the exodus (Gen 15:13–14; 50:24–25; cf. Exod 13:19), and Israel's deliverance from Egypt is seen to be in accordance with God's covenant commitment to Abraham and his descendants (Exod 2:24; 3:16–17; 6:2–8).

7. Cf. Exod 29:46, "I am the Lord their God, who brought them out of the land of Egypt so that I might dwell among them" (see also, e.g., Lev 22:33; 25:38; Num 15:41; Deut 5:6; Judg 2:1; 1 Sam 10:18; 1 Kgs 8:16, 21, 51; Ps 81:10; Jer 16:14; 23:7; 32:21; Ezek 20:6, 9–10; Hos 11:1; Amos 2:10; Mic 6:4). Unless otherwise stated, all references are from the NIV.

8. For discussion of the historicity of the exodus in some form, see, e.g., James K. Hoffmeier, *Israel in Egypt: The Evidence for the Authenticity of the Exodus Tradition* (New York: Oxford University Press, 1996); Kenneth A. Kitchen, *On the Reliability of the Old Testament* (Grand Rapids: Eerdmans, 2003) 241–312; cf. John Bright, *A History of Israel*, 4th ed. (Philadelphia: Westminster John Knox, 2000) 133–43. However, see, e.g., William G. Dever, *Who Were the Early Israelites and Where did They Come From* (Grand Rapids: Eerdmans, 2003); Israel Finkelstein and N. A. Silberman, *The Bible Unearthed: Archaeology's New Vision of Ancient Israel and the Origin of Its Sacred Texts* (New York: Free, 2001). See also Nadav Na'aman, "The Exodus Story: Between Historical Memory and Historiographical Composition," *JANER* 11 (2011) 39–69; Ronald Hendel, "The Exodus in Biblical Memory," *JBL* 120, no. 4 (2001) 601–22.

Israel up from Egypt point to the significance of the exodus, both in revealing God as Savior and Redeemer, and also in the nation's understanding of
itself as the special object of God's saving and redeeming activity.

Alongside the promise to make of Abraham a great nation, God promises an ongoing relationship with those descended from him: "to be your
God and the God of your descendants after you" (Gen 17:7). This, too, was
fulfilled in connection with the exodus, in God's announcement to Moses:
"I will take you as my own people and I will be your God" (Exod 6:7). This
formula—which here anticipates the Sinaitic covenant (cf. Lev 26:12)—is
repeated elsewhere in the OT in slightly variant forms as an expression of
the covenant ideal.[9] It is associated with God's continuing commitment to
his people, despite their sin, and with the promise of a new, restored relationship. Jeremiah views this in terms of a new covenant (Jer 31:31–34) in
which God's תורה will be written on human hearts, thus enabling the people
to meet the demands of being in covenant relationship with God (31:33).[10]
Ezekiel attributes that new ability to fulfill God's requirements directly to
the activity of God's Spirit (Ezek 36:27). It seems likely that these things
are parallel: both point to the future renewal and inward transformation
of God's people, which has as its goal the restoration of the relationship
promised to Abraham and embodied in the Sinaitic covenant: "you will be
my people and I will be your God."[11]

Another important expression linked with the exodus is God's description of Israel as "my firstborn son" (בני בכרי, Exod 4:22). The idea of God as
the father of his people is relatively rare in the OT (and certainly rarer than
it is in the NT), though it may be found in several OT passages.[12] Passages
that refer specifically to Israel as God's son are even less frequent; and most
appear to be linked with the exodus.[13] Jeremiah 31:9—in a passage referring
to the hope of deliverance from Babylonian exile that prepares the way for the
promise of the new covenant and using language reminiscent of the exodus
from Egypt—includes the only other reference to the people as "my [God's]

9. E.g., Jer 11:4; 30:22; 31:1, 33; Ezek 36:28; cf. Hos 2:23. For further discussion,
see Rolf Rendtorff, *The Covenant Formula: An Exegetical and Theological Investigation*,
OTS (Edinburgh: T. & T. Clark, 1998).

10. See, e.g., Routledge, *OT Theology*, 271–72.

11. Cf. Robin Routledge, "The Spirit and the Future in the Old Testament: Restoration and Renewal," in *Presence, Power and Promise: The Role of the Spirit of God in the
Old Testament*, eds. David G. Firth and Paul D. Wegner (Nottingham: Apollos, 2011)
346–67, esp. 357–59.

12. E.g., Deut 1:31; 32:6, 7; Isa 9:6; 63:16; Jer 3:19; cf. Mal. 1:6; 2:10.

13. Several passages refer to the people of Israel as God's children, e.g., Deut 14:1;
32:20, 43; Isa 1:2, 4; 43:6; 45:11; Jer 31:20—in most cases in the context of exodus or
second exodus language. See further, Keesmaat, "Exodus," 38–39.

firstborn" (בכרי) in the OT; and it links the hope of future deliverance with the special relationship established in the exodus.[14] In Hosea 11:1, a recalcitrant Israel is further referred to as the son that God brought out of Egypt, provided for, and even taught to walk, again pointing to the crucial role of the exodus in establishing the relationship between God and the people.[15]

The special relationship between God and Israel is also portrayed in terms of a marriage bond; and that, too, is linked with the exodus, and particularly with the Sinaitic covenant, where the marriage relationship between God and his people is deemed to have its beginnings. Thus, for example, Jer 2:2 idealizes Israel's desert wanderings following the making of the covenant at Sinai as a honeymoon: "I remember the devotion of your youth, how as a bride, you loved me and followed through the desert, through a land not sown." Furthermore, when Hosea points to the restoration of the broken relationship between God and Israel, he also looks back to the time of the exodus: "she will sing as in the days of her youth, as in the day she came up out of Egypt" (2:15).[16]

The ongoing significance of the exodus for the self–understanding of Israel is evident, too, in the fact that several of Israel's major festivals, including the three pilgrim feasts of Passover (and Unleavened Bread), Weeks, and Tabernacles, are closely linked with it. It seems possible that Passover and Unleavened Bread may have had a pre-history as spring festivals linked with the pastoral and agricultural year.[17] These were, though, reinterpreted in the light of the exodus. Similarly, the feast of Weeks (Pentecost), which was also an agricultural festival, became associated in later Jewish tradition with the anniversary of the Sinaitic covenant.[18] This reinforces the significance of the

14. The link with the exodus is reinforced by the LXX translation of verse 8, which suggests the returning exiles will be gathered "in the Passover feast."

15. Matt 2:15 quotes Hos 11:1 in relation to Jesus' "exile" in Egypt following Herod's threat on his life. It is unlikely that Hos 11:1 is prophetic (however, see John H. Sailhamer, "Hosea 11:1 and Matthew 2:15," *WTJ* 63 [2001] 87–96). Rather, this is a typological correspondence; see, e.g., James M. Hamilton, "'The Virgin Shall Conceive': Typological Fulfillment in Matthew 1:18–23," in *Built on the Rock: Studies in the Gospel of Matthew*, eds. Daniel M. Gurtner and John Nolland (Grand Rapids: Eerdmans, 2008), 228–47, esp. 230–32. Jesus in his life and ministry fulfills the narrative of Israel, and so presents himself as the ideal Israel; see R. T. France, *The Gospel of Matthew*, NICNT (Grand Rapids: Eerdmans, 2007) 80–81. N. T. Wright suggests that in the ministry of Jesus we see "the history of Israel in miniature," including an exodus, evident here in Matt 2:15. See N. T. Wright, *The New Testament and the People of God*, vol. 1 of *Christian Origins and the Queston of God* (London: SPCK, 1992) 402.

16. See also, e.g., Jer 31:32; cf. Jer 3:14; Ezek 16:8

17. See, e.g., Hayyim Schauss, *The Jewish Festivals* (London: Jewish Chronicle, 1986) 38–43

18. The OT does not link the Feast of Weeks directly to the Exodus; though it is

exodus event for later generations. Indeed, the liturgy associated with the annual celebration of the Passover requires participants to think of themselves as having been personally present at the exodus: "in every generation a person is duty-bound to regard himself as if he personally has gone forth from Egypt, since it is said, 'And you shall tell your son in that day saying, it is because of that which the Lord did for me when I came forth out of Egypt' (Exod 13:8)."[19] This sense of re-actualization is evident in Deut 5:2–4. Moses describes the new generation of Israelites, who are preparing to go in to take possession of the land, as those to whom God spoke at Horeb (Sinai): "the LORD our God made a covenant with us at Horeb. Not with our ancestors did the Lord make this covenant, but with us, who are all of us here alive today. The LORD spoke with you face to face out of the fire on the mountain." The generation that God met with at Horeb had passed away (cf. Num. 14:22–23). However, that event had lasting significance for the people as a whole, and future generations of Israelites were to identify with those who had gone before as those who had themselves received God's promises and experienced his deliverance. Moreover, each year, through the annual celebration of festivals, and particularly the Passover, the people of Israel re-lived the events of the exodus, and so confirmed their identity as the chosen, called, and redeemed people of God.

Some of the things linking Israel's identity as a nation with the events of the exodus are picked up in the NT—though now in reference to the Church. A key text is 1 Pet 2:9–10, "But you are a chosen people, a royal priesthood, a holy nation, a people belonging to God, that you may declare the praises of him who called you out of darkness into his wonderful light. Once you were not a people, but now you are the people of God; once you had not received mercy, but now you have received mercy." These verses quote Exod 19:5–6, which is directly related to the election of Israel at the exodus; and, they allude to Hos 2:23, which concludes the passage that points to Israel's restoration as a renewal of the relationship between God and Israel in the desert, and maybe also to Isa 43:21,[20] which also relates to the exodus. The re-iteration of the covenant formula provides a further important link between the people of

---

closely associated with divine covenants from Noah to Sinai in *Jubilees* (e.g., 6:17–22). See Schauss, *Jewish Festivals*, 89; Wright, *NT People of God*, 234.

19. Jacob Neusner, *The Babylonian Talmud: A Translation and Commentary* (Peabody, MA: Hendrickson, 2011) 4:537. See also, e.g., Robin Routledge, "Passover and Last Supper," *TynBul* 53, no. 2 (2002) 203–21 [218–19].

20. See, e.g., Paul J. Achtemeier, *1 Peter*, Hermeneia (Minneapolis: Fortress) 163–64. This link is strengthened by the reference to "chosen people" (1 Pet 2:9), which is present in Isa 43:20 but not in Exod 19:5.

God in the Old and New Testaments[21]; and, Paul's identification of believers as "sons of God" (Rom 8:14) may also allude to references to Israel as (albeit unfaithful) children in Deut 32:5, 19–20.[22]

There is considerable debate about the way OT passages may be properly applied to the Church; and there is an understandable tendency to shy away from the suggestion that the Church "replaces" national Israel.[23] However, by relating these and other key OT passages that are foundational for Israel's understanding of her own identity as the people of God to the Church, the NT writers appear to present the Church—understood as the inclusive community of those who have faith in Christ—as continuous with the people of God in the OT. Furthermore, because the exodus is so vital to Israel, it is understandable that it will also figure prominently in the self-understanding of the Christian community.

The identification of Jesus with the Passover Lamb[24] also points to a link between the people who were spared during the last plague in Egypt and who subsequently took part in the exodus and the covenant at Sinai, and those who now receive salvation through Christ's sacrifice, and enter into a new covenant relationship (cf. Luke 22:20).[25] Reinforcing that connection, it seems likely that the last supper that Jesus shared with his disciples was a Passover meal,[26] in which key events of the exodus were recalled, but

21. The covenant formula is clear in Hos 2:23, though not as clear in Peter's use of it. The formula also appears in relation to the Church in 2 Cor 6:16; Heb 8:10 (cf. Rev 21:7). For further discussion, see Elmer A. Martens, "The People of God," in Hafemann and House, *Central Themes*, 225–53.

22. See Keesmaat, "Exodus."

23. Space simply does not permit further discussion here. It seems significant, though, that the OT never wholly equates the "people of God" with the nation. In the exodus period, those who are disobedient may be "cut off from the people" (e.g., Exod 31:14; Lev 17:4, 9, 10; Num 9:13); the prophets refer to a "remnant" (see Routledge, *OT Theology*, 266–67) who are set apart from the nation as a whole by their faith (e.g., Isa 10:20–21; 37:31–32; Jer 23:3; Zeph 3:12–13); and this emphasis on faith and obedience rather than ethnic origin opens the way for other nations to be included among God's people (e.g., Isa 56:3–8; 66:19–21; see Routledge, *OT Theology*, 319–33). It can be argued that the Church saw itself in terms of this ethnically inclusive community of faith (cf., e.g., Rom 9:25–26; Gal 3:26–28; Eph 2:11–22).

24. E.g., John. 19:36 (cf. Exod 12:46); 1 Cor 5:7–8. For discussion of the significance of the Passover for Paul's theology, see Tom Holland, *Contours of Pauline Theology; A Radical New Survey of the Influences on Paul's Biblical Writings* (Feam: Mentor, 2004).

25. There also seems to be an implicit link between the exodus and baptism in 1 Cor 10:1–4.

26. In the Synoptic Gospels, the last supper appears as a true Passover meal (Matt 26:17–19; Mark 14:12–16; Luke 22:7–13, 15). John's chronology seems to be theologically motivated, demonstrating the correspondence between Jesus and the Passover lamb by placing the crucifixion concurrent with the slaughter of Passover lambs. See

in which, too, the significance of some traditional elements—in particular the unleavened bread and the (third) cup of wine that was drunk after the meal—were transformed in the light of Jesus' approaching death.[27] And just as participants in the Passover were invited to re-live the events of the exodus, and in so doing not only to remember what God had done for them, but also to affirm their solidarity with past generations of God's people, so too, through the continuing remembrance of that Last Supper—in what is variously termed the Lord's Supper, Communion Service, or Eucharist— successive generations of Christian believers recall Christ's sacrifice and also affirm their common heritage and their common identity as the people of God. They are, as Ciampa and Rosner suggest, "a group whose identity is formed in light of that which they all share together—namely, the redemption won through Christ's death on our behalf."[28]

Living as the People of God

As noted already, there is, in the OT, a close correlation between identity and activity. God is known through what he does; and that same correlation should be evident in the life of God's people: who they *are* should be reflected in what they *do*. Through the events of the exodus, God called Israel into a special relationship with himself, as his own treasured possession (Exod 19:5). However, that call to be the covenant people of God must be reflected in the way they conduct themselves—in relation to God, to each other, and to the rest of the world.[29]

A key expression of God's requirements for his people was the Law, which was closely associated with the Sinaitic Covenant. In the OT, the Law was viewed positively. It gave instruction in godly living, provided the opportunity to respond to God in loving obedience, and was the means by which the distinctive character of the people was preserved. As such, OT saints could take delight in it (e.g., Ps 19:7–11). Contrary to the way it is sometimes presented, the Law was not given as a means by which the people

further Routledge, "Passover," 205–6.

27. For discussion of the elements that may have been part of the Passover meal in the first century CE, see Routledge, "Passover," 208–18.

28. Roy E. Ciampa and Brian S. Rosner, *The First Letter to the Corinthians*, PNTC (Grand Rapids: Eerdmans, 2010) 552.

29. Terence E. Fretheim suggests that God's relationship with the people was already established through the Abrahamic covenant and the Sinaitic covenant was more about Israel's vocation: "to specify more closely the responsibilities of the descendants of Abraham for the sake of all the families of the earth." See Fretheim, "The Reclamation of Creation: Redemption and Law in Exodus," *Int* 45, no. 4 (1991) 354–65, esp. 361.

could earn salvation: those present at Sinai were already redeemed through the events of the first Passover; thus the Law was a basis not for *becoming*, but for *living as* God's people.[30] It does, though, emphasize the importance of obedience for that ongoing relationship. The Law also expresses God's character and will for his people, and shows his people how they can be more like him. Through the covenant, Israel was brought into fellowship with a holy God, and as a consequence was called to be holy too. A key expression of this is Lev 20:26, "You are to be holy to me because I, the LORD, am holy, and I have set you apart from the nations to be my own" (see also Lev 11:44–45; 19:2; cf. 21:8; 22:32). Of course the people of Israel had much to learn in their relationship with God over the coming years; however, the key indicator of what was required of them in that relationship was the character of God revealed, primarily, through the events of the exodus. That pattern is also evident in the NT, where Peter charges the Christian community with the same imperative (1 Pet 1:15–16); and, again, points to the link both between calling and right action and also between what God requires of his people and the nature and character of God himself.

Also important in providing an incentive to right living is the narrative of Israel's own history—, here again, the events of the exodus are particularly significant. As one aspect of this, obedience to God is seen as a grateful response to what he has done for the people by bringing them out of slavery (e.g., Deut 5:15; 16:12). Sometimes required action is more directly related to the people's own experience. So in Exod 23:9, they are commanded not to oppress an alien living in the land because they were aliens themselves and know how such oppression feels. Instructions about the redemption of Hebrew slaves are linked with the people's experience both of slavery, giving empathy with those who are enslaved, and also of their redemption by God, giving them a pattern to follow (Deut 15:12–15).

The covenant relationship between God and Israel has been compared, helpfully, to international treaties between a suzerain and a vassal.[31] God,

30. Sanders argues that this distinction, characterized as that between "getting in and staying in," still held within what he terms the "covenantal nomism" of Palestinian Judaism at the time of the NT writers, and is reflected in Paul's view of the law. See E. P. Sanders, *Paul and Palestinian Judaism* (London: SCM, 1977) 17, 180–82, 422–28, *passim*; and Sanders, *Paul, the Law, and the Jewish People* (Minneapolis: Fortress, 1985) *passim*. See also James D. G. Dunn, *The New Perspective on Paul*, rev. ed. (Grand Rapids: Eerdmans, 2008) 142.

31. See, e.g., George E. Mendenhall, "Covenant Forms in Israelite Tradition," *BA* 17, no. 3 (1954) 49–76, reprinted in Mendendall, *Law and Covenant in Israel and the Ancient Near East* (Pittsburgh: Biblical Colloquium, 1955). See also Peter C. Craigie, *The Book of Deuteronomy*, NICOT (Grand Rapids: Eerdmans, 1976) 22–24; Kitchen, *Reliability*, 283–312; Jon D. Levenson, *Sinai and Zion: An Entry into the Jewish Bible*, New Voices in

as suzerain, commits himself to the welfare, blessing, and protection of his people; and the people are called to respond with loyal and loving obedience. The outcome of such obedience is blessing and prosperity. Disobedience results in covenant curses, which involve the reversal of that blessing[32] and include eventual exile from the land. These "two ways" are set out in the book of Deuteronomy (e.g., Deut 30:15–18) and may be seen to provide a theological basis for interpreting the nation's history as set out in the books of Joshua to Kings, the so-called "Deuteronomistic History."[33] In particular, this provides an explanation of the exile in terms of God's clear statement that, as a consequence of disobedience, the people would "not live long in the land" (Deut 30:18).[34]

The pre-exilic prophets also challenge the people to live up to the obligations demanded by their special (covenant) relationship with God. They also point to judgment—in the form of defeat and exile—if they fail to do so.

For Hosea, Israel's apostasy results in a reversal of the covenant formula—"you are not my people, and I am not your God" (Hos 1:9)—and will lead to exile in Assyria, which is characterized as a "return to Egypt" (11:5; cf. 11:1). Hosea also points to the people's failure to display חסד (translated "love") towards God (6:4). The term חסד is difficult to translate adequately in English. It occurs in the OT within the context of relationships—particularly ones based on a covenant—and expresses the goodwill, loyalty, and dutiful action that the relationship demands.[35] In the case of the covenant between God and Israel, the focus of the OT writers is, usually, on the חסד shown by God. In Hos 6:4, however, the emphasis is on the חסד that God has a right to expect from the people (but which, sadly, is not forthcoming).

Biblical Studies (Minneapolis: Winston, 1985) 23–56; John A. Thompson, *Deuteronomy*, TOTC (Leicester: IVP, 1974) 14–21.

32. For further discussion see Robin Routledge, "Blessings and Curses," in *Dictionary of the Old Testament: Prophets*, eds. Mark J. Boda and J. Gordon McConville (Downers Grove, IL: IVP Academic, 2012) 60–64.

33. The term "Deuteronomistic History" is attributed to Martin Noth. See Noth, *The Deuteronomistic History*, JSOTSup 15 (Sheffield: JSOT Press, 1981).

34. See Routledge, *OT Theology*, 261–63. For discussion of the exodus motif in parts of the Deuteronomistic history, see Amos Frisch, "The Exodus Motif in 1 Kings 1–14," *JSOT* 81 (2000) 3–21; Lee Roy Martin, "'Where are all his wonders?' The Exodus Motif in the Book of Judges," *JBPR* 2 (2010) 87–109.

35. See further, e.g., Gordon R. Clark, *The Word Ḥesed in the Hebrew Bible*, JSOTSup157 (Sheffield: Sheffield Academic, 1993); Robin L. Routledge, "Hesed as Obligation: A Re-Examination," *TynBul* 46, no. 1 (1995) 179–96; Norman H. Snaith, *Distinctive Ideas of the Old Testament* (London: Epworth, 1953) 94–130; H. J. Zobel, "ḥesed," *TDOT* 5:44–64; B. Britt, "Unexpected Attachments: A Literary Approach to the Term ḥesed in the Hebrew Bible," *JSOT* 27, no. 3 (2003) 289–307.

Amos condemns the social and religious sin of Israel and challenges the complacency of the people. They assume that, because of their election by God, their future is secure irrespective of their behavior. The truth is just the reverse. The advantages associated with election should result in a greater level of commitment. The failure of the people to respond as they should increases their culpability: "you only have I chosen of all the families of the earth; therefore I will punish you for all your sins" (Amos 3:2). This follows the indictment of Israel in Amos 2:6-8 as one of seven kingdoms under God's judgment. Israel's sin is made worse in the light of what God has done for his people, primarily in the events of the exodus (2:9-10). Being chosen by God and given such privileged treatment by him brings responsibilities; and Israel's failure to fulfill those responsibilities in their dealings with God and within society brings divine punishment. There is a further, somewhat surprising, reference to the exodus in Amos 9:7: "'Are not you Israelites the same to me as the Cushites?' declares the Lord. 'Did I not bring Israel up from Egypt, the Philistines from Caphtor, and the Arameans from Kir?'" This verse likens the people of Israel, who feel secure in their wealth and status, as "notable men of the foremost nation" (6:1), with the Cushites, who may be mentioned here because they were regarded as distant and obscure.[36] It goes on to compare the exodus—which undoubtedly provided a basis for Israel's complacency—with the national migrations of the Philistines and the Syrians. This should not be taken to suggest that the exodus is not unique: as noted already, Israel's liability to punishment is predicated on their special calling by God, which finds its focus in the events of the exodus. The exodus *is* unique; however that uniqueness does not lie solely in the physical movement of Israel from one place to another, but in the relationship with God established in and through those events. By ignoring the demands of that relationship, the Israelites were reducing their journey from Egypt to just one more national migration. The absurdity of that conclusion reaffirms the importance of living out the calling associated with the exodus event.

---

36. This is the generally held view. See, e.g., Francis I. Andersen and David Noel Freedman, *Amos*, AB 24A (New York: Doubleday, 1989) 867-69; David Allan Hubbard, *Joel and Amos*, TOTC (Leicester: IVP, 1989) 233-34; James L. Mays, *Amos*, OTL (London: SCM, 1969) 157; Hans Walter Wolff, *Joel and Amos*, Hermeneia (Philadelphia: Fortress, 1977) 345. However, cf. Regina Smith, "A New Perspective on Amos 9:7a 'To Me, O Israel, you are just like the Kushites,'" *JITC* 22, no. 1 (1994) 36-47. Smith claims that, at the time of Amos, the Cushites had wealth and status. If so, their mention here may be to challenge Israel's mistaken belief that prosperity was a unique indicator of God's blessing and favor. Though not widely held, this view fits with the rest of the verse, which also notes similarities between Israel's experience and that of other nations.

While the main purpose of this text may be rhetorical, it also indicates God's interest in other nations.[37] Through the exodus, God established his relationship with Israel; and the correlation here between Israel's experience and God's involvement in other national migrations suggests that, in those events, God also entered into a relationship with those nations. The level of belonging is different: Israel remains the nation specially chosen by God (Amos 3:1–2), and the demands of the relationship are greater. Nevertheless, God's care and concern—including direct involvement in their history—extends to other peoples too.[38] We see a similar recognition of God's interest in all nations, again in connection with the exodus, in Exod 19:5. There God declares that, although Israel has been specially called, the whole earth belongs to him. Through the events of the exodus, God has entered into a unique, covenant relationship with Israel; but Israel is God's *special*, not his *sole*, possession; and, as the following verse indicates, their responsibility as a "kingdom of priests" includes a ministry to the nations.[39]

God's indictment of the people because they have not lived up to their covenant obligations is also evident in the "covenant lawsuit" (ריב) that God brings against the nation (e.g., Hos 4:1–3; Mic 6:1–8; cf. Jer 2:4–13).[40] The link with the Sinaitic covenant sets the covenant lawsuit

---

37. See, e.g., Hubbard, *Joel and Amos*, 234; Mays, *Amos*, 157–59; Wolff, *Joel and Amos*, 347–48.

38. See Routledge, *OT Theology*, 317–19; see also, e.g., Terence E. Fretheim, *God and World in the Old Testament: A Relational Theology of Creation* (Nashville: Abingdon, 2005) 24; James Chukwuma Okoye, *Israel and the Nations: A Mission Theology of the Old Testament* (Maryknoll, NY: Orbis, 2006) 75–77; Christopher J. H. Wright, *The Mission of God: Unlocking the Bible's Grand Narrative* (Downers Grove, IL: IVP, 2006) 96–98, 465–67.

39. See Routledge, *OT Theology*, 170–73; Wright, *Mission*, 332–33; see also Daniel Block, "The Privilege of Calling: The Mosaic Paradigm for Missions (Deut 26:16–19)," *BibSac* 162 (2005) 387–405; Terence E. Fretheim, "'Because the Whole Earth is Mine': Theme and Narrative in Exodus," *Int* 50, no. 3 (1996) 229–39. According to Frisch, in 1 Kgs 8:41–43 "the Exodus also serves . . . as a catalyst for the proclamation of God's name in the world" ("Exodus Motif," 11). A similar theme is seen in passages that suggest the transference of traditions associated with Sinai (and thus with the exodus), where they were associated specifically with Israel, to Jerusalem, where they take on universal significance; e.g., the Law (Isa 2:2–4) and the covenant meal eaten by Israel's elders, as representatives of the nation, on Sinai (Exod 24:11) but now shared with all peoples (Isa 25:6–8); see J. Gordon McConville, "Jerusalem in the Old Testament," in *Jerusalem Past and Present in the Purposes of God*, ed. P. W. L. Walker (Cambridge: Tyndale House, 1992) 21–51, esp. 25–27; Routledge, *OT Theology*, 276, 329.

40. On the covenant lawsuit, see, e.g., Leslie C. Allen, *The Books of Joel, Obadiah, Jonah and Micah*, NICOT (London: Hodder and Stoughton, 1976) 363–67; Richard M. Davidson, "The Divine Covenant Lawsuit Motif in Canonical Perspective," *JATS* 21, no. 1 (2010) 45–84; H. B. Huffmon, "The Covenant Lawsuit in the Prophets," *JBL* 78 (1959) 285–95; H. Lalleman-de Winkel, *Jeremiah in Prophetic Tradition: An Examination of*

generally within an exodus context. In Mic 6:1–8, though, the exodus is more specifically in view; and God's case against his people is related, directly, to their failure to respond to what he did for them at this key time in their history.[41] Significantly, that proper response includes חסד (translated "mercy" in Mic 6:8; cf. Hos 6:4).

Failure to meet the demands of the Sinaitic covenant is also an important feature of Jeremiah's prophecy. Jeremiah 2:4–13 describes God bringing a charge against Israel because of covenant unfaithfulness and links that charge directly with the exodus events (Jer 2:6–7; cf. 2:1–3).[42] He notes the people's disobedience in the light of all that God has done for them (e.g., 32:20–23), reiterates the covenant curses threatened in Deuteronomy (e.g., 11:3–8), and points to the inevitability of Babylonian exile. His message, though, is not all negative. As we have seen, Jeremiah also sees a future hope in terms of a new and better covenant relationship (31:31–34; cf. 32:40–41).[43]

The challenge to God's people to live a life worthy of their calling continues into the NT (e.g., Eph 4:1; 1 Thess 2:12; 2 Thess 1:11). As we have seen, NT writers use exodus motifs to emphasize continuity between the people of God in the Old and New Testaments. It is therefore unsurprising that those motifs appear in the call to the Christian community to right living. Thus, as noted above, Peter urges believers to holy living on the basis of God's command in Leviticus (1 Pet 1:15–16; cf. Lev 11:44); and 1 Peter 2:9–10, which has clear echoes of the exodus, is also linked with the need for the obedience and right living that should accompany the call to be God's people, which then points others to him (1 Pet 2:11–12). The covenant formula, "I will be their God, and they will be my people," also occurs in 2 Cor

the Book of Jeremiah in the Light of Israel's Prophetic Traditions (Leuven: Peeters, 2000) 171–72; James L. Mays, *Micah*, OTL (London: SCM, 1976) 128–36; Kirsten Nielsen, *Yahweh as Prosecutor and Judge*, JSOTSup 9 (Sheffield: JSOT Press, 1978).

41. See further, e.g., Allen, *Joel, Obadiah, Jonah, Micah*, 367–75; Stephen Cook, *The Social Roots of Biblical Yahwism*, Studies in Biblical Literature (Leiden: Brill, 2004) 75–78.

42. See also, e.g., Jer 7:21–26; 32:20–25; 34:13–22.

43. See below. For further discussion of the significance for the exodus for pre-exilic prophets, see, e.g., Richard J. Clifford, "The Exodus in the Christian Bible: The Case for 'Figural' Reading," *TS* 63 (2002) 345–61, esp. 350–52; Rebecca G. S. Idestrom, "Echoes of the Book of Exodus in Ezekiel," *JSOT* 33, no. 4 (2009) 489–510; Corrine Patton, "'I Myself Gave Them Laws That Were not Good': Ezekiel 20 and the Exodus Traditions," *JSOT* 69 (1996) 73–90; Gary Yates, "New Exodus and No Exodus in Jeremiah 26–45: Promise and Warning to the Exiles in Babylon," *TynBul* 57, no. 1 (2006) 1–22. For more general discussion of the exodus motif and godly living see, e.g., Richard D. Patterson and Michael Travers, "Contours of the Exodus Motif in Jesus' Earthly Ministry," *WTJ* 66 (2004) 25–47, esp. 29–32.

6:16[44] and, with a small variation, in Rev 21:7. In both cases it sets out behavior that is inappropriate for those called to be the people of God. The call to right living is also associated with the exodus narrative in 1 Cor 10:1–21. Also, in 1 Cor 5:6–8, in the light of the death of Christ as the Passover lamb, believers are urged to clear out the "yeast of malice and wickedness" (5:8) and become what they "really are" (5:7).

The Exodus and Redemption

As we have seen, the events of the exodus were foundational for the people's understanding of the nature and character of God and their relationship with him. Because a central element of this was God's action on behalf of his people in bringing them out of slavery in Egypt, the exodus—which Chris Wright describes as the first act of divine redemption described as such in the Bible—became paradigmatic: setting "the contours for what God himself means by redemption."[45]

The exodus demonstrates that God is willing and able to deliver his people, and so provides a basis for hope in the face of current and future threats.[46] There is a frequent call for God to act again as he did in the events of the exodus. Faced with a national crisis, the psalmist pleads with God, "have regard for your covenant" (Ps 74:20). Habakkuk, looking back on God's mighty acts in the past, calls on him to "renew them in our day" (Hab 3:2). These are expressions of trust in God, but the implication that God needs to be reminded of his past commitment indicates the relationship is

---

44. The reference to "come out from among them" (6:17) and to God as "father" and the people as his "sons and daughters" (6:18) might also allude to the exodus. For discussion of these verses in relation to Paul's "new exodus" theology, see William J. Webb, *Returning Home: New Covenant and Second Exodus as the Context for 2 Corinthians 6:14—7:1*, JSNTSup 85 (Sheffield: JSOT Press, 1993).

45. Wright, *Mission of God*, 275. The Hebrew terms used, primarily, in this context are גָּאַל (and the related noun, גֹּאֵל) and פָּדָה (sometimes translated "ransom"). Their usual sense implies rescue or release on the basis of a payment, including release from slavery. In the relationship between God and Israel, whist the connection with release from slavery in Egypt is clearly present (though by God's intervention, rather than payment), the terms denote more general deliverance. See, further, e.g., Robert L. Hubbard Jr, "גָּאַל," *NIDOTTE* 1:789–94; Hubbard, "פָּדָה," *NIDOTTE* 3:578–82; Helmer Ringgren, "גָּאַל," *TDOT* 2:350–55; H. Cazelles, "פָּדָה," *TDOT* 11:483–90; Jeremiah Unterman, "Redemption," *ABD* 5:650–54.

46. This seems particularly evident in psalms of lament, e.g., Pss 44:1–3; 74:12–17; 77:11–20; 80:8–11; see also, e.g., Neh 9:9–15; Ps 89:9–10; Isa 10:24, 26; 63:7–14; Jer 16:14–15; Ezek 16:59–60; 20:33–38; Hab 3:2–15.

not, now, as it should be.[47] Sometimes this is attributed to Israel's failure to meet her covenant obligations, one result of which is God's anger (e.g., Pss 74:1; 77:9; 80:4; Hab 3:2).[48] Nevertheless there is the confidence that God's mercy will finally prevail. For example, in Ps 77, the psalmist, after complaining that God appears to have rejected his people (77:7) and withdrawn his חסד (77:8), goes on to recall God's mighty acts (77:11–20) and, as John Goldingay notes, "never moves back again."[49]

God's desire to renew the relationship established through the exodus is evident in Hos 2:14–23. God will lead Israel back into the desert to the place where the relationship first began; and he will bring about a new covenant with them. The somewhat unorthodox restatement of the covenant formula (2:23) points both to God's continuing commitment to his people and to the renewed commitment of the people to God. In this passage, "the desert" is a place of new beginnings; but it also represents God's judgment (cf. 2:3). As noted above, that judgment will take the form of exile in Assyria, here depicted as a "return to Egypt" (Hos 11:5). God's purpose, though, in allowing such a disaster is to bring an apostate people to their senses and open the way for their restoration and renewal.

Jeremiah's promise of a new covenant (Jer 31:31–34) will also be fulfilled on the far side of divine judgment. Apostasy, this time of Judah, will result in exile in Babylon; but, following that judgment, which is intended to purge and refine the people, God will act once again to redeem, restore, and renew them, and to re-establish his covenant relationship with them.

The depiction of the return from Babylonian exile as a second or new exodus is evident, particularly, in Isa 40–55.[50] Watts suggests that "exodus

47. Clifford suggests that the events of the exodus need to be "re-activated" ("Figural Reading," 349–51).

48. Sometimes God's failure to act on behalf of his people does not appear justified (e.g., Ps 44). For further discussion of lament psalms see, e.g., Claus Westermann, *Praise and Lament in the Psalms* (Edinburgh: T. & T. Clark, 1981); see also Walter Brueggemann, *Theology of the Old Testament: Testimony, Dispute, Advocacy* (Minneapolis: Fortress, 1997) 374–81. Nevertheless, despite the questions and apparent contradiction, the psalmist continues to call on God for help.

49. John Goldingay, *Psalms* (Grand Rapids: Baker, 2006–2008) 2:459–60.

50. See, e.g., Bernard W. Anderson, "Exodus Typology in Second Isaiah," in *Israel's Prophetic Heritage: Essays in Honor of James Muilenburg*, eds. Anderson and Walter Harrelson (New York: Harper & Brothers, 1962) 177–95; Anderson, "Exodus and Covenant in Second Isaiah and Prophetic Tradition," in *Magnalia Dei, the Mighty Acts of God: Essays on the Bible and Archaeology in Memory of G. Ernest Wright*, eds. Frank Moore Cross et al. (New York: Doubleday, 1976) 339–60; Carroll Stuhlmueller, *Creative Redemption in Deutero-Isaiah*, AnBib 43 (Rome: Biblical Institute Press, 1970) 59–98; Rikki E. Watts, *Isaiah's New Exodus in Mark*, BSL (Grand Rapids: Baker Academic, 1997); Watts, "Consolation or Confrontation: Isaiah 40–55 and the Delay of the New

typology . . . is central to the salvation theme" of these chapters.[51] Isaiah 43:16 and 51:10 refer to the pathway through the sea (cf. 44:27; 50:2). God will once again make a highway in the wilderness (40:3; 43:19) and guide his people to their destination (42:16). As he made water flow from a rock during the exodus from Egypt (48:21; cf. Exod 17:2–7; Num 20:8), God will once more provide food and drink for his people on their journey (Isa 41:17–20; 43:19–20; 49:10). The glory of God seen on Sinai and in the Tabernacle (e.g., Exod 24:16–17; 40:34–38) will again be revealed, though now for all to see (Isa 40:5). Just as God delivered his people from the Egyptians with an *outstretched arm* (Exod 6:6; Deut 4:34; 5:15; 26:8), in the new exodus God's *arm* will again be revealed (Isa 40:10; 51:9; 52:10). The reference to God going before the people and acting as their rear-guard (52:12) also echoes exodus language (Exod 13:21–22; 14:19–20). Some passages suggest an easier and more glorious journey than before (cf. Isa 55:12). The people will not leave in haste (52:12; cf. Exod 12:11; Deut 16:3), the unwelcoming desert will be transformed (Isa 41:18–19; 49:9–10; 55:13), and the difficult terrain will be made passable (40:4; 49:11). This coming salvation is described as a "new thing" (42:9; 43:19; cf. 48:5)—in contrast to the "former things" (41:22; 42:9; 43:9, 18; 46:9; 48:3), which probably refer to the events of Israel's salvation history including the escape from Egypt (43:16–18)[52]—and points to the promised deliverance from Babylon as a new and better exodus.[53]

Exodus," *TynBul* 41, no. 1 (1990) 31–59. References in Isa 1–39 also point to a second exodus; e.g., Isa 11:11–16; 19:19–25; see, e.g., Fishbane, "Exodus Motif," 126–29 (though there is not space to develop that discussion here).

51. Watts, *New Exodus*, 79.

52. See, e.g., Anderson, "Exodus Typology," 187–89; Clifford, "Figural Reading," 352; cf. John N. Oswalt, *The Book of Isaiah: Chapters 40–66*, NICOT (Grand Rapids: Eerdmans, 1998) 101–2. Another view is that the "former things" relate to the judgment announced in Isa 1–39; see, e.g., Walter Brueggemann, *Isaiah 40–66* (Louisville: Westminster John Knox, 1998) 44–45; Brevard S. Childs, *Introduction to the Old Testament as Scripture* (Philadelphia: Fortress, 1979) 328–30; Fishbane, "Exodus Motif," 132–33; though this seems less likely. "Former things" refers to the exodus in Isa 43:16–18 (Brueggemann, *Isaiah 40–66*, 58).

53. See, e.g., Anderson, "Exodus Typology," 187; Brueggemann, *Isaiah 40–66*, 59; Brevard S. Childs, *Isaiah*, OTL (Louisville: Westminster John Knox, 2001) 336–37; Clifford, "Figural Reading," 352; Peter E. Enns, "Creation and Re-creation: the Interpretation of Psalm 95 in Hebrews 3:1—4:13," *WTJ* 55 (1993) 255–80, esp. 258–60; Charles A. Packer, "An Unfamiliar Wilderness: The Rhetoric of Reorientation in Second Isaiah," *ICJ* 10, no. 1 (2011) 91–108; David W. Pao, *Acts and the Isaianic New Exodus*, BSL (Grand Rapids: Baker Academic, 2002) 52–55; Carroll Stuhlmueller, "The Theology of Creation in Second Isaias," *CBQ* 21 (1959) 429–67.

The link with the exodus in Isa 40–55 also occurs in frequent references to divine redemption,[54] particularly in the characteristic designation of God as "Redeemer" (גאל).[55] There is a close relationship, too, in these chapters between redemption and creation. One aspect of this is to emphasize God's power to rescue his people: the God who created the heavens and the earth is able to deliver them.[56] Drawing together creation and redemption themes also suggests a more direct correspondence between them.[57] There is an explicit link between God's redemption of his people at the exodus and the divine power in creation in Isa 51:9–10. The reference to the "road in the depths of the sea so that the redeemed might cross over" (51:10b) points to the exodus, while "the waters of the great deep" (תהום; cf. Gen 1:2) allude to God's victory over the waters of chaos at creation.[58] "Rahab" (51:9b–10a) is probably to be understood in the same context—as a chaos monster defeated by God (cf. Job 26:12). Isaiah 44:27 makes further reference to God drying up the "watery deep," which again appears to bring exodus and creation traditions together,[59] though now in the context of the

54. Isa. 43:1; 44:22, 23; 48:20; 51:10; 52:3, 9.

55. Isa 41:14; 43:14; 44:6, 24; 47:4; 48:17; 49:7, 26; 54:5, 8.

56. E.g., Isa 40:12–31; 42:5; 44:24; 45:9–13, 18; 48:12–13; 51:13, 16.

57. See further, Routledge, *OT Theology*, 136–38; Stuhlmueller, *Creative Redemption*; Stuhlmueller, "Creation in Second Isaias"; Gerhard von Rad, "The Theological Problem of the OT Doctrine of Creation," in *Creation in the Old Testament*, ed. Bernhard Anderson, IRT 6 (London: SPCK, 1984) 53–64; see also Peter Enns, "Creation and Re-creation," 261.

58. See, e.g., Brueggemann, *Isaiah 40–66*, 129–30; Childs, *Isaiah*, 403; Fishbane, "Exodus Motif," 135–36; Susan R. Garrett, "Exodus from Bondage: Luke 9:31 and Acts 12:1–24," *CBQ* 52 (1990) 656–80, esp. 663–64; Oswalt, *Isaiah 40–66*, 341–43; Claus Westermann, *Isaiah 40–66* (London: SCM, 1969) 241. For discussion of creation as divine victory over the waters of chaos, see Routledge, *OT Theology*, 124–30; see also, e.g., Bernhard W. Anderson, *Creation Versus Chaos: the Reinterpretation of Mythical Symbolism in the Bible* (New York: Association, 1967); John Day, *God's Conflict with the Dragon and the Sea: Echoes of a Canaanite Myth in the Old Testament* (Cambridge: Cambridge University Press, 1985); Fretheim, *God and World*, 43–46; Pao, *Acts*, 56–57; Robin Routledge, "Did God Create Chaos: Unresolved Tension in Genesis 1:1–2," *TynBul* 61, no. 1 (2010) 69–88. For an alternative view, see David T. Tsumura, *Creation and Destruction: A Reappraisal of the Chaoskampf Theory in the Old Testament* (Winona Lake, IN: Eisenbrauns, 2005); Rebecca S. Watson, *Chaos Uncreated: A Reassessment of the Theme of "Chaos" in the Hebrew Bible*, BZAW 341 (Berlin: de Gruyter, 2005).

59. A similar correspondence between the waters of creation and the waters of the Red Sea is seen in, e.g., Pss 74:12–17; 77:16–20; cf. Hab 3:3–15. Several commentators also see links between Exod 15:1–18 and ANE creation myths; see, e.g., Peter C. Craigie, "The Poetry of Ugarit and Israel," *TynBul* 22 (1971) 3–31, esp. 19–26; Fretheim, *God and World*, 123.

coming Babylonian deliverance.[60] This close link between exodus and creation suggests that the exodus may be seen as a creative act by which God's people were brought into being.[61] By relating this to the deliverance from Babylon, that event, too, is also portrayed as a creative act, one which will result in the re-creation and renewal of Israel.[62]

The close link between exodus and creation might also allow us not only to see the exodus as a creative act, but also to view creation as a salvific act in which God rescues the cosmos from chaos.[63] This points to a divine commitment to the redemption of the whole of the created order; and it has significant implications for the OT view of world mission.

The use of exodus traditions in the later prophetic writings points to a typological correspondence between the people of God in Egypt and those languishing in exile in Babylon—and their respective deliverances.[64] This is not simply calling to mind an example of God's redemptive power in the past in order to give reassurance for the future. It is that; but, it also points beyond it to the ongoing purpose of God for his people. The God who redeemed and created them in the exodus events continues his work of

60. Further links between the exodus and creation may be evident in the idea of "rest" (e.g., Exod 33:14) seen in the institution of the Sabbath and the construction of the Tabernacle/Temple (see, e.g., G. K. Beale, *The Temple and the Church's Mission: A Biblical Theology of the Dwelling Place of God* [Leicester: Apollos, 2004] 32–36; R. E. Clements, *God and Temple* [Oxford: Blackwell, 1965] 65–69; Fretheim, *God and World*, 128–29; Okoye, *Israel and the Nations*, 31–32; John H. Walton, *The Lost World of Genesis One: Ancient Cosmology and the Origins Debate* [Downers Grove, IL: IVP, 2009] 87–92), and also associated with the settlement in Canaan (see, e.g., William J. Dumbrell, *Covenant and Creation: A Theology of the Old Testament Covenants*, Biblical and Theological Classics Library [Carlisle: Paternoster Press, 1997] 121–23; Fretheim, *God and World*, 61–64).

61. See, e.g., Clifford, "Exodus as Figure," 348–49; Enns, "Creation," 258; Fretheim, "Reclamation"; Fretheim, *God and World*, 109–33; Bernard Och, "Creation and Redemption: Towards a Theology of Creation," *Judaism* 44, no. 2 (1995) 226–43.

62. This is in line with the view that the exile represents a return to chaos/uncreation. In Jer 4:23, coming judgment results in a world that is "formless and empty" (תהו ובהו)—the same expression that describes the pre-creation state in Gen 1:2; see, e.g., Walter Brueggemann, *Jeremiah: Exile and Homecoming* (Grand Rapids: Eerdmans, 1998) 59–60; Michael Fishbane, "Jeremiah IV 23–26 and Job III 3–13: A Recovered Use of the Creation Pattern," *VT* 21, no. 2 (1971) 151–67; Hetty Lalleman, "Jeremiah, Judgement and Creation," *TynBul* 60, no. 1 (2009) 15–24, esp. 18–20. The terms תהו and בהו appear in Isa 34:11, again in the context of uncreation (cf. 34:4). Zeph 1:2–3 also depicts divine judgment as a reversal of creation.

63. See, e.g., Fretheim, "Reclamation"; Okoye, *Israel and the Nations*, 24–34; Robin Routledge, "Mission and Covenant," in *Bible and Mission: A Conversation between Biblical Studies and Missiology*, eds. Peter F. Penner et al. (Schwarzenfeld, Germany: Neufeld, 2008) 8–41.

64. See, e.g., Clifford, "Figural Reading."

redemption, renewal, and (re-)creation—in order that the people should be what they were called to be.

As noted, a key aspect of that renewal is the internal transformation that will enable God's people to be obedient. Jeremiah links that transformation with the new covenant (Jer 31:33; cf. 24:7). Ezekiel attributes it to the work of the Spirit (Ezek 36:26–27), though his use of the covenant formula (36:28) suggests that he also has a renewed covenant relationship in mind. In Isa 40–55, the primary agent of renewal is the Servant of the LORD.[65] The identity of this figure has been much debated, though the link with Torah and the fact that passages referring to the Servant appear in the immediate context of second exodus imagery suggest a Moses type of figure.[66]

References and allusions in the NT both to the exodus from Egypt and to the new exodus also suggest a typological correspondence between the OT people of God and the Church.[67] The Christian community is made up of those who have been redeemed through the sacrifice of Christ, the Passover Lamb, and brought out of slavery to sin and into a new covenant relationship with God. This points to continuity between Israel and the Church; though there is also the sense that hopes associated with the exodus motif are only fully realized in Christ.[68]

One important aspect of this is the NT writers' use of second exodus imagery. N. T. Wright argues that, in the minds of many first-century Jews, there was a sense in which the exile still continued.[69] Geographically, the people were back in their own land; but, the great promises of restoration had not yet been fulfilled. The NT writers set the coming of Jesus against that

65. References to the Servant appear primarily in four so-called "Servant Songs," Isa 42:1–9; 49:1–6; 50:4–9; 52:13—53:12. For an overview of the Servant, See Routledge, *OT Theology*, 291–96; for discussion of the Servant's role in renewal see, e.g., Robin Routledge, "Is There a Narrative Substructure Underlying the Book of Isaiah," *TynBul* 55, no. 2 (2004) 183–204.

66. See Gordon P. Hugenberger, "The Servant of the Lord in the 'Servant Songs' of Isaiah: A Second Moses Figure," in *The Lord's Anointed: Interpretation of Old Testament Messianic Texts*, eds. Philip E. Satterthwaite et al (Carlisle: Paternoster Press; Downers Grove, IL: IVP, 1995) 105–40.

67. See, e.g., Clifford, "Figural Reading," 353–58; Richard B. Hays, *Echoes of Scripture in the Letters of Paul* (New Haven: Yale University Press, 1989); Patterson and Travers, "Contours," 37–47.

68. See, e.g., Fred L. Fisher, "The New and Greater Exodus: The Exodus Pattern in the New Testament," *SWJT* 20, no. 1 (1977) 69–79; Matthew Thiessen, "Hebrews and the End of the Exodus," *NovT* 49 (2007) 353–69; see also the discussion below.

69. Wright, *People*, 268–72, 299–301; see also Clifford, "Figural Reading," 352–54; Pao, *Acts*, 143–46. In Thiessen's view it is the exodus rather than the return from exile that has not been completed, and so "new exodus" language is inaccurate ("Hebrews," 355); however, cf. Enns, "Creation."

background. In his life and ministry, he re-enacts the Israel's narrative in order to bring Israel's history to a climax and end its long bondage.[70] This he offers through a second exodus, effected through his death and resurrection.[71]

The idea of Jesus as the ideal Israel also relates to his portrayal in the NT as God's Servant.[72] In Isa 40–55, the Servant is sometimes identified with Israel;[73] however, Israel has failed in that role, and God has appointed another Servant who embodies what Israel was meant to be[74] and through whom Israel will be restored.[75] Christ fulfills that role in the NT.[76]

As we have seen, God's Servant in the OT is also associated with Moses; and NT writers also note typological correspondences between Moses and Jesus, the one who will lead Israel in a new exodus.[77] This correspondence is highlighted in the reference to Jesus' own "exodus" in Luke 9:31. This could simply refer to his coming death; however, other allusions to the exodus in Luke's gospel, and particularly the occurrence of this statement in the context of a conversation with Moses, also suggest a link with the deliverance of Israel from Egyptian bondage.[78]

70. Wright, *People*, 401–3.

71. Ibid., 388–89.

72. E.g., Matt 12:18; Acts 3:13, 26; 8:32–35; Phil 2:6.

73. E.g., Isa 41:8–9; 42:19; 43:10; 44:1–2, 26; 45:4.

74. This seems the best way of interpreting the reference to the Servant as "Israel" in Isa 49:3. See, e.g., Routledge, *OT Theology*, 292; Childs, *Isaiah*, 383–85; John Goldingay, *God's Prophet, God's Servant: A Study in Jeremiah and Isaiah 40–55* (Exeter: Paternoster, 1984) 127–29; Oswalt, *Isaiah 40–55*, 291; cf. Wright, *People*, 388.

75. Isa 49:5–6; see also Routledge, "Narrative Substructure."

76. See, e.g., Goldingay, *God's Prophet*, 79–80; C. R. North, *Isaiah 40–55: The Suffering Servant of God*, TBC (London: SCM, 1966) 29–36. Keesmaat, "Exodus," 40–41, further notes a correspondence between Christ as God's "firstborn" (Rom 8:29) and Israel as God's "firstborn" (Jer 31:9; cf. Exod 4:22).

77. As well as direct comparisons (e.g., John 1:17; 3:14; Heb 3:1–6), there are allusions and intertextual links; see, e.g., Enns, "Creation," 270–72; Fisher, "New and Greater Exodus," 75–77; Patterson and Travers, "Contours," 39–42; Kurt Queller, "'Stretch out Your Hand!' Echo and Metalepsis in Mark's Sabbath Healing Controversy," *JBL* 129, no. 4 (2010) 737–58.

78. See Garrett, "Exodus"; David Ravens, *Luke and the Restoration of Israel*, JSNTSup 119 (Sheffield: Sheffield Academic, 1995) 128–29; Joel B. Green, *The Gospel of Luke*, NICNT (Grand Rapids: Eerdmans, 1997) 381–82. For Garrett, this has implications for Luke's soteriology, which she views as deliverance from bondage to Satan. Something of this may be indicated, too, in the reference to the "finger of God," which occurs in the exodus narrative (Exod 8:19) and in Jesus' casting out demons (Luke 11:20), which demonstrates his power over "the strong man" (Luke 11:21–22).

Several recent investigations discuss the significance of the new exodus for NT writers.[79] Rikki Watts explores the significance of the new/second exodus for Mark's gospel. He argues that the introductory sentence (Mark 1:1–3; cf. Isa 40:3) sets out the conceptual framework of the book.[80] Watts also notes the sense of disappointment that followed the return from exile[81] and the hope of a new exodus—whose fulfillment is inaugurated through Christ's ministry.[82] David Pao looks at the new exodus particularly in relation to Acts. Like Watts, he notes the significance of the quotation from Isa 40:3–5 (Luke 3:4–6), describing it as the "hermeneutical lens"[83] for Luke's writings. His discussion has implications for the Church's identity: God's continuing purposes for his people, being worked out through the book of Acts, include Jews and Gentiles, and thus the Christian community as a whole may be properly construed as "the true people of God."[84]

This new exodus, enacted through Christ, is also related to the work of the Spirit. In Isa 63:7–14, God's leading of his people through the desert is closely associated with presence and activity of the Spirit (cf. Neh 9:20).[85] Sylvia Keesmaat sees an intertextual link between this and the reference to being "led by the Spirit" in Rom 8:14.[86] As noted above, she also argues

79. E.g., Andrew C. Brunson, *Psalm 118 in the Gospel of John: An Intertextual Study of the New Exodus Pattern in the Theology of John*, WUNT 2/158 (Tübingen: Mohr/Siebeck, 2003); Garrett, "Exodus"; Sylvia C. Keesmat, *Paul and His Story: (Re)interpreting the Exodus Tradition*, JSNTSup 181 (Sheffield: Sheffield Academic, 1999); Dave Mathewson, "New Exodus as a Background for 'the Sea was no More' in Revelation 21:1c," *TrinJ* 24NS (2003) 243–58; Rodrigo J. Morales, *The Spirit and the Restoration of Israel: New Exodus and New Creation Motifs in Galatians*, WUNT 2/282 (Tübingen: Mohr/Siebeck, 2010); Pao, *Acts*; Patterson and Travers, "Contours"; Watts, *New Exodus*; Webb, *Returning Home*; William N. Wilder, *Echoes of the Exodus Narrative in the Context and Background of Galatians 5:18*, Studies in Biblical Literature (New York: Lang, 2001).

80. Watts, *New Exodus*, 370.

81. Ibid., 67, 73, 104.

82. Ibid., 383.

83. Pao, *Acts*, 37, 45

84. Ibid., 5, 65, 83, 249. This argument is developed throughout his discussion.

85. According to Richard J. Sklba, Isa 63:11–14 and Neh 9:20 are post-exilic retellings of the exodus story, giving prominence to the Spirit, who will also take an active role in Israel's restoration; see Sklba, "'Until the Spirit from on High Is Poured out on Us' (Isa 32:15): Reflections on the Role of the Spirit in the Exile," *CBQ* 46 (1984): 1–17 [13]. Paul appears to do something similar in 2 Cor 3:16–18, where he links the 'Lord' in the exodus narrative (3:16; cf. Exod 34:4) with the activity of the 'Spirit'; see, e.g., Paul Barnett, *The Second Epistle to the Corinthians*, NICNT (Grand Rapids; Cambridge: Eerdmans, 1997) 199–202; C. K. Barrett, *The Second Epistle to the Corinthians*, 2nd ed., BNTC (London: A. & C. Black, 1973) 122–23.

86. Keesmaat, "Exodus," 40. The Greek verb, ἄγω, occurs in Isa 63:14 (LXX) and Rom

that there are further echoes of exodus language in the designation "sons of God"[87] and in the reference to God's "firstborn,"[88] which in Rom 8:29 refers to Jesus. Keesmaat further notes allusions to the exodus in the contrast between "sonship" and slavery in Gal 4–5.[89] Rodrigo Morales, too, notes the contrast between slavery—as a result of being under the curse of the law—and sonship through the Spirit. The possible link with Isa 63:14 suggests that Paul saw this restoration in terms of a new exodus.[90] Like Keesmaat, he further notes the link between being "led by the Spirit" (this time in Gal 5:18) and Isa 63:14. Following Wilder, Morales also points to Ps 143:10, which may also include exodus typology.[91] However, Morales does not see restoration as a return from exile. Rather, echoing the curse/blessing language of Deuteronomy, he argues that the curse of the law brings death. Redemption from that curse, through the outpouring of the Spirit, results in life.[92]

The significance of the exodus as a paradigm for redemption is evident in both testaments. Through the exodus, God demonstrated his commitment to his people and his power to act on their behalf. Following the exile, God promised a new exodus: a new act of redemption that will also bring about a new creation of Israel and of the whole created order. That promise has been fulfilled in Christ, the new Moses who leads his people—now made up of Jews and Gentiles—in a new exodus: out of slavery and death and into new life as the children of God and with the blessings of a new age.

Conclusion

As we have seen, the exodus plays an important part in the development of key biblical themes. It was the creative event through which God chose and established the nation of Israel as his own people. As such, it was crucial for their understanding both of their own identity and of their responsibility to God. Also, and very significantly, the exodus was a paradigm for

---

8:14 (and Gal 5:18). The link is even closer in the LXX which refers to the Spirit giving "guidance" (MT: "rest"). For a textual discussion, see, e.g., Oswalt, *Isaiah 40–66*, 609.

87. Keesmaat, "Exodus," 38–39; see notes 13 and 76, above.

88. Ibid., 40–41.

89. Sylvia C. Keesmaat, "Paul and His Story: Exodus and Tradition in Galatians," in *Early Christian Interpretation of the Scriptures of Israel: Investigations and Proposals*, eds. Craig A Evans and James A. sanders (Sheffield: Sheffield Academic, 1997) 300–333.

90. Morales, *Spirit*, 127–29, 149.

91. Ibid., 146–51; see also Wilder, *Echoes*.

92. Morales, *Spirit*, 86–131.

redemption. God, who had delivered his people in the past, would act in the future to bring them back from exile in a new exodus—which would also be a creative act that would result not only in the restoration of Israel, but also the re-creation of the whole world. The NT sees the work of Jesus in terms of this new exodus, which will bring God's purposes for his people—which now includes Jews and Gentiles—to a glorious conclusion. This, though, is not just a matter of NT writers finding OT texts to support their position; rather, they see in the new exodus the continuation and final fulfillment of God's creating and redeeming activity.[93] As such, the exodus motif may be seen to be an important unifying theme within biblical theology.

93. Wright notes this, in relation to Matthew's Gospel, as "the continuation and proper completion of the whole of history itself" (*People*, 389). See also Peter E. Enns, review of *Paul and his Story*, by Sylvia Keesmaat, *BBR* 10, no. 1 (2000) 151–53. Enns suggests, "Paul's letters are an effort to understand Israel's traditions in light of the death and resurrection of Christ . . . He is defining the present, post-resurrection cosmos by bringing all of Scripture to bear on this central, climactic event" (151).

Made in the USA
Middletown, DE
17 November 2017